PRAGMATIC CHORAL PROCEDURES

by
Russell A. Hammar

The Scarecrow Press, Inc.
Metuchen, N.J., & London
1984

Library of Congress Cataloging in Publication Data

Hammar, Russell A.
  Pragmatic choral procedures.

  Bibliography: p.
  Includes index.
  1. Choral singing. 2. Conducting, Choral. I. Title.
MT875.H18 1984   784.9'6   84-5332
ISBN 0-8108-1698-9

This book is affectionately dedicated
to my wife, Mickey, and to
all of my singing companions
who have taught me more
than I can ever acknowledge.

● ACKNOWLEDGMENTS

This book could not have been written without the encouragement from the choristers with whom I have worked during the past forty-five years in the field of choral endeavor. Their patient support--even indulgence at times--has helped me to recognize the conditions under which the choral singer functions. My wish is that the ideas expressed in this manuscript will assist other conductors as they labor in the field to become more efficient and, most of all, understanding of the needs of the singers in their ensembles.

I want to acknowledge the loving support of my wife, who not only has sung in my choirs, but has patiently encouraged me to finish this project. Her valuable insights and challenges often have led to clearer statements and a more rational discussion of topics.

Finally, I wish to thank Eleanor Vander Linde, who typed and aided significantly in editing the manuscript.

● TABLE OF CONTENTS

Acknowledgments   v
Preface   xiii
Introduction   xv

PART I: BASIC CONSIDERATIONS FOR
THE CHORAL CONDUCTOR

CHAPTER 1: A BRIEF HISTORY OF CONDUCTING   3
    Ancient Practices   3
    Medieval Practices   5
    Renaissance Practices   6
    Seventeenth and Eighteenth Centuries   7
    Nineteenth Century: Advent of the "Full-
        Blown" Conductor   10
    Twentieth-Century Demands upon the Conductor   14

CHAPTER 2: MUSIC EDUCATION THROUGH THE
            CHORAL EXPERIENCE   19
    Learning Readiness   20
    The Paths of Musical Growth   20
    The Paths of Growth Applied to the Choral
        Situation   24
    The Need for Effective Vocal Pedagogy in
        Training Choral Ensembles   26
    Principles of Teaching Sight-singing in Choral
        Ensembles   27

CHAPTER 3: THE CONDUCTOR'S ROLE:
            SERVING THE SINGER'S NEEDS   31
    Motivation   31
    The Drive Toward Success   33
    The Drive Toward the Familiar   35
    The Drive Toward New Experiences   35
    Derived Drives   35
    Goals   37

vii

Whole Versus Part Learning (S-A-S) 38
Individual Differences 42
Summary--Principles of Learning 49

PART II: CONSIDERING THE ROLE OF
THE CHORAL SINGER

CHAPTER 4: VOCAL DEVELOPMENT OF THE
CHORAL SINGER 55
Textures of Sound 55
Resonance 63
Volume 64
Aural Image 65
Breathing and Posture 67
Approaching Vocal Pedagogy Through Diction 74
The Vowel as the Basis of Vocal Production 77
The Vowel Spectrum 78
The Shape of the Buccalpharyngeal Cavity 80
Using the Vowel Spectrum 87
Vowel Derivations 91
The Sub-vowel 97
Modified Vowels 99
Treatment of Diphthongs 100
Treatment of Consonants 101
Singing in the Extremes of the Vocal Range 104
Tone Placement 105
The Passaggio 105
The Male Falsetto and the Head Voice 106
Intonation Problems 111
Physical Vocal Maladies Often Overlooked 117
Summary 120

CHAPTER 5: MUSICAL DEVELOPMENT OF
THE CHORAL SINGER 125
The Basic Problem of Sight-singing: Self-
reliance 125
Other Aids in Sight-singing 131

PART III: CONSIDERING THE ROLE OF
THE CHORAL CONDUCTOR

CHAPTER 6: THE CONDUCTOR FACES THE
CHORAL ENSEMBLE 141
Profile of Singers 141
Auditioning Singers 145

Seating Arrangements 147
Attendance Checking 151
Grading Systems 153
Personal Relationships with Singers 157
Personality Characteristics of the Conductor 159
The Importance of an Affirmative Attitude 160
Choice and Preparation of the Music 165
Introducing New Music 165
Pacing of the Rehearsal 167
Drilling 173
Memorizing 174
Making Mistakes 177
Interpretative Factors 178
Concert Protocol 180

CHAPTER 7: SOME TECHNICAL CONSIDERA-
            TIONS FOR THE CONDUCTOR 185
Beginning the Rehearsal on Time 185
Physical and Psychological Condition of the
    Singers 185
Pedagogical Uses of Repertoire 187
Body Posture and Movements of the Conductor 191
Facial Expressions 193
Baton or Hands 194
The Preparatory Beat 195
The Ictus 196
The Attack 196
The Anacrusis 197
The Release 199
Conveying Musical Ideas and Meanings 200

CHAPTER 8: SOME INTERPRETATIVE CON-
            SIDERATIONS FOR THE CONDUCTOR 203
Vocal Texture Relating to Historical Periods 203
Legato 213
Staccato 214
Marcato 215
Crescendo and Diminuendo 216
Phrasing 217
Rubato and Tenuto 218
The Fermata 219
Horizontal Movement of the Music 222
Blend and Balance 223
Rushing and Dragging of Tempi 229
The Hemiola 232
Long Notes: Their Expressive Potential 232
Melismas: Maintaining Tonal Consistency 235
Summary 236

CHAPTER 9:   REHEARSAL ROOM CONSID-
             ERATIONS   239
  Decor   239
  Ventilation and Temperature   239
  Room Set-up   240
  Room Acoustics   240
  The Use of Recording Equipment   241

          PART IV: CONSIDERATIONS RELATING TO
                     CHURCH CHOIRS

CHAPTER 10:   CHURCH CHOIR ORIENTATION   247
  Worship and Music   247
  Historical Perspective   247
  The Twentieth Century   276
  Summary   280

CHAPTER 11:   CONTEMPORARY CHURCH
              MUSIC CONCEPTS   285
  Defining Worship   285
  Music and Worship   286
  Musical Performance and Worship   290
  The Ministry of Music   297
  Areas of Scope and Function   298
  The Role of the Minister of Music   301
  The Church Choir   305
  The Choir Member   307
  Factors Necessary for Serving Choir
    Members' Needs   311
  The Administration of Church Choirs   317
  Recruitment   321
  Auditions   324
  Rapport with the Congregation   326
  Planning the Musical Program   327
  Paid Singers   331
  Multiple Choirs   332
  Care of Music   334
  Conclusion   335

Bibliography   341

Index   351

● LIST OF ILLUSTRATIONS

Figure   Page

1.   The Ear and Eustacian Tube   66
2.   The Diaphragm   68
3.   The Lungs and Diaphragm   68
4.   The Breathing-Posture pyramid   69
5.   Correct and Incorrect Posture   71
6.   Lower Breathing Posture   73
7.   Focal Points of Resonance--"AH" Vowel   81
8.   Focal Points of Resonance--"AY" and
       "EE" Vowels   82-83
9.   Focal Points of Resonance--"OH" and "OO"
       Vowels   84-85
10. Vowel Spectrum Relationships   86
11. Complete Vowel Spectrum   88
12. Vowel Spectrum Vocalized in Unison   89
13. Vowel Spectrum Vocalized in Harmony   89
14. Vowel Relationships   92
15. Losing the Core of the Vowel   94
16. Vowel Focus   94
17. Vowel Focus   94
18. Correct Vowel Focus   95
19. Short Vowel Formation   96
20. Short Vowel Pronunciation   97
21. The Use of the Short Vowel "uh"   98
22. "Zipper Action" of the Vocal Folds   106
23. Cycles per Second of Tuning Temperaments   114
24. Comparison of Equal and Just Temperaments   115
25. Vocal Cord Nodules   117
26. Vocal Cord Nodules   117
27. Vocal Cord Nodules   117
28. Aid to Note Detection   132
29. Aid to Note Detection   133
30. Aid to Note Detection   134
31. Aid to Note Detection   136
32. Rhythmic Aid   137

Figure		Page
33.	Vertical and Horizontal Pacing Graph	172
34.	Use of Chorale as Warm-up Exercise	188-189
35.	Preparatory Beat	195
36.	The Anacrusis	198
37.	Crescendo and Diminuendo	216
38.	Chorale Illustration of Fermata	221
39.	Reinforcing Vocal Sections	228
40.	Reinforcing Vocal Sections	230
41.	Reinforcing Vocal Sections	231
42.	The Hemiola	233
43.	The Hemiola	234
44.	The Trope	252
45.	Organum at the Fourth and Fifth	255
46.	Conductus	257

● PREFACE

The purpose of this book is to examine the pertinent practical elements and experiences which I have found to be useful and necessary in working successfully with singers. My work in the field of music spans more than forty years with amateur and professional choral groups. I have also taught studio voice for more than thirty years. My approach to choral tone combines an understanding of the needs and demands that the vocalist experiences, whether it be as a choral singer only, or also as a soloist.

Many excellent books have been written about conducting gestures, i.e., the physical patterns and mannerisms relating to this art. Therefore, I find little need to stress these points of reference, except to provide illustrations for discussion of technical and interpretative conducting gestures. This book was prepared to be of practical use to both beginning choral directors and established conductors. Chapters ten and eleven are written mainly for church choir directors and clergymen; however, these two chapters also contain material which is pertinent for all choral conductors.

The material in this book deals with historical facts, tried and proven music education principles, practical advice about rehearsal problems, some ideas about the all-important interpretative aspects of choral music, and the problems facing choral music education.

It appears to me that not enough thought is given to the psychological concerns of singers, who must function in the group dynamic. I do not profess to be a psychologist; yet, during my four decades of experience in this field, dealing with almost every kind of choral group, I find that we conductors often exhibit a lack of awareness of the subtle personal needs of our singers. I have made my share of mistakes in dealing with my "charges." The school of hard knocks has brought to my attention many problems--and some solutions to them--which I want to share with my readers.

Some of these ideas may help others avoid a bit of the trauma I have experienced. Thus, chapters two and three will address some of the basic principles of learning which affect the overall morale and performance of ensemble singers. Usually, these persons are not soloists and, consequently, they are motivated to seek artistic expression within the security of the group dynamic so as to fulfill this musical desire. It is the conductor's responsibility, therefore, to help them find satisfaction of that need through thoughtful leadership and understanding.

The reader will find some statements repeated throughout the chapters of this book. These basic concepts are purposely reiterated in various contexts in order to emphasize their importance to the conductor. It is analogous to a wheel with spokes; the spokes converging at the center to give support to the entire wheel. On the other hand, I have made a special effort to include only the most practical matters which should concern the choral conductor. Many details omitted are to be left to the instincts and inclinations of the readers, who must develop and/or solidify their own techniques in keeping with their individual proclivities.

I wish to thank the persons, too numerous to list, for their contributions to my thinking and experience during the years in which I have worked in this rewarding--and, at times, frustrating--activity. There are "lows" along with the "highs" for the conductor. It is also hoped that the experienced choral directors who read this book will find some new insights into their work; or if they differ at times with what I have to say, their own ideas may be strengthened. It is my desire, in the final analysis, that my ideas will stimulate all readers (tyros and veterans alike) to become more effective leaders in their chosen field.

Russell A. Hammar
April 15, 1983

● INTRODUCTION

The responsibility which an individual assumes for the performance of a choral or instrumental ensemble is an awesome
one. It is rare, and likely impossible, to find a conductor
who can be all things to all people. There will always be
critics. In no way can one expect to find agreement at all
times within a group of musicians. Yet, the person who
leads others must attract a significant number of followers
in order to be successful. Even if the ensemble members
cannot agree with all of the director's decisions, mutual respect must exist. Thus, a further and most important ingredient of the leader's personality is to be alert and willing
to learn from mistakes. Committing the same errors repeatedly in music, or in dealing with others, breeds lack of respect on the part of the group for the person in charge.
Again, to be respected as a director, one must exhibit respect in all ways for the singers and instrumentalists.

In the final analysis, the effective conductor of any
musical ensemble must be able to mold it into a unit which
successfully translates the abstract score into meaningful
sound. The listeners, as well as the participants, should
be able to grasp some of the intrinsic qualities lying dormant in the musical language called notation.

Lazare Saminsky's profile of an orchestral conductor
certainly applies to the choral director as well. He states
that a conductor is a peculiar complex of artists. He is all
in one:

   --a psychophysical metronome;
   --a pedagogue amalgamated with virtuoso handling [of]
      a gigantic instrument;
   --a mime, but one whose gesture is for the orchestra
      only. *

---

*Lazare Saminsky, Essentials of Conducting (London: Dennis
Dobson, 1958), p. 61.

Whatever the personal reasons that lead individuals into the music leadership field, the responsibility reaches far beyond the glamour of the public performance. Yet, there are many inherent rewards to be experienced, such as these:

> Personal satisfaction achieved from a successful performance;
>
> The buoyant feeling resulting from a rehearsal in which much progress has been made;
>
> The satisfaction of working together toward an experience which is more significant than any one individual in the group can achieve alone (including the conductor);
>
> The satisfaction gained from non-verbal communication between leader and singers.

The latter item is one of the most significant points to be made in this treatise--that of achieving the level of communication whereby the ensemble and the director are working together. The singers should never feel that they are working for the conductor; rather, that they are working with the conductor to reach the highest level of achievement of which the group is capable. The director must "roll up his or her sleeves" and work as an integral part of the unit --neither above, nor as a separate part of it. As cited above, the group must admire and respect the personal and professional qualities of its leader. There must exist a mutual respect between the director and the singers.

The conducting (leading) of ensembles has come a long way since the early efforts of group endeavors, when the leader waved his hand, or beat time with a large stick, or tapped his foot while sitting at the harpsichord in an effort to keep the performers together.

At the writing of this book the entire world is in a state of great upheaval and uncertainty about values and commitments--as well as economic survival. Young people, preparing to enter the professional world, rightly have a great sense of apprehension. Those desiring to enter the teaching profession are told by demographers that the pool of students in the 1980's will greatly diminish as a result of the zero or possible minus population growth in the Western world. This condition underscores the need for courageous, dedicated musician-teachers (including church choral directors) to develop into superb and sensitive musicians who will also be able to work effectively with both their charges and their employers--school principals, music committees and the public at large. In the next decade or two there will emerge a great opportunity for choral directors to capitalize upon the opportunity to organize community choruses since there may well be a great lack of artistic activity in the schools owing to the financial crunch which is already occurring.

It is also of prime importance that these future conductor-teachers attain a broad, liberal education, so as to cope with our radically changing society. Superb technicians who can function brilliantly only in a narrow and limited area of activity surely will be frustrated by problems that cannot be anticipated during their years of preparation. Therefore, the successful choral director must be able to understand and handle a wide variety of issues relating to our society in addition to possessing a comprehensive understanding of musical styles. He or she must be capable of working with persons whose attitudes are very diverse and be sensitive to their needs and desires. The "revolutionary" attitudes of students, who face such an unstable world in both economic and social terms, will constantly present unpredictable challenges to their leaders. The students' tastes in music will reflect the nature of the society in which they have been reared. Their motivation to sing--or lack of it--and their backgrounds (including poor musical training because of budget cuts in schools) will sharply reinforce this unstable feeling of what the future holds for them. Adolescents are increasingly rebellious of authority, constantly questioning the ability and decisions of their elders. This is not all bad in the final analysis, because young people need to have the freedom to develop into independent, creative persons. Moreover, students are becoming more and more discerning and vocal about the kind of education they are receiving and the uses of their own time to pursue the ends they desire.

Thus, the personally tactful and well-qualified teacher-musician will be the individual who will be able to cope with the situation described above. He or she must be dynamic in all phases of work with young people as they attempt to adjust to the life-style of the future.

Specifically, it is more important than ever before that choral conductors attain a comprehensive knowledge of their

field including how to teach "class voice" to the members of
their ensembles, whether it be the public or private grade
school or high school, college-university or community choral
organizations.   Certainly, church musicians will continue to
be confronted with similar problems, even more than they
have experienced in the past.   They will need to be able to
teach elements of music as well as to prepare choirs for
church services.

PART I:

BASIC CONSIDERATIONS FOR
THE CHORAL CONDUCTOR

- Chapter 1:
A BRIEF HISTORY OF CONDUCTING
PRACTICES

Early historical facts concerning the conducting of musical ensembles are somewhat difficult to document. Most of the existing information has been gained by inference from the writings about group efforts to make music. In addition, drawings, paintings, stone and wood carvings that depict the activity of coordinating the performances of singers and instrumentalists have contributed to the limited knowledge about early conducting practices.

ANCIENT PRACTICES

The Old Testament writings (particularly the Psalms) make ready reference to the Hebrew people's expression of religious customs through instrumental and vocal music. According to the Bible, King David was especially influential in cultivating musical expression. The belief that many Psalms were sung, as well as spoken, is a commonly accepted premise. The responses of the Hebrew people to their leaders (cantors) came first in the form of "Amens" and "Hallelujahs." Later, the practice is believed to have become more sophisticated, developing into chanting whole responsorial phrases, such as is found in Psalm 136. Here, the same phrase was repeated after each statement of praise or supplication chanted by the cantor:

> Cantor: O give thanks unto the Lord; for he is
> good:
> Response: for his mercy endureth forever.
> Cantor: O give thanks unto the God of gods:
> Response: for his mercy endureth forever.
> Cantor: O give thanks unto the Lord of lords:
> Response: for his mercy endureth forever, et
> cetera. [King James Version]

The Psalm contains twenty-six verses in the above manner and includes historical material as well as expressions of thanks and praise. Thus, the antiphonal and responsorial expressions have deep roots in the historical heritage of the Judeo-Christian liturgy.

A recent discovery of early Hebrew musical custom has been unveiled by a music scholar in France, Suzanne Haik-Vantoura. Since 1940, she has worked at deciphering what biblical scholars originally thought were accent marks and symbols in Aramaic, the language spoken in western Asia during the Middle Ages. She found that these marks were words with meanings, such as "rest," "end," "jump," and "succession." From these starting points, this music theorist and composer has assembled what she believes to be biblical music sung nearly three thousand years ago. She has reconstructed what she believes to be the music of several Psalms and the Ten Commandments. Moreover, Miss Haik-Vantoura believes that the entire Old Testament was sung or chanted in some manner, singing being the best means of perpetuating folk-lore messages.[1]

Clay tablets of the ancient Sumerians, who were part of the Babylonian empire (now part of southern Iraq), indicate that in the fourth and third millennia B.C. there were religious services employing liturgists, psalmists, priests, and someone especially in charge of the choir.[2] Egyptian paintings of the era about the fourteenth century B.C. reveal persons playing instruments. It is also common knowledge that speaking and singing choruses were part of the Grecian cultural expression. Further, hand clapping was used to undergird the rhythmic structure of the music.

Ancient Greek law demanded the use of choruses for semi-religious festivals. The Romans, whose indigenous musical heritage was sorely lacking, employed Greek singers and instrumentalists for their pleasure. Obviously, then, someone was needed to coordinate (lead) those efforts--a conductor of sorts. Rhythm (keeping singers together) was of prime importance. Melodies were transmitted by Grecian hieroglyphics and by oral transmission. Scholars have deciphered these codes and have constructed modern equivalents to early Greek music. The Greeks also conducted singers by using a method called "chironomy." This style was highly developed in the later use of plainchant. It became the established method of conducting Gregorian Chants. Chironomy consists of graceful arcs described by the hand and arm to

show the contour of the melodic line along with specific angles
or stops to indicate tempi or note values.

The early Christians perpetuated the Hebrew responsorial religious tradition. These responses were monotone,
simple recitation. By the end of the fourth century A.D.,
there had emerged a more florid style of responses which
required better training among the singers. A school of singing called the Schola Cantorum had been founded early in that
century by Pope Sylvester. As the Roman liturgy became
more sophisticated, the need for the chanting to develop further became very important. Great progress was made under
Pope Gregory (A.D. 590-605) when he reorganized the Schola
Cantorum into a well-established training school for use in
the Church.

MEDIEVAL PRACTICES (A.D. 700-1500)

We know that during medieval times there were some efforts
to conduct church music ensembles, but these barely matched
our contemporary concepts of conducting. The church choir
of this era had professional musicians designated to train the
singers and coordinate the responses. Chironomy (hand gestures), nodding of the head, tapping of the foot, or waving an
abbot's or bishop's staff were the chief means of indicating
tempi and any interpretative features of the music. Choral
leaders in the church (singer-cantor or director-precentor)
used a shepherd's staff or cantor's stick to show authority.
An associate director (succentor) was used for split choir
work. His main function was to set tempi, indicate pauses
and rests, and give pitches to the singers. Also, the pre-
centor reminded his singers what notes of the scale to sing
by pointing to various parts of the thumb and the fingers and
knuckles of the palm side of the left hand facing the singers.[3]
Modal (melodic) notation gave way to mensural (rhythmic) notation, which in turn paved the way for the mature polyphonic
music of the sixteenth century. Eventually polyphony assumed
dominance in church music, causing plainchant to fade away
over the succeeding generations.[4] In the late fifteenth century some art works pictured an ensemble leader holding a
stick in the right hand, the predecessor of our contemporary
baton.

In the latter part of the medieval era, with the development of stringed instruments, winds (recorders, sackbuts and
shaums), as well as percussion (cymbals, castanets, etc.), a

designated leader took charge of setting and maintaining the
proper tempo by whatever means seemed appropriate to him.
He was also responsible for the general outcome of the music.
These were usually secular groups, however,

There is more evidence by way of late medieval paintings that musicians and singers of secular music (including
madrigals) had someone beating time, at least for rehearsals.
Where singers and/or instrumentalists performed together for
secular purposes, a conductor was present with a long stick
to thrash out the meter and sometimes the rhythm. [5]

According to Grove's Dictionary, as far back as the
fifteenth century it had become customary to beat time for
the Sistine Choir singers in Rome with a roll of paper called
the "sol-fa." The process was called "tact" (pronounced
tAHkt) which was the motion used by the chief singer to coordinate the efforts of the ensemble. The "tact" (or "tactus")
was given according to the pulsations of the music or the
word emphases without a pattern; just up and down motions. [6]

These early time beaters probably did no more than
establish the right tempo and then hold a pulse.
The practice seems to have been universal up to
at least the first part of the eighteenth century. [7]

Conducting of church music during the seventeenth and
eighteenth centuries continued, for the most part, to use audible means of time beating, i.e., wooden sticks, paper rolls
and pieces of tin fastened to music racks. [8]

RENAISSANCE PRACTICES

The term "Renaissance" literally means "rebirth" of Greco-
Roman glories in the field of art, and it has no exact parallel in music. Grout refers to the period as "... a rebirth
of the human spirit, a revival of standards of culture."[9] Yet,
the term in musical context refers to a period in Northern
and Southern Europe which introduced a new and fresh sense
of harmony and polyphony significantly different from the medieval period. The development of new instruments and the
perfection of existing ones led to melodic and harmonic experimentation effecting a radical change in musical texture
during the 150 years from around 1450 to 1600.

The new sense of freedom introduced the concept that

instruments and voices could be interchangeable--doubling or substituting for each other except in cathedrals, where accompanying instruments were traditionally forbidden. Another major contribution to the mercurial growth of music during the Renaissance was the birth of printing with movable type perfected by Johann Gutenberg circa 1450. This invention led to the printing of individual voice parts, a practice that continued in Europe through the nineteenth century; this in contrast to the full scores with which we are most familiar today. It was a marvelous innovation for singers to have their own individual scores. No longer did several choristers have to share one lone copy of music. Printed manuals on how to sing, play, and compose now became available, thus improving the level of musical performance. However, as in all periods of music, change was gradual, so even though the music of the Renaissance had its distinctive qualities, medieval practices often continued alongside of newer forms. "[W]hat was then exceptional now became typical."[10]

There were two additional features of Renaissance music which are noteworthy: 1) the equality of voices which gave important melodic material to all voice parts, and 2) the gradual introduction of bar lines that came late in the era. This innovation assisted in stabilizing the ensemble efforts of the performers.

The refinement of keyboard instruments--harpsichord and organ--permitted the ensemble leader to control the performers more authoritatively. Still, foot-tapping and hand-beating were the basic conducting gestures used during this period. It seems wise to recognize that

> [I]n general, it is not unfair to say that up to the middle of the 19th century a fairly correct performance was all that a conductor expected of his players [or singers]. Now, correctness is the minimum from which he starts.[11]

SEVENTEENTH AND EIGHTEENTH CENTURIES

With the decline of Renaissance polyphonic music, and the loss of a great deal of rhythmic subtlety, the office of "time-beater" became less important. Consequently, the practice fell into disuse. The refinement of the harpsichord gradually led to the practice of placing that instrument in the role of

"percussionist." The plucking of the strings by the instrument's plectra served to produce the needed percussive effect, which became the rhythmic base for singers and instrumentalists. As instruments were further developed and orchestras began to expand in size during the seventeenth century, the harpsichord became the focal point of these larger
ensembles. However, when the harpsichordist could not com-
municate adequately with the continually growing orchestral
forces, a combination harpsichordist leader and "time-beater"
emerged. He used a cane to tap out meter to begin a musical selection, and then occasionally tapped out changing
rhythms, meters, ritardandos and accelerandos, even during
the actual performance of the piece! Jean Baptiste Lully
(1632-1687), the Italian-born French composer of operas, is
reported to have stabbed his foot so hard with a cane while
sitting at the harpsichord and beating time that he eventually
died from the infection which resulted from the blow.

It became customary at the Paris opera in the eighteenth century for the ensemble leader, sitting at a desk, to
beat time audibly by striking a stick of some sort against the
desk top or any object that would transmit sound. This custom was particularly prominent during the late seventeenth
and eighteenth centuries. Eventually, the noisy stick became
so obnoxious to listeners, that the practice fell into disuse
and the control of the orchestra was jointly assumed by the
first violinist (later called the concertmaster) and the person
at the keyboard. [12] Quite naturally, the hands, the fist, the
head, the roll of paper, and the stick were all exploited by
various musical leaders to control the music-making forces.

History tells us that Johann Sebastian Bach directed
his choirs from the organ or harpsichord simply by using
body movements and nodding his head. He is, however, re-
puted to have used a roll of paper as a baton on occasion.

By the end of the seventeenth century instrumental
groups were getting larger. The four-part string orchestra,
consisting of violins, violas, cellos and basses had become
the core of the instrumental forces. To strengthen the vocal forces, flutes or recorders, the double reed family, brass
and timpani were added totaling perhaps about 20 to 25 players. However, substitutions were often made for missing
instruments, a recorder being used instead of a violin, for
instance. Bach continually complained to the ecclesiastical
authorities and town council about his lack of adequate instrumentalists, qualitatively and quantitatively. However, he was
usually ignored.

On the other hand, the domineering Handel, with his huge physique and confident manner, was able to engage and control large forces of singers and instrumentalists, particularly for his oratorios.

> During rehearsals he could be a tyrant, giving offenders a fearful tongue-lashing. [13]

There is no specific evidence as to how Handel conducted rehearsals. Yet, we may assume that generally he followed the current Baroque custom of "presiding" from the harpsichord.

> However, there seems to be some evidence that he [Handel] did some manual conducting from time to time, depending on general conditions. [14]

With the death of Bach and Handel, the consensus in the musical world seemed to be that Baroque musical form had expressed just about everything that could be "said" by this style of composition. (Ironically, J. S. Bach was not universally recognized as a great composer until 75 to 100 years after his death.) As new forms of musical composition emerged, with Mozart and Haydn dominating the field, inevitable changes in ensemble directing were to be made, though these innovations manifested themselves very gradually.

In time, standardization of the orchestral size and balance was established. Previously, any number of violins from about six to twenty-eight were used, along with varying numbers of wind instruments. Until the mid-nineteenth century the composer himself was usually the leader (director) of the musical forces, and he determined the particular balance which he deemed best for his composition. In addition to the composer's advice and/or leadership, the concertmaster entered the fray, and soon the practice of using the violin bow as a quasi-baton emerged as a mildly effective tool for controlling the ever-growing forces. At other times the person at the keyboard, during the early stages of this transition period, shared the "conducting" responsibilities with the concertmaster. Still, there was merely metronomic leadership rather than an interpretative direction of the music.

At this point the reader may be asking, "What about the choral conductor? Where was he?" Until the nineteenth century, when community choruses began to emerge in England and Germany, choral work was predominantly church oriented, except for madrigal and other informal singing. The leader, naturally, was the church organist, who accompanied the singers with an organ continuo (figured bass) part --primarily a chordal support for the voices. The singers followed the lead from the keyboard as to tempi, attacks, and releases.

With the compositional development becoming more complex in texture during the high Baroque period (the first half of the eighteenth century) and with the instrumental forces becoming larger, the need for more control over the entire group of singers and players emerged as a primary concern.

NINETEENTH CENTURY: ADVENT OF THE "FULL BLOWN" CONDUCTOR

Conductors of the early nineteenth century were content to use a large stick simply to control the ensemble by indicating pulse, while the expressive and musical side of the work was shown by the left hand or word of mouth in rehearsal. [15]

> In the case of conducting, there was a tendency to direct from the bench of a keyboard instrument even after the superiority of the use of the baton over the older method had been conclusively demonstrated. [16]

However, the baton, as a reliable tool for manipulating or controlling orchestral forces, still was not utilized during Haydn and Mozart's time.

> ... Strange to say, even at this late date, the baton was very little used. [17]

Undoubtedly, the early nineteenth-century conducting technique was so crude that the traditional means of control from the keyboard was considered to be the superior method for leading ensembles. (Yet, even now, persons who are very secure at the keyboard, have a tendency to rely upon that instrument as the best means of establishing and maintaining control of the performing forces--especially in rehearsal.) We know that the "stick" in the eighteenth and early nineteenth centuries was very large and cumbersome to maneuver. However, a factor which influenced the progress of the use of the baton began to assert itself.

> The alternative practice of leaving the direction to
> the first violin aroused objections on all sides.   It
> was ridiculous for a violinist to move the neck of
> his fiddle up and down while playing ... or stop
> playing and beat time with his bow. [18]

Moreover, the violin bow, used as a baton, was a
very awkward conducting stick.   Also, as orchestral size
grew, it was apparent that a more satisfactory and definitive
means of coordinating the efforts of the players (and singers
in large choral works) was needed.   In addition to that,

> ... The improved instrumentation tended to make
> useless the keyboard in the orchestra.   Then, the
> appearance of the full score paved the way for the
> interpretative conductor. [19]

Mozart was regarded as a very capable conductor,
even during his youth.

> Perhaps no musician ever started his career as a
> conductor so young as did Mozart.   He was com-
> missioned to write music for the Mass, and in ad-
> dition, an offertory and a trumpet concerto to cele-
> brate the dedication of the Chapel. [20]

This boy of twelve years of age received universal applause
and admiration from his audiences.   Obviously, his reputa-
tion was enhanced by his genius as he matured.

> There was strong evidence that Mozart at times
> conducted in the modern manner, and by so doing
> pointed the way toward the reintroduction of the
> baton. [21]

It is axiomatic then, that as orchestral conducting developed into an art, choral conducting would emerge following the same basic patterns of behavior.

The Lutheran tradition of chorale singing was an integral part of the church liturgy.   Therefore, the congregation developed into a kind of large chorus.   Out of this experience the informal Singkreis (singing circles or community
choruses) began to emerge in Germanic countries.   English
universities began to develop "glees"--the forerunners of our
modern collegiate glee clubs.   The popularization of choral
singing in Europe led to the inclusion of women in these

choruses and eventually composers began to write for this
medium of vocal expression. Some of the compositions were
simple folk songs; others were ambitious choral works for
the growing sophisticated choirs and choruses.

> ... [C]horal activity after 1800 shifted from the
> church to the public choral concert, an activity in
> which the amateur choral society played a promi-
> nent and active role.[22]

During the late eighteenth and the entire nineteenth
centuries choral societies emerged in the United States as
well as in Europe. Larger cities in New England and New
York City were pioneers in this field of endeavor. The Moravian influence in Pennsylvania spawned the famous Bethlehem
Bach Festival, which was begun in 1898 under the leadership
of Frederick Wolle. The New York (City) Oratorio Society
dates back to 1873, whereas the Stoughton Massachusetts Musical Society began in 1786. The famous Handel and Haydn
Society of Boston was organized in 1815. Thus, we can observe that the amateur singing societies' emergence was the
catalystic force which became the seed of the art of contemporary choral singing in the Western world. The "grass
roots" influence has brought ensemble singing from the early
church and the hymn singing of the Reformation Church to
its present state of maturity. As a result, choral conducting has achieved par with that of the instrumental field in
training and leadership.

By the latter half of the nineteenth century the world
of musical composition had become so complex that it was
absolutely mandatory for the conductor to respond interpretatively, i.e., to go far beyond the mere technicalities of time
beating. From Beethoven's earliest classical symphonies to
his massive romantic "Ninth Symphony," we can observe the
emergence of conducting as an art. According to composer-
violinist, Ludwig Spohr (1784-1859), Beethoven was hardly a
graceful conductor. The softer the music, the lower he bent;
the louder the music, the more he rose up as tall as he
could stand. His sforzando gestures were made by his "tear-
ing apart his arms from a previously crossed position on his
breast."[23] He also shouted wildly. Beethoven's conducting
antics became so acute that in his later years (being deaf),
the concertmaster and a pianist were employed to keep the
performance under control--even though there was no piano
part in the score.

By the time of Beethoven's death in 1827, the orchestra had developed in stature resembling its present form. The basic difference was in tuning, which was considerably below the present concert pitch of 440 or 444 cycles (English) per second for the tuning pitch of "a^1." By 1825 wind instruments were keyed instead of having only holes to be stopped; the brass instruments were now given valves. These refinements in intonation led to much more sensitive interpretation of the music. (It is no wonder that during J. S. Bach's time his complex music was ignored! His music couldn't be played in tune then, and even today the modern brass players often have some difficulty playing his compositions with good intonation.) The new refined violins had longer necks, giving the players more tolerance for proper intonation. It became imperative now for the conductor to learn to manage these improved forces with intellectual sensitivity, expressed through his physical gestures in order to achieve artistic results.

It was Hector Berlioz (1803-1869), the French composer-conductor, who greatly enhanced the art of conducting. By 1855 he had brought the orchestra and conducting to unprecedented heights. He diagrammed beats and spoke of conserving arm and body movements to properly express the nature of the music. Mendelssohn also had been influential in establishing the true role of the conductor. Ludwig Spohr in the 1820's was one of the first modern conductors to use the baton as we know it today--a smaller, lighter stick that behaved very well in the hand of the director. Spohr also made a great contribution to more efficient rehearsal procedures in that he was the first to introduce bar numbers and letters to the score and parts. [24]

By mid-nineteenth century, the art of conducting became a focal point of discussion among composers and conductors. As cited previously, until this time composers primarily had conducted their own works. Now, the spread of musical activity was becoming so great that they were conducting each other's compositions, and even non-composers were conducting orchestras and choruses. Thus, the original control over the compositions was being eroded and the musical scores had to contain more precise directions for preparation and performance. Consequently, the art of conducting became more exacting, paving the way for the "full-blown" maestro of the baton in the twentieth century.

The modern conductor, using a smaller, lighter stick,

which can be guided with the fingers, instead of grasping it
with the whole hand, makes the baton an extension of the arm
and hand.   It allows for reflective and graceful gestures in
conducting.   So here we observe the transition, from rather
primitive efforts to conduct ensembles, to the concept we
now have of the modern conductor.   Every choral conductor
should become familiar with using a baton, in order to be
comfortable when needing it for conducting choral-orchestral
compositions.

TWENTIETH-CENTURY DEMANDS UPON
THE CONDUCTOR

As we consider the role of the contemporary choral conductor, we observe that musical scores have become more and
more complex.   This is a natural phenomenon as we note the
progression of musical composition from the ancient chanting
through the age of polyphony and the opening of new doors of
experimentation to what appears today as extremely complex
rhythmic, dynamic, and melodic contours.   Perhaps, by the
middle or late twenty-first century our present seemingly
"complex" musical idioms will be commonplace to the composers of that era.

Our present avant-garde compositions again require
new concepts of conducting gestures.   These ultra-modern
scores require tutelage in interpreting their "language."
Many scores resemble road maps of a sort, rather than the
traditional notation of music to which we have accustomed
ourselves.   Accompaniments for choral works often call for
improvised instruments, including sounds on tapes.   Thus,
our traditional patterns of conducting must be extended to
embrace almost any physical movement which will dramatize
the "far out" expressional needs demanded by these new compositions.

Specifically, we have observed that the art of conducting has progressed from primitive gestures, through plainchant chironomy, to time beating; from organized patterns of
controlling ensemble forces employing compound and uneven
rhythmic accoutrements to the extreme freedom needed to express radical ideas of the present complex musical scores.

Practically speaking, however, contemporary society,
at large, is generally conservative and tends artistically to
thrive in the past.   While Beethoven was considered to be

radical in his day, his music is readily accepted by the public today. Undoubtedly, J. S. Bach's complex polyphony was too far ahead of his time and his musical forces usually were too incompetent to reveal the intrinsic values of his music. It was not really appreciated until two centuries later. Today, choral conductors are generally confined to the music of the Renaissance, Baroque, Classical and Romantic Periods, and contemporary compositions which reflect neo-classic styles, rather than music of the avant-garde. Audiences and most singers are unprepared to accept complex contemporary harmonies and rhythms.

The terms "conductor," "director" and "teacher" will be used interchangeably since they refer to one and the same person in the ensemble situation.

NOTES

1. Feature story (United Press International), The Fresno Bee, December 29, 1979.
2. Ray Robinson and Allen Winold, The Choral Experience (New York: Harper's College Press, 1976), pp. 32-33.
3. Clyde W. Holsinger, A History of Choral Conducting with Emphasis on the Time-beating Techniques Used in the Successive Historical Periods, Ph. D. dissertation, Evanston (Illinois), Northwestern University, 1954, p. 110.
4. Ibid., pp. 117-118.
5. Harold Schonberg, The Great Conductors (New York: Simon and Schuster, 1967), pp. 26-27.
6. Eric Blom, ed., Grove's Dictionary of Music and Musicians, 5th edition (New York: St. Martin's Press, 1955, Vol. II), pp. 397-398.
7. Schonberg, op. cit., p. 28.
8. Holsinger, op. cit., p. 236.
9. Donald Jay Grout, A History of Western Music, 3rd edition (New York: W.W. Norton, 1980), p. 170.
10. Ibid., p. 176.
11. Blom, ed., Grove's Dictionary, loc. cit., p. 404.
12. Ibid., p. 398.
13. Paul Henry Lang, George Frideric Handel (New York: W.W. Norton), 1966, p. 541.
14. Richard Coar, The Masters of the Classical Period as Conductors, privately published (Sarasota, Florida: 1949), p. 34.

15. Blom, ed., Grove's Dictionary, loc. cit., Vol. I, p.
        501.
16. Coar, op. cit., p. 60.
17. Ibid., p. 71.
18. Ibid., p. 71.
19. Ibid., p. 74.
20. Ibid., p. 87.
21. Ibid., p. 91.
22. Robinson and Winold, op. cit., p. 25.
23. Schonberg, op. cit., p. 59.
24. Ibid., p. 86-87.

REVIEW QUESTIONS FOR CHAPTER 1

(1) Why is it difficult to document early conducting prac-
     tices?

(2) Describe ancient practices of chanting among the Hebrew
     people.

(3) Why was hand-clapping used in early music practices?

(4) Describe early conducting gestures.

(5) What is chironomy?

(6) What was the Schola Cantorum?

(7) What was the role of the cantor?

(8) What was the role of the succentor?

(9) What development paved the way for the emergence of
     mature polyphonic music of the 16th century?

(10) What was the "sol-fa" of early times?

(11) What is "tact"?

(12) What was the role of the harpsichord in early music
     ensemble efforts?

(13) How did Bach and Handel conduct their choral groups?

(14) What was the role of the concertmaster in early times?

(15) How did early 19th-century conductors lead their forces?

(16) What was (is) the Singkreis?

(17) Cite some early choral groups in the U.S.

(18) Describe conducting practices by the latter half of the 19th century.

(19) What influence did Berlioz, Mendelssohn, and Spohr have upon conducting?

(20) When did the art of conducting seem to emerge?

● Chapter 2:
MUSIC EDUCATION THROUGH
THE CHORAL EXPERIENCE

The successful choral conductor understands that his or her
essential role is that of an educator, whether directing a
church choir, community chorus or school ensemble. It is
important to recognize that in the various grades of public
or private school instruction, ensemble singing provides an
excellent opportunity to teach basic concepts of musicianship.
In view of any ensemble activity (on whatever age level) the
objective should be for the singers to become sensitive to the
intrinsic values of the music to which they are exposed, "...
for we are dealing with the essential aesthetic responsiveness
of human beings."[1]

Two general modes of teaching exist: one is mechanistic, the other, developmental. The mechanistic approach
to teaching assumes that a process of assembling and accu-
mulating facts or knowledge is the manner in which people
learn. That is to say, knowledge or skill is attained by ac-
quiring specific information and then assembling it in some
logical manner, just as a wall is constructed out of bricks,
or an automobile is built by putting the parts of it together
in the right order on an assembly line.

In contrast, the developmental approach to learning
stresses the essence of the music during the process of working out the details, rather than the mere accumulation of
facts or motor skills. The first objective, then, is to make
the learning experience enjoyable. In doing this, there must
be a flexible plan for the process, since people obviously differ in the sequence and length of time of their musical development.

The acquisition of technique should result from the
attack upon such problems which are both musical
and technical, and technique itself should be re-

garded as the ability to translate musical conceptions adequately and satisfactorily into sound. [2]

In music education we often structure our learning
around attempting to teach facts, such as notes, theoretical
rules and manipulative techniques, while we neglect tonal de-
sign and the expressive values of the music at hand. However, if we fail to relate factual material to the whole of the
music, we commit a grave error. What is important is how
we relate factual material to the learning process. There
are no fixed rules that govern going from one step to the
next, except in general terms, as will be discussed later in
this chapter.

How much of the theory of music we teach in any
given situation depends upon the time frame and circumstances
under which we operate. What is of prime importance is presenting the ensemble situation itself as a means of providing
a host of rewarding experiences for the musical development
of its participants. These experiences can and should follow
certain paths of musical growth.

LEARNING READINESS

No matter how much the leader of a group of singers (or
any leader, for that matter) desires his or her followers to
move along a progressive path of learning, it must be recognized that the learners will progress only when they have
gained enough insight to achieve the desired skill. Therefore, choral conductors should organize their objectives in
a manner which will lead to discovery on the part of the singers. They must never entertain the notion that all persons
learn the subject matter at the same rate. It is most important that directors know that the paths of learning are
extremely complex, and that no simple technique will accomplish all of the desired goals. That is why the theory of
learning espoused by James Mursell's classic book, Education for Musical Growth, seems to outline the learning process in a realistic fashion and is as pertinent today as it was
in mid-century.

THE PATHS OF MUSICAL GROWTH

In his book, cited above, Dr. Mursell outlined what he called
"Avenues of Musical Growth." They identify the learning ex-

perience in a manner which forms a profile for all learning
experiences. In terms of music, they are as follows:

> Growth in musical <u>awareness</u>
> Growth in musical <u>initiative</u>
> Growth in musical <u>discrimination</u>
> Growth in musical <u>insight</u>, resulting in
> Growth in musical <u>skill</u>

Careful examination of these elements will reveal their
value in structuring the ensemble experience so that musical
growth can be accomplished.

> The five broad avenues of musical growth are by
> no manner of means mutually exclusive or separable
> from one another.... They are simply aspects of
> outer manifestations of the same thing, namely, de-
> veloping a musical responsiveness. [3]

Careful examination and thought reveal that all five
paths or avenues are dependent upon one another, interacting
and embellishing each other. They are analogous to a five-
lane highway, which may be illustrated as follows:

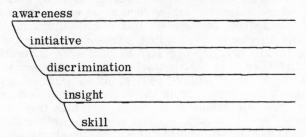

The lanes of this highway provide the learner with the opportunity to switch back and forth on the "freeway of learning"
as the need presents itself. Herein lies the role of the teacher
(director); that is, to help the singers shape attitudes which
will motivate them toward seeking further experiences in music. This objective is accomplished by the director's being
a totally effective leader technically and psychologically.

Musical Awareness

Mursell's idea of awareness concentrates upon enlightenment regarding the opportunities available to an individual
in a given situation including a wealth of musical experiences

evolving from expressive meanings of the music. Musical
awareness should be arresting, impelling and revealing.[4] By
the term "arresting" we may conclude that something found
in the music causes the individual to want to take a second
look at it; "impelling" should cause the learner to be drawn
into some positive action of further experience with the music; "revealing" should be the unfolding of new insights into
the aesthetic qualities and technical matters necessary to realize the essence of the music being studied.

Pursuing these clues further in terms of the ensemble
experience, one may recognize that this notion can be refined
to identify such a response as awareness of specific problems
in a piece of music. Further, one's attention can be arrested
by theoretical problems, such as intervals, strange and/or
satisfying harmonies, rhythmic problems or attractive rhythmic figures, interesting or difficult melodic lines, just to
name a few possibilities. These points of awareness, then,
lead to the next logical response on the part of the singer.

Musical Initiative

When the singer's attention is arrested by awareness
in any of the several areas of thought or experience mentioned, the natural response is that of initiating some action
to further inquiry or exploration. One must strike out for
oneself toward fulfilling a desire to gain more understanding
and satisfaction. In the ensemble situation, the singers will
want to refine their ability, as a group and individually, to
"negotiate" the notes, and in the process, experience the
deeper, intrinsic values of the music to which they have been
exposed. This is a further illustration of the "impelling"
factor which Mursell suggests above. It produces initiative
on the part of the learner. Musical initiative will lead to
self-discovery, self-revelation and a growing resourcefulness,
even in the group dynamic. Mursell goes on to state that
growth in musical initiative is a continuous process which
leads naturally to musical independence.[5] In other words,
one is impelled farther along the "musical expressway."

Musical Discrimination

The action of musical initiative logically leads to musical discrimination, i.e., the pursuit of improved tone quality, vocal technique, sight-singing, etc.

> There is only one possible basis for musical dis-
> crimination, and that is responsiveness to the con-
> stitutive values of the art of music.... The great
> obstacles to the acquisition of musical skills are
> not manipulative, but psychological. 6

This process of discrimination will also lead to preferences,
such as "I like this selection very much," or, "I don't think
this piece has as much to offer as I would like."

In terms of the technological aspect of learning, discrimination should lead to the discernment of factors, such
as, "I sang that note too high or too low"; or, "Now I have
a better understanding of the distance between those two
notes." Moreover, in learning how to sing more efficiently,
ensemble members may begin to discriminate between a tight
jaw resulting in a pinched tone and the new experience of how
to release tension in the oral cavity. There are many other
examples of musical discrimination available if the reader
will contemplate the responses and applications to this concept. Being able to discriminate is the natural path of re-
vealing--a development which leads to the next lane of the
highway.

Musical Insight

This concept might be described as "Aha, now I see
what it is all about!" It is the culmination of the three previous experiences cited above, which reveal the deeper values
inherent in the music, or the better understanding of the technical factors which improve one's performance of the music.
In other words, the light begins to dawn in areas where the
singers are still striving to improve their understanding and
skills. An example of this might be to encounter an elusive
intervalic skip in the choral score and become aware of the
fact that one now understands a method by which that interval
can be identified. Other illustrations might be to imagine the
emotional quality of the tone which the director is seeking;
or that the correct posture can lead to more efficient vocal
production; or to understand the correct rhythmic feel of the
music.

Musical Skill

The final consequence of experiencing these paths of

musical growth is skill. Skill is achieved as a result of the
natural evolution described above. It cannot be realized before insight takes place. Optimal learning is emphasized
only when there is practical application of the preceding experiences on the part of the learner.

> ... [T]he process of learning must be the process
> of clarifying that goal, not merely stumbling in a
> fog. 7

Lasting skill must emerge from the musical experiences,
ideally, from the music itself.

THE PATHS OF GROWTH APPLIED TO
THE CHORAL SITUATION

In further identifying the paths of musical growth with the
choral ensemble, let us construct some hypothetical experiences as examples:

1. Musical Consciousness (Awareness). The choir
is introduced to a new musical selection which is contemporary in harmonic texture--a distinct departure from the
Baroque, Classic and Romantic repertoire which they feel
secure in singing. This "new style" of music calls for careful planning on the part of the director. He or she must explain that the sound will have a different texture and will be
more difficult to read--and learn--because of the complexity
of the "awkward" intervals and close harmony. The singers
need some orientation as to why this music is more difficult
to "digest"; that the close harmony is a result of the series
of natural overtones carried to much further development
than the music of the Romantic period; that these overtones
transposed down next to the fundamental tones from which
they derived and cause the so-called dissonances. They need
to be challenged to master the more difficult music to which
they are now exposed. They also need to be able to per-
ceive the composition as a whole--although it may be only a
rough "picture" of the work at this point in their exposure.
(This theory will be discussed in its application in Chapter 3
as the concept of synthesis-analysis-synthesis is discussed.)
The consciousness (awareness) of various aspects of the whole
(composition) should initiate a positive response to this experience.

It is important again at this juncture to recognize that

musical growth is a gradual, evolving process which requires
time, with each person learning at his or her own pace. "Instant learning" may only appear to happen. Rather, learning
is only achieved when insight has been gained; when there has
been mastery through experience and when all of the parts
are recognized as a whole. This is what is meant by the
term "learning readiness."

2. Musical Application (Initiative). Ideally, the response to this musical selection should evoke a desire on the
part of the singers to explore it further. The teacher must
guide the choristers toward keeping the "whole" in mind, as
the separate parts are examined and problems are being
solved. The director should always return to the "whole"
(synthesis) after pursuing the analysis process; that is, concentrating upon any one or more problems in the music during
the analysis (problem-solving) efforts, yet keeping in mind
that the view of the whole piece is the most important objective. At this juncture, motivation of the singers is of vital
importance. (This will be further developed in Chapter 3).
Individual work on the music by the singers is most desirable, but should always be done in the context of how their
part relates to the other voices in the ensemble.

3. Musical Discernment (Discrimination). Here, the
singers begin to discern the correct from the incorrect notes;
or what may be the preferable tempo or dynamic range of a
phrase; or how to negotiate notes properly with acceptable
vocal technique. It is highly unlikely that optimum results
will be achieved immediately, but efforts should continually
be made by the director to assist the singers in developing
their discriminitive powers.

4. Musical Cognition (Insight). At last the singers
are consciously experiencing the proper response to the conductor's demands in terms of correct notes and musical expression. They are now able to solve the mental and physical requirements necessary to sing this complex style of
music.

5. Musical Proficiency (Skill). Finally, the singers
are able to approach the music with confidence. While not
every note may be perfectly produced or negotiated, the overall experience is a satisfactory one, producing a sensitive
reading of the musical selection.

It is of utmost importance here to recognize that these

areas of growth interact, and that as proficiency (skill) is
achieved in some spheres, the various paths will produce
new responses. That is to say, development of proficiency
(skill) in one area produces new consciousness (awareness),
further application of effort (initiative), a new sense of discernment (discrimination), additional cognition (insight), leading to further proficiency (skill). The paths of the five-lane
highway constantly interact and change lanes, progressively
revealing new musical knowledge.

THE NEED FOR EFFECTIVE VOCAL PEDAGOGY
IN TRAINING CHORAL ENSEMBLES

On the surface, the title for this section seems ridiculously
obvious. Of course, choral ensemble members as well as
their conductors readily admit that good choral sound is fundamental to the basic morale of the group as well as to its
audience. Yet, many choral directors are significantly ignorant as to the function of the voice. The need for more
intensive training in vocal pedagogy, particularly in better
understanding of the vocal mechanism and its limitations,
is underscored by Leon Thurman in an article in the American Choral Directors Journal. He laments the neglect of
proper training among choral directors by concluding:

> We need to learn as much as we can about good,
> healthy singing techniques and teach them as the
> core of our vocal-choral program. [8]

There exists a wide variety of concepts of good choral
tone and how to achieve optimum results. Many high school
conductors utilize what may be termed the "soft-tone" approach, so that the voices may not be abused. Other directors tend to drive the young voices very hard, producing
harsh, strained tones in an attempt to get larger, more mature sounds.

Choral tone or timbre may be categorized into three
broad areas of identification:

1. "Straight tone"--no vibrato permitted
2. "Laissez-faire"--vibrato encouraged, even re-
    quired
3. "Sonorous-blend tone"--controlled vibrato tone
    through accurate vowel production.

Chapter 4 will elaborate on this subject. A specific approach to vocal pedagogy will be discussed which is based upon the pure vowel concept as described in number three above.

PRINCIPLES OF TEACHING SIGHT-SINGING IN CHORAL ENSEMBLES
And Improving the Ability (Skill) to Sing at Sight

Often, the approach to sight-singing by choral directors is mechanical and boring for the singers whose raison d'être is to SING. Learning to sight-read and improving the skill for an understanding of the basic theory of music are parts of a long-term process--one which requires time, patience and, above all, practice.

Many choral directors set aside rehearsal time to "teach" sight-singing. Actually, every new song should be utilized to teach sight-singing rather than learning it by rote. Instead of relying upon the pianist to play the notes for the choir, the singers should be encouraged to become more independent of the keyboard and to be aggressive in pursuit of the notes--even at the risk of making mistakes. The choristers should be taught to identify such intervals as octaves, seconds, thirds, fourths, fifths, and so on. For instance, the director should call attention to thirds as line to line or space to space, or seconds as a line to a space or a space to a line on the staff of their choral scores, hearing--then identifying--these intervals. Moreover, as they are singing, the director should verbally identify the skips with their intervalic names so as to be constantly reinforcing the concept of thinking and hearing intervals. The singers should progress slowly and carefully as they proceed over the notes to be learned. They should be told to listen very carefully in order to determine whether or not they are singing the correct pitches.

A further practical comment should be made, however. In instances in which the piano has always been used as a crutch for the singers, there should be a gradual withdrawal, so as not to leave them floundering. Instead, the keyboard can be used to outline harmonic contours in diatonic music or to reinforce certain awkward intervals, or to aid singers when the musical progression tends to break down altogether. The main point to be stressed to the singers is that they are not considered to be stupid if they cannot read musical notation very well--or at all. It should be explained to them that learning to read music is analogous to learning a new language. This is the point at which the teacher (director) must turn salesperson by pointing out that, if one can hear well enough to repeat a melody correctly, one is already on the road to understanding how to read music by sight. Hearing intervals (note relationships) is the first step to sight-singing. The Five-Lane Highway sequence of learning outlines the sequence of learning in the process of learning to sing at sight. It needs to be stressed repeatedly that proficiency in sight-singing takes time, perseverance and patience on the part of both student and teacher (choral director).

Improving Sight-singing Skills

When the basic theory of sight-singing is within grasp of singers who have not yet developed this skill, the director needs to patiently nurture their growth. Many choral singers have been exposed to the basic theory of sight-singing sometime during their lives, but rarely have they been encouraged to develop a clearer understanding of how to apply it to the abstract grouping of notes. Moreover, they have not been encouraged to be aggressive about sight-singing because they and the director fear they will make too many mistakes. Since someone has always been at the piano "plucking out" their notes, they have probably memorized the music by rote --never having exercised their knowledge of spatial or rhythmic relationships. They should be encouraged to "sing out" and hear their mistakes, since that is the means by which they can make a comparison, i.e., "Did I sing too high or too low?" When this approach to sight-singing (reading) is utilized, the singers begin to develop confidence in their ability to read the notes, rather than to learn them by rote.

One very important psychological point to emphasize again is that a conductor should never imply that any one person or the group as a whole is rather dull. A remark about a notational or rhythmic problem, such as, "That's easy! Why can't you get that?!" insults the singers and erodes their self-confidence. Instead, a remark to the effect that, "This is a bit tricky, isn't it? Let's analyze it and figure out where the problem is," can keep the singers' egos intact. It is effective pedagogy to have the group as a whole (or section) gather insight as to how to solve a given problem, i.e., all sections join in singing the problem area if the tessitura permits; or altos with basses and tenors with sopranos, helping each other with their parts.

Various aids in notational or rhythmic problems will be cited in Chapter 5 to reinforce learning.

It should be stressed that the choral experience can be a valuable and enjoyable means of teaching the elements of music and also advancing concepts of music theory in addition to preparing music for concert performance.

NOTES

1. James R. Mursell, Education for Musical Growth (Boston: Ginn, 1948), p. v, Preface.
2. James R. Mursell, Basic Concepts in Music Education, Fifty-seventh Yearbook of the National Society for the Study of Education, Nelson B. Henry, editor, distributed by University of Chicago Press, 1958, p. 148.
3. James R. Mursell, Education for Musical Growth, loc. cit., p. 126.
4. Ibid., pp. 144-146.
5. Ibid., pp. 166-167.
6. Ibid., p. 174.
7. Ibid., p. 222.
8. Leon Thurman, "Voices," The Choral Journal, Lawton, Oklahoma, H. Judson Troop, ed. (October 1979), Vol. XX, No. 2, p. 11.

REVIEW QUESTIONS FOR CHAPTER 2

(1) Define the "mechanistic approach" to (music) education.

(2) Define the "developmental approach" to (music) education.

(3) What is meant by the term "learning readiness"?

(4) Cite the five avenues of musical growth and the five-lane highway of learning.

(5) Cite some individual (personal) examples of the five avenues of musical growth which you can identify in your past training and experience.

(6) What are the applications of these avenues to the choral situation?

(7) Why is there a specific need for effective vocal pedagogy in training choral ensembles?

(8) What is the basic reason why singers do not sight-read music readily?

● Chapter 3:
THE CONDUCTOR'S ROLE:
SERVING THE SINGER'S NEEDS

The topic of motivation embraces a very complex set of concerns that tend to influence the attitudes of ensemble singers. The aim of this chapter is to examine motivation in a simple and usable manner as it applies to the choral situation.

MOTIVATION

A fundamental concept of human relationships is that everyone has a basic desire to be accepted and loved. In the hierarchy of our needs are five categories which may be defined as these:

1. "Physiological" needs--those basic biological needs that when satisfied, permit us to seek "higher" social goals.
2. Safety needs--those concerns which may affect us from our environment, and also, when not threatening, permit us to seek "higher" social goals.
3. Love needs--to gain affection from family and peers.
4. Esteem needs--to gain acceptance from other persons in our environment leading to self-confidence.
5. Self-actualization--to become everything that one is capable of being. [1]

In most instances, persons who sing in choral groups are relatively free of physiological and safety concerns. Their drives tend toward gaining love and esteem and achieving self-actualization.

Stacey and DeMartino have developed the concept above into another pattern which brings this discussion into sharper

focus.   They outline three types or levels of driving forces
or urges, which are recognized as human needs:

> I.   Fundamental characteristics of adjustment:
>   a) drive toward success
>   b) drive toward the familiar
>   c) drive toward new experiences
>
> II. Appetites and aversions:
>   a) food-hunger
>   b) sex-hunger
>   c) excretion-hunger
>   d) specific contact-hunger
>   e) rest-hunger
>   f) sensory motor-hunger
>   g) fright (injury-avoidance)
>   h) pugnacity (interference-avoidance)
>
> III. Derived drives:
>   a) desire to be with others
>   b) desire for attention from other persons
>   c) desire for praise and approval
>   d) desire to be a cause
>   e) desire for mastery[2]

In this book we shall be concerned primarily with items I
and III and how they apply to the choral situation.

Further consideration of this subject should include
success and failure as it involves the choral experience in
terms of aspiration.

> Not only is the level of aspiration fundamental for
> the experience of success and failure, but the level
> of aspiration itself is changed by success and fail-
> ure. [3]

Stacey and DeMartino claim that after success, a person
usually tends to set a higher goal, and if there is failure
in an endeavor, the level of aspiration generally diminishes. [4]

We have stated previously that the physiological needs
of the individual, such as hunger, safety, etc., are of less
concern to this discussion than are the psychological ones.
In the realm of group activity, the psychological needs, however great in number and magnitude, basically involve acceptance by peers and leader, along with a "sense of belonging, "

i. e. , being an accepted member of the group. 5 This involves
the concept of self-esteem (self-respect) and self-actualization; that is, "what a person can be, he must be, " according
to Maslow. 6 Thus, we may conclude that certain conscious
and unconscious needs elicit drives toward determined goals,
which in turn become motives for particular actions and reactions.

Another view of this complex subject might be to re-
group them in the following manner:

1. Success/mastery/new experiences
2. Attention/praise/approval
3. Enjoyment of being with others

These are the items of motivation that strongly influence the
reasons for persons to join together in the activity of group
singing.

The desire to move from the known to the unknown
and again to the known, must be recognized as a strong motivating force in education (including the church choir experience). We progress from previous knowledge to the new
problem (unknown), which, when solved (known), provides
the initiative to once again seek the unknown.

Of further concern to the choral director are the various levels of aspiration of the singers. The homogeneous
ensemble can be expected to have a somewhat equal level of
aspiration, whereas the heterogeneous group of singers may
vary widely in their expectations. As an example, this writer's Bach Chorus is a homogeneous group of singers dedicated
to singing the compositions of the Bach family of musicians.
In contrast, his College Singers entertain a wide variety of
tastes and abilities. This condition demands an entirely different set of plans and functions through a variety of compositions of many periods and styles of music. The conductor
who is sensitive to the various capabilities and tastes among
the ensemble members can avoid some serious mistakes in
planning and working with non-specialized ensembles.

THE DRIVE TOWARD SUCCESS

Following the outline of Stacey and DeMartino, the element
of success holds a top priority of need for the average chorister as he/she seeks a successful, rewarding experience
through the group dynamic.

The need for individual aesthetic expression in the arts
is greater than appears on the surface. For most individuals
the group dynamic supplies the security which all "grass
roots" singers need in order to realize success in their quest
for artistic expression. Most of these singers would be reluctant to stand alone and sing a solo. However, in the security of the group, their inadequacies are absorbed by the
total efforts of the ensemble. This kind of effort toward
self-expression becomes a non-threatening opportunity to realize aesthetic experiences on a level which most singers
can never achieve alone.

A case in point is the example of classic works, such
as Handel's MESSIAH or J. S. Bach's Mass in B-minor.
Very few individuals in choral groups that perform these
works could sing the solos and duets effectively. Yet, as
members of a fine ensemble, they can perform the choruses
at a level equaling--or sometimes surpassing--that of the
professional soloists. Thus, "ordinary" singers can achieve
a degree of artistic expression far above their individual capabilities. It may be said that this is the raison d'être for
ensemble participation.

Expressing oneself in music via the group dynamic
acts as an integrating and socializing agency. It provides
a suitable, concerted effort to achieve a specific goal. The
non-threatening atmosphere of the ensemble can be intimate,
enjoyable and expressive, thus serving many ancillary needs
of the individual member with the group. This underscores
the joy of working together in the group dynamic.

The successful concert performance is a kind of communal reward for the participants. The group has worked hard
to prepare the music for presentation to an audience. Thus,
the performance is the apex of all of the effort expended to
seek the enjoyment of the music's message. Also, there is
a natural desire to celebrate--to experience an after-glow
together. To go directly home or to one's home or room
immediately following a public performance is to invite lone-
liness and possible depression--a sudden "let-down." People
need to share their reactions concerning the good or even
not-so-good moments during the concert. The director might
do well to arrange for a post-performance "get-together" of
some sort with refreshments for the group.

The realization of learning something new and valuable
in the rehearsal situation provides strong impetus for good

morale and certainly a reward for the singers, Fortunate, indeed, is the choral director whose members fear missing a rehearsal lest they are deprived of some valuable information regarding vocal pedagogy, music history, theory or style-- and the sheer pleasure and satisfaction of progressing musically.

THE DRIVE TOWARD THE FAMILIAR

Despite the fact that choristers may seek to learn something new and valuable, there is still a need to experience the familiar. This element reinforces the personal egos of the singers in contrast to a continuous diet of new, unfamiliar musical confrontations. Interspersing music which may be rather easily "digested," serves to alleviate some of the frustrations of the unfamiliar, difficult selections in a given repertoire. It permits the ensemble to delve more readily into interpretative elements of the music and thus gain satisfaction (again reflecting the element of success-reward) for their efforts.

THE DRIVE TOWARD NEW EXPERIENCES

The feeling of success derived from learning something new finalizes the trio of fundamental characteristics of adjustment. However, this realm of activity requires the ensemble director to be astute in selecting repertoire that will challenge the singers, yet not be too difficult for them to envision a concept of the whole--rough though it might be. Therefore, it is imperative that the choice of music be suitable to the vocal and musical capabilities of the group. The director must also develop the technique of rehearsing the music efficiently, so as to maintain interest while solving the problems encountered in the musical score. The director must figuratively roll up his/her sleeves and work with the ensemble to achieve the goal of mastering the technical elements of the music, then moving on to the intrinsic, interpretative aspects lying inherent on the printed page. This is not to suggest that some interpretative factors be left until all of the technical elements are mastered. The egos of the singers must always be kept in mind and preserved as much as possible.

DERIVED DRIVES

1. Desire to be with other persons. The social setting of

the choral ensemble should be of utmost concern to the director.   In all choral situations, the element of social inter-
course is derived from the fact that in a successful choir,
the singers must lose their individual identities in their efforts to achieve a successful whole.   Ensemble singers, who
are unable to experience this condition, are usually frustrated
members of the group.   The choir must be a "melting pot"
wherein the more proficient singers recognize that they are
no more important than the less skilled members.   The
"stars" should not be entitled to any special treatment by
the director or the rest of the singers.

2.   Desire for attention from other persons.   Even
the "lowliest" of the singers ideally should be accepted by
his or her peers.   However, in some school choirs persons
feeling inferior to other singers may present problems by
exhibiting behavior which attempts to draw attention to themselves, such as excessive talking to neighbors and making
unnecessary comments or criticisms about the director, the
music or the other singers.   This condition may well present
the director with some difficult discipline problems, which
likely will require special attention on an individual basis
with an offender.

3.   Desire for praise and approval.   It is of utmost
importance for the director to compliment the ensemble as
a whole for even the smallest evidence of achievement.
Ideally, something positive can be said about every rehearsal,
and certainly every performance.   Approval for efforts expended is a significant need for each individual as he/she
feels a part of the group's achievement.   However, compli-
menting (singling out) individuals for specific reasons should
be handled with care.   When a soloist performs outstandingly
in rehearsal or concert, it is often proper to acknowledge
the effort with a verbal comment by the director or applause
by all.   In principle, the compliment must be deserved.

4.   Desire to be a cause.   When a choral ensemble
achieves a certain level of success in a rehearsal or presents a satisfactory program, each member has a right to
feel part of what caused the success.   Every person, regardless of ability, should share in the feeling of the ensemble's
achievement.   The entire group should receive any accolades.

5.   Desire for mastery.   This condition refers specifically to an earlier comment cited by Stacey and DeMartino,
wherein a person usually tends to set a higher goal after

realizing success in a given sphere of activity, then going on to additional achievements. Conversely, failure usually diminishes the level of aspiration. Everyone desires to be a part of a successful venture with which he/she is associated. Constant failure or disappointment is ruinous to anyone's morale.

However, a tangential factor should be considered here. That is, how strong is the drive toward one's goal? Is the reward for successful achievement sufficient to cause the individual(s) to continue to pursue a goal for the sake of the prized reward? It is possible that initial failure may intensify an individual's drive to reach a certain highly desired goal. For instance, if an individual fails to qualify for a select group of singers, he or she may work more diligently so as to be selected for the ensemble at the next audition; or an ensemble might work much more diligently to achieve a higher festival rating or approval from an audience.

GOALS

Choral directors should have specific long and short term goals for themselves and their ensembles. These goals should be realistic--within the realm of the singers' abilities.

1. The long term goals should include such objectives as improved tone quality and intonation, ensemble feeling, correct phrasing, clear enunciation and improved sight reading ability. Also, an appreciation for varied styles in the successive periods of music should be emphasized by the conductor.

2. The short term goals may be identified as rehearsal techniques to perfect the performance of the music: finding correct notes, solving specific vocal problems, dynamic ranges of the music being rehearsed, introducing theoretical concepts found in the music, and in general, utilizing the music itself to achieve progress toward the long term goals. Specific application to these matters will be considered in future chapters.

However, there are some by-product factors which may emerge in the pursuit of these goals. These factors may lead to frustrations among the singers, especially in ensembles in which there is a wide diversity of talent or training:

1. Goals that are too far advanced for some singers
    may cause them to become discouraged and drop
    out. The alert director will need to sense this
    condition in some members of a heterogeneous
    ensemble. Attention to individuals in small groups
    in "therapeutic" rehearsal sessions (or individual
    tutelage) may be needed.

2. Goals that do not permit some of the advanced
    singers to perform at their level of expertise,
    can be exasperating for them. These persons
    could be employed as remedial workers for the
    singers who need special help.

3. Some ensemble singers may not be satisfied with
    what may appear to be a lack of personal and/or
    group success--recognition by others. These are
    persons who find it to be difficult to lose their
    singular identities in the group dynamic--particu-
    larly large choral forces, in contrast to small
    chamber choirs. When a large choral ensemble
    achieves outstanding recognition for its achieve-
    ments, these persons may then find satisfaction
    in being a part of the endeavor. Otherwise they
    will drop out of the group.

WHOLE VERSUS PART LEARNING
(Synthesis-Analysis-Synthesis)

This subject plays a significant role in the continued motivation of the singers. It involves the notion of the Gestalt
theory of learning (see Chapter 2). As we know, the general concept of the Gestalt approach is that the whole is
greater than the sum of the parts. It may be illustrated
by the example of three workers who were asked what they
were doing. One said, "I am laying bricks"; the second
said, "I'm building a wall"; the third said, "I am building a
house." All three of them were adept at laying bricks. However, the first two had not perceived their efforts in terms
of the whole.

Likewise, the choral singers' overall view of their
efforts should be to experience a complete synthesis of the
music--a concept of the whole composition. This whole, although only roughly comprehended at first, must be refined
through each encounter with the music. The "vision" of the

tout ensemble must not be lost while seeking to solve the specific problems found in the music--as important as these
problems may be. In analogous terms, the director and the
singers must not lose sight of the proverbial forest because
of seeing only the individual trees. Again, this underscores
the need to understand the process of Synthesis-Analysis-
Synthesis in learning. To assume that an individual or group
can "polish up" a few bars of music, or develop a specific
skill, and then put it "on the shelf" to be utilized later, is
an entirely false concept. What is referred to here is the
practice of some directors who frequently work on minute
details or errors before the composition has been sung
through (synthesized) for the first time. The singers need
to experience an over-all view of the whole before working
on the parts. Some directors rehearse a musical selection
by "polishing" each phrase chronologically, assuming that a
phrase learned early in the sequence of rehearsals will still
be fresh in the singers' minds at a later time. They do not
realize that there is loss of memory and skill when parts
are not reviewed from time to time. (Specific application
and illustrations of S-A-S will be discussed in Chapter 6.)

Human beings are very complex entities--far more
so than science has been able to decipher. The aspects of
human personality are not fully understood by the psychological and physical sciences. Our bodily cells are composed
of atoms which are really nothing more than energy. We
are the mystery of electromagnetism. We have conflicting
responses to our daily life experiences of joy, awe, wonder,
love, compassion, tenderness, etc. We also have feelings
of anger, greed, anguish, terror, lust, gluttony, envy, jeal-
ousy, pride and vanity. Therefore, we must seek to become
sensitive to the creative forces within ourselves so as to experience the higher values in life, such as artistic endeavor.

These feelings (emotions), as related to musical in-
volvement, revolve uncontrollably around the events in our
various life-activities. We find tensions and resolutions of
them in our everyday experiences. However, they may be
more "programmed" for us in artistic expression, such as
through music wedded with text. For instance, there are
musical "dissonances" and harmonic suspensions, which give
added dimension to the total effect of a choral composition.
The text of choral and vocal compositions provides a dimension beyond the scope of instrumental compositions. The
harmonic, melodic and rhythmic components of the music
emphasize (deepen) the message of the text. Therefore, the

choral director must capitalize upon this opportunity to achieve artistic expression, bringing to the surface the intrinsic values of the composite whole--music and text; this to be accomplished without becoming bogged down in sentimentality or over-indulgence in technical maneuvering.

Earlier statements in this book have referred to the need for the choral conductor to consider the relationship of emotion to learning.   Examining in further detail some of the factors that influence learning through emotions, we may recognize the following:

1.   A positive response to the learning situation is undoubtedly viewed by educators as being a fundamental requisite to effective learning.   Yet, in rehearsal, the director's role is essentially a negative one, pointing out errors of omission and commission.   Therefore, the conductor must seek to couch his attitude and remarks in as positive a manner as possible, avoiding ridicule or the "putting down" of the group or individuals in it.

The director should always avoid remarks such as, "What is wrong with you?" or "That's easy to get," implying that the group, or some individuals in it, are unintelligent --or at best, rather slow.   Often, asking a constructive question will help singers solve their own problems, such as, "What is the correct note for you tenors to sing at bar fifteen?"   This approach will tend to help singers develop sharper insight into the process of sight-singing and still maintain their self-confidence and personal integrity.

2.   If the rehearsal is boring to the group, the cause may stem from any number of factors.   It may be that

a.   as cited above, the music may seem to be too difficult for the group to grasp in stride.   Consequently, the director must develop a repertoire of effective rehearsal techniques to maintain interest while the ensemble labors to learn the music.   (If the score is unquestionably beyond the ability of the ensemble's potential, the director's choice has been wrong.)

b.   the music and/or text may not be interesting to the singers.   Thus, the choice of repertoire is crucial to the intellectual and technical level of the ensemble.

    c. a director's lack of enthusiasm for the music being studied can elicit boredom. Hence, his or her enthusiasm for seeking the intrinsic values of the music (and text) over and above the technical elements is of vital importance.

    d. the pace of the rehearsal may be too slow because the director is not adept at solving problems accruing in the rehearsal. The conductor must develop the skill to keep the rehearsal moving by avoiding long pauses while making decisions or by talking too much.

The director's ability to anticipate, identify and resolve problems, which may occur in the rehearsal, is crucial to the morale of the ensemble. Technical proficiency (musicianship) has a great influence upon the attitude of the learners, and it behooves the director to develop his/her musical savvy and techniques of problem-solving to a significant degree so as to avoid boredom and discouragement among the singers.

3. Creative teaching through sensitive interpretation of the music should generate positive emotional responses. In the area of performance, the aesthetic values of the music, expressively presented, become a capstone of satisfaction for the hours of labor which are required for preparation of a program. The director, who leads with vitality, enthusiasm and a sense of discovery, surely will elicit positive emotional responses. The conductor must determine how a particular phrase or section of a composition should be interpreted, and then attempt to bring the group's performance to that level of expression.

The optimum learning situation is a gradual, cyclical exposure of the whole. The Synthesis-Analysis-Synthesis approach to learning enables the ensemble members to experience gradual improvement in the music being studied as they keep the total composition in mind. By synthesizing the entire selection at appropriate times, the ensemble's morale is enhanced, because the members can recognize and appreciate their progress in terms of the whole composition. Consequently, the concept of the whole musical work is maintained all the while the parts are being learned. (See Chapter 6 for more discussion of this topic.)

INDIVIDUAL DIFFERENCES

Of prime concern to the conductor-teacher is the recognition
that a group of singers may be comprised of individuals whose
talents and attitudes differ substantially from one another.
This condition presents special problems and/or concerns
for the director.

In reflecting upon the average group of singers, we
find that the ability of the members to sing with good or acceptable tone quality can range from poor to outstanding.
Also, the ability to sing the music at sight varies widely.
We can compare the gradation of musical talents analogously
to sports activities. Those with a natural proclivity toward
the use of their muscles in football, baseball, tennis or golf
are able to perform acceptably--even without special tutoring.
However, with proper instruction, these athletes usually become outstanding sports performers. Conversely, muscularly
uncoordinated persons in sports activities require a great
amount of instruction to be able to function at a satisfactory
level. Even then, they usually do not excel to the degree
of distinction comparable to the naturally coordinated athlete.
It is rare when such persons rise to the level of the "natural" athlete, even though the instruction may have improved
their actions to a noticeable degree. On a scale of 0-100,
the person beginning at 50 or above certainly has a better
chance of reaching near the 100 mark than the person beginning much lower on the scale. Likewise, applying the
singer-musician to this analogy, the level of achievement
ratio is similar. Certain singers will never be especially
outstanding, but all of them can improve with good instruction. Thus, they will enjoy a significant degree of satisfaction from their efforts.

As cited previously, the outstanding singer-musicians
usually become the leaders of their sections, and if they are
not conceited or arrogant about their abilities, they will be
admired by their peers. They may assist the progress of
their ensemble in several ways:

1. Leading section rehearsals, if this technique is
   utilized by the director;

2. Vocalizing the group in warm-ups;

3. Generally acting as a catalyst for a positive feeling toward the rehearsal situation;

4. Singing solos where needed, or participating in soli groups and smaller ensembles;

5. Acting as tutors to those who need extra help.

Directors should provide the means by which the singers can voice their opinions and concerns. All too often the conductor is unaware of the negative feelings which may develop among members of an ensemble. These feelings of frustration may simmer for long periods of time, often leading to attrition from the organization. Some means for solving this problem are these:

1. Establishing regular office hours when members may come in for conversation or confrontation with the director about their concerns or grievances;

2. Allowing or encouraging singers to make suggestions during rehearsals. However, this must be handled carefully, because it can impede rehearsal efficiency. It can also cause some psychological problems as to who is in charge of the group. It all depends upon the kind of questions asked, or the suggestions given, as well as the manner in which the person presents them. If the singer who speaks up in rehearsal exhibits respect for the director in tone and manner, the director can utilize the comment(s) in a positive way. Conversely, negative criticism may invoke a strained atmosphere, which needs to be handled personally at a later time with the "attacker." The director, encountering this situation, needs to assess his or her own capabilities regarding the situation as to whether the "attacker" has a valid criticism. Yet, this policy works well for some directors, who are able to adroitly handle suggestions and questions from their members during rehearsals;

3. Encouraging members to air their concerns to the organization's officers, or to an ombudsman selected for that purpose;

4. Having a suggestion or "gripe" box for members to express their concerns. Most ensemble members who feel the need to express their opinions, gripes, etc., prefer anonymity, so the suggestion or "gripe" box provides an ideal outlet for them.

Singers in ensembles that have rigid requirements for membership may be reluctant to complain or offer suggestions to the director. Some fear that they will be dismissed from the organization if they ask questions or appear to be critical of the director or organization. However, the conductor who is in full control of the group can encourage comments which are emphasized as being made for the welfare of the group and not the individual member.

The most significant point to remember is that the conductor must respect each member of the organization as an individual, especially since it is necessary for each singer to submerge his or her personality in the effort to achieve ensemble unity. This notion needs to be underscored again and again, for it is one of the most important aspects of the group dynamic that any director must embrace. The conductor must have a positive approach in making corrective comments in a rehearsal. Above all, having a good sense of humor and being able to laugh at oneself is imperative. These are all-important ingredients necessary for establishing and maintaining a good rehearsal atmosphere.

Special Concerns

In choral situations in which there are persons on a membership waiting list, the director has significantly different motivational concerns from the conductor who must rely upon the "good will" of those who are recruited to sing with few, if any prerequisites. If the director must labor under the realization that some members think they are so advanced and are doing everyone a favor by singing in the group, that conductor's position of leadership is surely threatened. If the ensemble is vocally and/or musically weak, these "special people" can pose a problem. In no way does this imply that all advanced singer-musicians will be a problem to a director. Yet every conductor should be aware of the possible threat of this problem occurring, particularly in the church choir situation.

Most choral directors must face the problem of motivating a group of "less talented" choral singers at some time during their careers. However, given time, an exceptionally resourceful musician-teacher can build an acceptable group of singers from even a poor ensemble.

Motivating the Select Ensemble Personnel

When a singing group has achieved enough distinction
to have more persons desiring to participate in it than can
be accommodated, motivational problems among the singers
may concern the following:

1. Equal opportunity to demonstrate their capabilities
for solos and leadership roles should be available to all members. Seniority may well be a strong factor in choosing soloists and section leaders. However, continually assigning
solos to the same persons, while ignoring others, could well
cause resentment if the "neglected ones" are also reasonably
strong, reliable performers. Obviously, there can be no
formula established for selecting soloists. That decision
must be carefully handled by the director in relation to the
personnel of the group.

One choral conductor, known to this writer, has members of his organization choose his soloists by secret ballot
vote. He has found this to be very successful in avoiding
"favoritism" in regard to the selection of his soloists. He
claims that his singers are very objective, and as a consequence, it is a much more democratic means of selection
than a director's "authoritarian" decisions. He states that
personal popularity is rarely a factor in the choices. In
fact, he utilizes this practice in all of his groups--not only
with his select ensembles. He asks for volunteers to audition for the solo parts of a piece, having them sing their
portion during rehearsals. This may occur over a period
of several rehearsals. Then, he asks the group to vote on
their choice, confident that they have good judgment in the
matter. Being part of the decision-making process eliminates negative competitive attitudes. A disadvantage of this
process may be that persons auditioning last have an advantage over the first or early aspirants in that the later audi-
tionees can profit by the performance of the earlier ones.
The main principle should be, however, to spread the solo
(soli) parts as widely as possible among the membership of
the group.

2. Maintaining high standards requires that the conductor must command the musical respect of the singers. A
thorough knowledge of the score and attention to detail set the
standard for the ensemble to follow. The group will aspire
only to the level of quality which the director sets, both technically and interpretatively. Thus, the conductor must be

more than a highly competent technician in the field of music.   One must also become a sensitive interpreter (of the
music), delving deeply into the intrinsic musical values of
the score--that abstract entity which "comes into being" only
after it is translated into sound.

3.   Performance opportunities of a reasonable number
are important in order to maintain a high degree of motivation.   However, some proud, eager directors schedule too
many performances, and sooner or later some members may
begin to resent this exploitation.   This situation sometimes
exists in outstanding high school ensembles.   As a result,
some students refuse to join college-university groups because
they fear repeated exploitation.

4.   A high degree of musical challenge in regard to
repertoire is necessary to maintain a consistent, intense
level of motivation.   That is, the level of difficulty of the
music should challenge them to work beyond their present
level of musicianship.   This is not to say that none of the
repertoire may be within a relatively easy grasp so as to
give them respite from the more difficult music.   The factor
of vertical and horizontal pacing of the rehearsals comes into
play here.   Horizontal and vertical pacing refers to the amount
of time allotted to rehearsals and the difficulty and number
of musical selections to be prepared.   (This will be discussed
further in Chapter 6.)

Motivating Non-selected Singers

1.   Attaining and maintaining a high level of motivation in an ensemble consisting of singers with varying degrees
of talent and experience may well be one of the most difficult
tasks confronting a director.   The leading musician-singers
must be relied upon to "pull" their section along.   Those who
are more musically and vocally advanced may tend to become
resentful or bored because of being held back by the slower
learners.   The leaders of such a group are usually the "work
horses" of the ensemble.   Their role is to lead the way until
the music is learned.   That is not to say that the rest of the
group may not be working hard, but the latter's slower pace
of learning may become an irritation for the more musically
proficient singers.   A way to resolve this situation is to utilize the advanced singers as teaching helpers, giving special
assistance to those who need it by means of small group rehearsals, special lessons in theory or voice culture, or as
leaders for the various sections in the choir.

Section rehearsals will aid the slower learners, but normally this technique should not be used solely for "pounding out" the notes of the individual parts. Section rehearsals present an opportunity for vocal pedagogy, for achieving vocal blend within each section, and for improving musicianship among the singers. Also, not to be overlooked is the sense of camaraderie that develops as each section is cloistered in separate rooms working in unison toward these goals.

However, it is the total rehearsal "climate" which is the fundamental factor in achieving and maintaining the interest of all of the singers. The level of difficulty of the repertoire ideally should strike a "middle ground" to challenge all members. Moreover, if all of the singers are stimulated or inspired by a sensitive interpretation of the score, their interest will usually remain at a high level, despite differences of talent and experience.

2. The choice of repertoire, as mentioned earlier, for a diverse group of singers requires extreme care. The director should spend many hours of research selecting a balanced program of music which will challenge and be of interest to the majority of singers in the ensemble. The texts of the selections are also of great importance. Vocal music can be a means of exposing singers to poetic and literary masterpieces to which the singers may not otherwise be introduced. Furthermore, familiar texts can be given new meaning when set to music.

3. Homogeneous groups of poor sight-singers, on the other hand, will really prove to be less difficult to motivate if the repertoire chosen is not beyond their level of achievement. Moreover, simple, homophonic-style music readily adapts itself to effective vocal pedagogy in the rehearsal atmosphere. An alert director can use chorales, simple harmonic music and unison singing to improve tone quality and intonation--two of the major problems of "grass roots" singers.

4. Church choirs represent a classic example of the wide variety of singing ability in ensembles--both musically and vocally. Therefore, church choir directors must develop effective methods of teaching vocal and theoretical skills which benefit their singers. (There may always be some singers who do not feel the need for further instruction in theory or voice, but that is something which the director must accept.) The concept of service to the church (stewardship or duty) can go only part of the way toward maintaining

the high degree of motivation needed to achieve good results. Since most church choirs are made up of volunteers, rehearsals and performances must always strive to be rewarding, enjoyable experiences. Humor in the rehearsal is always an added catalyst for any satisfying choral experience.

5. Use of keyboard and other instrumental forces to compensate for vocal and/or musical weaknesses of choral groups needs careful consideration by the director. The temptation for many conductors is to rely too heavily upon instruments--especially the keyboard--to compensate for lack of reading skills among the singers. Thus, their growth in sight-singing tends to be stunted. Withdrawing the piano or organ from doubling the notes of the singers in rehearsals may be traumatic for them at first, but removing support will eventually enhance their ability to become more independent readers of the score. However, this keyboard withdrawal should be applied by degrees as the singers become more and more self-reliant.

6. Performances play a large role in the motivation of any ensemble. The adult church choir generally has a regular schedule of "performance" for the services. Therefore, the obligation to present inspiring musical experiences for the singers and congregation is prescribed for them. On the other hand, younger choirs frequently do not have this "built in" opportunity. To motivate these young people to sing, there is a need for them to perform in a regular place in the church service. This could be once a month singing the anthem, or more often singing choral responses, depending upon the choir's ability. In school situations the opportunity to perform for assemblies, give concerts, and even take tours, usually provides the motivation necessary to reach the goals set by the director.

Audience Appeal

The two-fold problem of music which appeals to the singers and that which receives a good response from the audience or church congregation is a significant challenge for most choral directors. The musical tastes of audiences are often at odds with the director and choir. Many conductors choose their repertoire on the basis of audience appeal only. Other conductors ignore the desires of their audience and program music only to suit their own tastes. Following are some criteria that are pertinent to the problem of balancing audience appeal with musical taste:

a.   Choose music which is within the scope of the en-
     semble's ability to perform well.   There is a vast
     resource of good music for all purposes available
     to the director who takes the time to research cat-
     alogues of publishers who will frequently send sam-
     ples of music on request or certainly single cop-
     ies of scores on approval.   Many will send sam-
     ples of their music voluntarily as it is published.
     A letter to publishers on school or church letter-
     head usually gets results in receiving sample cop-
     ies or copies on approval, except major works.
     In fact, it is advantageous to keep in mind that
     publishers are in business to sell their music,
     so they are eager to make it available to direc-
     tors.

b.   Sensitive interpretation of the music beyond the
     mere technical manipulation of attaining accuracy
     and good tone quality should be the highest objec-
     tive of every conductor; i. e. , seeking to discover
     the intrinsic values inherent in the music.

c.   Appropriate choice of church music to enhance the
     liturgical theme is most desirable.   This requires
     the cooperation of the clergy and will be discussed
     more thoroughly in Chapter 11.

d.   Aesthetic appeal is surely one of the most elusive
     elements to define for practical purposes.   The
     items (a), (b), and (c) above combine to aid in
     the audience's acceptance of the selections pre-
     sented by a given ensemble.   Moreover, the com-
     bination of audience acceptance and satisfaction by
     the ensemble that the musical performance was
     worthwhile provide the impetus for continued high
     morale for all concerned.

SUMMARY--PRINCIPLES OF LEARNING

Applying the principles related to learning which are described
in Chapters 2 and 3 is a challenging assignment.   The developmental approach to learning is much more subtle than the
"mechanistic" way, though the latter may seem more orderly
at an initial glance.   Therefore, a summary of some of the
ideals cited above may be valuable for the readers, who can
then adapt them to their own individual techniques of directing
ensembles.

From Crudeness to Precision

First of all, we should regard the rehearsal situation
as one which moves from crudeness to precision; from roughly
perceiving the whole to refining it through developing insights
into more clearly conceived patterns of action. The initial
efforts should involve the concept of synthesis-analysis-
synthesis, as has been cited in both Chapters 2 and 3. This
approach to learning tends to undergird the positive motivation of the singers. These early efforts to establish the profile of the musical selection (or a movement from a large
work) should provide a crude synthesis (view) of the composer's musical intent. Each subsequent effort to analyze specific problems during rehearsals should provide a clearer
synthesis of the whole. The application of the S-A-S principle should become a significant factor in achieving a high
level of motivation during each rehearsal. (Examples of
how this is accomplished will be shown in Chapter 6.)

Gestalt Versus the "Mechanistic" Approach

The Gestalt concept of learning states that the whole
is greater than the sum of the parts, whereas the "mechanistic approach" assumes that specific learnings and skills can
be accumulated and then utilized when needed. This latter
practice can be demoralizing because singers are not given
the opportunity to assess their progress in terms of the
whole. Moreover, when they try to employ what they thought
they had already learned, they often find that the concept or
skill has become stale. They have been merely working on
little parts of the musical selection, whereas what they should
be doing is continually experiencing an improved view of the
whole composition.

Therefore, in applying S-A-S to rehearsal technique,
the conductor should return from the analysis effort periodically to sing the entire selection (or movement), so as to
assess and experience progress in terms of the whole. We
should repeatedly synthesize the composition (the whole) as
we rehearse. It is this gradual and continual reshaping of
mental patterns which develops insight and subsequently skill.
The five-lane highway should be the subconscious format of
musical growth, cited in Chapter 2, which outlines the sequence of learning: awareness, initiative, discrimination,
insight, and finally, skill.

Again, it should be emphasized that this developmental process of learning requires patience and perseverance. Moreover, the process recognizes that individuals learn at different rates of speed, and the faster learners, particularly, need to have the satisfaction of "tasting" the whole periodically.

Again it should be emphasized that the director must be aware of the importance of recognizing individual differences in the precarious task of making the choral singers' role an overall satisfying one.

Thus, the conductor's role in serving the needs of all the singers rests upon a high degree of motivation toward their learning the music--most importantly experiencing the subtle, intrinsic values within the score. Consequently, the feelings of success can reward their efforts. Their emotions, governed by their feelings, then should be generally positive in nature.

NOTES

1. Don E. Hamachek, Human Dynamics in Psychology and Education (Boston: Allyn and Bacon, 1972), pp. 131-137 (abridged).
2. Chalmers L. Stacey and Manfred F. DeMartino, eds., Understanding Human Motivation (Cleveland: Howard Allen, 1958), p. 21.
3. Ibid., p. 224.
4. Ibid., p. 224.
5. Ibid., p. 35.
6. Ibid., p. 39.

REVIEW QUESTIONS FOR CHAPTER 3

(1) Define motivation in practical terms for yourself.

(2) What is the hierarchy of individual basic needs?

(3) What are the three types or levels of "driving forces" for an individual?

(4) Cite "derived drives" of the individual.

(5) Relate the "sense of belonging" to self-respect and self-actualization.

(6)   What are some of the frustrations experienced by en-
      semble singers?

(7)   How is the individual's ego involved in the choral en-
      semble situation?

(8)   State some motivation problems which might occur in
      a) an unskilled (weak) ensemble, b) a strong select en-
      semble.

(9)   Articulate in your own words the need for individual
      aesthetic expression.

(10) How does reward for successful ensemble experience
      relate to the individual's ego?

(11) What is significant about the individual finding aesthetic
      expression through the ensemble experience?

(12) List some long term goals of choral experience which
      enhance each individual member's motivation.

(13) List some short term goals of choral experience which
      enhance each individual member's motivation.

(14) Describe some positive approaches to the learning sit-
      uation in the choral ensemble.

(15) How should the choral director concern himself/herself
      with individual differences among the members?

(16) What is meant by the phrase "crudeness to precision"
      in regard to the musical progress of an ensemble?

PART II:

CONSIDERING THE ROLE OF
THE CHORAL SINGER

● Chapter 4:
VOCAL DEVELOPMENT OF
THE CHORAL SINGER

The choral director who knows little or nothing about vocal
pedagogy is certainly at a great disadvantage in the field,
unless the ensemble happens to be comprised of all professional singers needing little or no vocal instruction. Yet,
even with highly proficient singers, problems will arise that
require knowledge of how the vocal mechanism functions.
Moreover, it is also of great importance for the choral conductor to know how to relate the important concepts of vocal
production in practical terms which can be comprehended by
tyro as well as more advanced singers. The role of the
choral director or Minister of Music is to educate beyond
merely drilling the notes of the music. This is an opportunity, and, in fact, it is a duty, to help improve vocal technique and to acquaint the singers with the great heritage of
music stemming from the Judeo-Christian religious tradition.

The purpose of this chapter is to present an approach
to vocal pedagogy which serves the needs of the gamut of
choral singers. This writer has developed a specific system of vocal pedagogy, testing it in the "choral laboratory"
over a period of more than twenty-five years with "grass
roots" church choirs, junior and senior high school and college age choral groups, community choruses, and professional groups. This approach to vocal pedagogy is based
upon the concept that vowel purity throughout the entire scope
of the vocal range is the chief means by which vocal production is enhanced. This system of vocal pedagogy utilizes the
music currently being studied to achieve specific as well as
broad goals. However, before discussing this pedagogical
approach to singing, it seems important to examine some
concepts of choral tone.

TEXTURES OF SOUND

Varieties of Tone Quality

Almost all listeners and performers will agree that

expressive tone quality is the basic attraction of any choral group. However, tastes vary so greatly that one cannot conclude that there is a particular texture of sound which appeals to everyone; nor is there one sound that is suitable for all musical styles representing the several periods of music.

First of all, the sound represented by pop, jazz, and rock groups is usually quite different from the traditional vocal sound produced by those choral ensembles which perform the so-called standard repertoire. Even within the "standard repertoire" of choral music, there is a great difference of opinion as to what constitutes "proper" or "ideal" tone for the various periods of music history. We should observe the following periods of Western Europe's music history.

Renaissance choral music (ca. 1250-1600) generally consists of four or more unaccompanied, homogeneous voice lines of similar character and equal importance[1] in contrast to earlier music of the Middle Ages in which the melodic line (principal voice) was embellished by organum. The net effect of the Renaissance style of music is that the harmonies are predominantly the result of the melodic contours. It is imperative, therefore, that the vocal texture of this musical style be "transparent" (sans wide vibrato in the voices). Since most of Renaissance period music was written for sacred services and performed in resonant stone churches and cathedrals, the rather "sterile" vocal timbre produced sounds that permitted the individual voice lines to remain unblurred.

The Baroque period music (ca. 1600-1750) mirrors the architecture, art work, and perhaps also science and philosophy of that era. [2] Baroque music is usually ornate with many embellishments, and also reflects identifiable nationalistic characteristics (such as Italian, English, German, French and Spanish styles). Variety is evident in that in some of the compositions the music itself dominates the text (florid melismas), whereas in other instances the text dominates the music (chorales, hymns, and homophonic compositions). The role of the thorough (figured) bass and counterpoint was developed to a very high degree during this period. Baroque music also requires a "clean, " "lean" vocal texture.

The Rococo style of music (beginning about 1720) reflects the style galant dominated by Italian and French composers of that period, such as Domenico Scarlatti and Couperin,

and also the more expressive Germanic music, as characterized by C. P. E. Bach, Haydn and Mozart in their earlier
years of composing. The galant style is "elegant, playful,
witty, polished and ornate."3 Thus, the choral director must
strive for vocal clarity in singing the florid passages of this
musical style. One must also recognize the emerging simplicity of melody and harmony found in other facets of the
music of this transitional period, where greater vocal sonority is required. The Rococo style, therefore, possesses
strong elements of both the late (High) Baroque and the early
Classical periods. The characteristics of this music are
summarized by Reinhard Pauly as "... an effort to overcome
even more formal and stiff setting of the previous age."4 It
was a very transient, short period embracing the gamut of
ornateness and simplicity and bridges the gap between the
Baroque and Classic periods. It manifested the escape from
the seriousness of the Baroque style.

The Classic period of music (ca. 1770-1820) in which
the mature Haydn, Mozart, Christian Bach and the youthful
Beethoven dominated the musical scene produced even more
melodic simplicity. This led to the demise of the strict contrapuntal style which dominated Baroque music. The growth
of opera and the eventual dominance of secular music influenced the composition of the so-called Classical period. The
evolution of this music was to become more concerted (concert music as opposed to church music). It is characterized
by great pomp and magnificence as illustrated by such works
as Haydn's "Creation," "The Seasons" and Mozart's "Corona-
tion Mass" and "Requiem." These dramatic works demand a
larger scale of choral texture than most Baroque and Renaissance music. Yet, this musical fabric requires a preciseness and clarity in the vocal forces rather than heavy, "thick"
textures of sound as found in music of the Romantic period.

The music of the nineteenth-century Romantic period
is probably the most familiar of musical textures to our contemporary ears in that it has lush--sometimes thick--harmonic
characteristics and soaring melodic lines. This music is
usually the easiest to master, because the more massive
harmonic structure tends to mask intonation problems, and
the sonority of sound is very gratifying to both singers and
listeners.

Contemporary music of the twentieth century presents
many problems for singers. In the first place, the harmonies are much more complex in that they consist of upper-

partial tones which are transposed down next to the fundamental tones. These "dissonances" and often "awkward" intervalic sequences or relationships present many musical and vocal problems for the singers who must hear (imagine) the pitch in the "mind's ear" before attempting to produce it. (In contrast, instrumentalists have the advantage of more mechanical means of producing pitches.) This insecurity of pitch tends to exacerbate vocal problems inherent to the singer. Without doubt, complex twentieth-century music assaults the egos of singers.

When working in this idiom, the choral director must nurture the singers carefully, being very aware of the tendency of the singers to develop extreme vocal tension which often results from high tessituras and "dissonances." In this style of music excessive vibrato in the voices will cause intonation and blend problems stemming from the close tonal relationship.

Choral tone should reflect the physical nature of each era's music, i.e., the chord structure and also the melodic and rhythmic characteristics. To assist us in our understanding of choral timbres, we can observe three broad categories of tonal concepts that exist.

The "Straight Tone" School

This concept envisions a choral tone which is entirely devoid of vibrato. It is usually the norm for jazz and rock ensemble singing. This tone quality can be described as brash or harsh, reflecting the mood of our times. (The arts have always been a mirror of the era in which they existed.) Even though this "straight tone" may seem harsh, bad vocally, and unpleasant to hear by some standards, the voices in these ensembles do generally blend.

There is another facet of "straight tone" production which is considerably modulated from the radically harsh tone quality described above. This concept of tone was established through the influence of the Christiansen (Choral) School. Its beginnings stem from Peter Lutkin, founder of the Northwestern University A Cappella Choir in 1906 and F. Melius Christiansen, who founded the St. Olaf Choir in 1911. [5] This style of vocal production (sans vibrato) dominated the midwestern choral tradition until the middle of the twentieth century, when Robert Shaw's influence began to manifest itself with its vibrant tonal elements.   The "straight tone" vocal production had its roots in the ancient Middle East and Far East.   It later became the accepted tone quality for the plainchant in the resonant stone cathedrals of Europe during the Middle Ages.   This tonal concept perpetuated itself through medieval times to the present as the "proper" sound for unaccompanied church choral music.

The "dry" tone production, devoid of any vibrato, provides a practical means by which blend can be achieved. When all the voices are denuded of their individual characteristics (the effect of which imitates an orchestral reed section), the homogeneity of sound is impressive.   However, what is lacking in this kind of tone quality is a dynamic fortissimo devoid of strain.   Also, the tendency to flat en masse in a cappella singing is another problem that accrues from this approach to tone production.   The entire choir will often flat as much as a half, or even a whole, step.   To remedy this situation, a great deal of effort needs to be expended by directors of these "straight tone" choirs to mechanically adjust the pitches; i. e. , slightly enlarging the intervalic steps on ascending passages and diminishing them on descending steps.   Another negative effect of vibratoless vocal production is that, in order to achieve the required straight tone, the laryngeal muscles must be held in a slightly fixed position, thus incurring a noticeable amount of tension in those muscles and, frequently, harsh tones.

There is no doubt that these "straight tone" choirs have contributed greatly to the development of choral singing in the United States.   As the "missionaries" were graduated from these midwestern colleges during the 1930's, they went on to establish the principles of superior balance and blend throughout the country.   The result of these efforts brought a higher consciousness in the public school sector as to the values of choral singing.   The choral literature of the Renaissance, Baroque and Contemporary periods was explored to a significant extent, although the Romantic period was certainly not excluded from the repertoire.   Even the Great Depression of the thirties did not significantly deter the development of the choral movement.   High schools and small colleges prided themselves in their choral singing achievements. Large a cappella choirs became the norm from the 1930's to at least mid-century.   Gradually, after World War II, musicologists began to exert greater influence on the choral field.   Baroque music in particular began to be reinterpreted, utilizing instruments and smaller, more select choirs.

Nevertheless, the sixty (and more) voiced a cappella choirs still remain dominant in America, particularly in the Midwest where it all began.

A significant conflict emerged from the "straight tone" school dominance. Many studio (private) voice teachers were (and still are) in complete opposition to this style of singing. In many instances, they discouraged their students from participating in these highly controlled choirs, some teachers absolutely forbidding their students to sing under such conditions. Thus, there arose a division in the vocal sector, which still remains in some places where the "straight tone" concept continues to be dominant. It should be emphasized, however, that this tonal concept has been tempered to some extent by many choral directors who were trained under the "straight-tone" influence. A "modest" vibrato is acceptable --and even welcomed--where once it was absolutely forbidden. Therefore, it should be noted that the extremely controlled tonal concept begun by Lutkin and Christiansen has moderated generally among their heirs, with the result that the "sterile" sound is no longer the absolute norm.

Somehow, an erroneous notion has been established that the "straight-tone" school approach to choral vocal pedagogy stressed the concept of "the vowel is the tone." Just the opposite was true. Having been reared in Minnesota during the thirties under the strong influence of the Christiansen tradition, this writer was taught that all vowels must sound as much alike as possible. In fact, Christiansen would have preferred to dispense with all vowel colors and use only one neutral vowel; this, to produce a homogeneous tone quality among the singers similar to reed instruments. However, the strong Lutheran influence of textual authority found in the scriptures prevented his fully realizing this objective. Often, he stressed this orchestral tone concept by de-emphasizing words (particularly consonants) so as to establish an instrumental aural image for his singers to emulate. The pure vowel was an anathema to his concept of choral sound because the wide spectrum of vowel color provides too much variety of tone color to coincide with this desire for consistently smooth and balanced tone.

The Laissez-faire School

In 1919 John Finlay Williamsom founded the Westminster Choir, and during the twenties another distinctive tonal

concept was added to the choral picture. What emerged was
a choral tone diametrically opposed to the "straight tone"
school. Development of individualized (solo) tone quality was
the main objective, the premise being that total freedom of
vocal production led to the best choral sound. Thus, the
label "laissez-faire school" succinctly describes the approach
to choral tone in which everyone is encouraged to sing as
though he or she were a soloist. In recent years this approach to choral tone has been modified toward less individualistic quality--moving toward a more controlled tone production.

Obviously, the fortes and fortissimos of these choirs
were far more dramatic than the vibratoless tones of the
"straight tone" ensembles. However, controlling these colorful voices in unaccompanied singing produced significant blend
and intonation problems. On the other hand, these choirs,
producing such free and vibrant sounds, fared extremely well
when singing with large orchestral forces--the voices com-
peting more successfully with the instrumental texture. This
condition was the result of each voice having an abundance
of overtones which the orchestral forces could not absorb.
Thus, choirs utilizing the Williamson approach to vocal pedagogy became the favorite ensembles of the major symphony
orchestras in the eastern part of this country, particularly
the New York Philharmonic and Philadelphia orchestras.

If one pursues the use of significant vibrato into the
arena of "grass roots" (non-select) choirs, it can be appreciated that vibrato present in some voices and absent in others causes significant problems in blending the choral sound.
This condition is frequently encountered in community and
church choirs. Thus, the question arises: Should the director attempt to denude the colorful voices of their vibratos
so as to achieve better blend, or attempt to improve the
"dry" voices so that they resemble the richer voices?

There is no single or complete answer to the question
above. The final decision as to tone quality must be made
in each local situation. For instance, the acoustics of the
church or concert hall affect the basic tone quality of a given
choir. This is of significant importance in any analysis of
choral tone. An acoustically "dry" room will more readily
accommodate a reasonable degree of vibrato in the voices
because of its tendency to absorb sound. Conversely, the
"live" room (with much reverberation) will be better suited
to those choral groups whose production is rather straight

or "dry." In a moderately balanced acoustical hall or sanctuary, a well-controlled choral tone, with some amount of
vibrato in the voices, should produce the most satisfactory
results for singers and listeners in terms of both blend and
sonority. The vocal pedagogy described later in this chapter
is designed to be of value to directors seeking to solve this
problem of blend--yet, encouraging freedom of vocal production.

The "Sonorous-Blend" School

        The emergence of Robert Shaw in New York after
World War II with his Collegiate Chorale and the Robert
Shaw Chorale, introduced what might be termed a "sonorous-
blend" tone quality. It strikes a middle ground between the
"straight tone" and "laissez faire" concepts of vocal production. Undoubtedly, this kind of tonal concept existed long
before Shaw's time. However, it was the great popularity
of his choral groups which focused attention on the vibrant,
yet controlled tone. His ensembles became a model for many
choir directors. During the war, Shaw had been the rehearsal director for the Fred Waring (radio) Glee Club. It was
here that he "learned the ropes" by being exposed to the tone
syllable concept, which has become the hallmark of Waring's
choral publications. Being an exceptionally creative person,
Shaw eventually developed his own set of standards and concepts centering around the notion that most singing problems
revolve around rhythmic details. From this approach, combined with a highly interpretative emphasis, he developed a
variety of tone colors. However, it should be cited here
that eventually Shaw's concert and recording groups were
composed entirely of highly trained professional singers whose
pedagogical needs were minimal. He had only to demand
certain effects from his singers and he got them. There
was little need to apply any remedial vocal efforts such as
those needed by high school, college, church, and community
choral conductors in order to achieve their desired results
with "grass roots" singers.

            This trained-voice influence was the point of de-
        parture for criticisms of the soft-tone approach
        to choral development, straight tone singing, and
        over-emphasis upon the blending of similar voices. 6

        Thus, a more generally acceptable concept of choral
tone, which can be adapted to all styles of choral singing, is

termed here as the "sonorous-blend" school. This middle ground tonal concept produces a choral texture which blends well, yet has the vitality to express a wide spectrum of dynamics without strain. One means of achieving this combination of blend and sonority is through the establishment of pure vowel production by every member of the ensemble. The "gospel of the vowel" approach will be discussed in detail later in this chapter.

Here is a summary of the three "schools" of choral tone:

1. Straight tone--dry, homogeneous sound, basically devoid of vibrato, whose primary goal is blend.

2. Laissez-faire--complete freedom of vocal production with emphasis upon soloistic quality from each singer; distinctive vibrato encouraged.

3. Sonorous-blend--disciplined singing, but permitting a reasonable amount of vibrato; strong emphasis upon mutual ensemble feeling.

RESONANCE

Dr. Estes D. Freud's article in the Archives of Otolaryngology states,

> In "acoustic science" resonance means the prolongation or increase of any sound by reflection. It is the property of sonorous bodies to vibrate in unison with the vibration of other bodies, and thus reinforce the original sound. As an example, the wooden body of a violin is the resonance box for the strings. Without its resonance body, the violin would be a very poor instrument indeed. 7

Likewise, any wind instrument, including the human voice, must have a resonating cavity to provide a specific character for the sound produced by the vibrator--metal or reed mouthpiece for instruments and vocal folds for singers. One additional factor to be considered is that, although the resonance chambers of all other instruments remain fixed in size and shape, the vocal resonator (buccalpharyngeal cavity) constantly fluctuates in size and shape. As a result of this movement to accommodate vowels and consonants, singers

incur many more problems in tone production than do the
instrumentalists.

In order to achieve resonance among the voices, the
proper aural image of the tone must be formed in the singers' minds (imagination).   The term "aural image" is used
here to describe the singers' ability to imagine the correct
tone quality to be produced.   The terms "forwardness,"
"head" and "nasal" resonance and imagining the tone to re-
verberate on the upper front teeth (the desire to produce a
brilliant tone quality) are also objectives which are frequently
stated.   We hear the terms "deep" and "rich."   Those directors, who desire a "dark" tone quality are prone to suggest
that there must be a significant yawning sensation for the
singers.   This action lowers the larynx, a good objective
if not carried to extreme.   The tone thus produced is "deep"
and "rich," but often tends to be "wobbly" with too large a
vibrato (tremolo).   This is usually the result of lowering the
larynx too far--caused by too much "yawn."

The combination of the slight yawn (rather than the
almost full yawn) with the "forward," "nasal" sensation will
likely produce the middle ground "sonorous-blended" vocal
quality described above.

One description as to how to achieve this "balance"
of bright tone, which is based upon the presence of a significant amount of high partials, is to instruct the singers to
mentally form a very clear vowel while still incorporating
the slight yawning sensation.   This action tends to produce
a deeply-set vowel, while avoiding the "woofy" tone quality
produced by the deep-throated yawning feeling.   A more detailed description of achieving this tonal resonance will be
made later in this chapter.

                            VOLUME

As mentioned in the discussion above concerning "schools"
of choral tone, volume is related to vitality of tone.   The
choral singers who are encouraged to produce free tones with
noticeable vibrato can achieve a great deal of volume.   The
"edge" produced by a variety of vibratos produces more
"carrying" power, unless the overall tone is too dark and
"woofy."   It is likely that, in decibels of sound, there may
not be a significant difference; yet, the "penetrating effect"
of tonal variety among the voices creates the impression of
greater volume--all other things being equal.   In other words,

Fulltone--considers sonority, resonance and depth above power.... The fullness of tone is secured by tone placement, breath support and vowel equalization. 8

Therefore, it seems safe to conclude that the volume necessary to express dynamically loud music can be best achieved by a vibrant tone which is controlled in blend by unified vowel production. Clearly produced vowels, containing proper depth (space), should be the first mental-physical concept introduced to singers as they strive to improve their tone quality, blend, and volume. This applies as well to advanced singers, whose voices may not blend well resulting from the individualistic quality of their voices.

It can be stated that an "impacted" tone is the result of a clearly-produced vowel of proper size and shape to reinforce the correct partials. This condition results in what is often referred to as a resonant tone. It is analogous to a rifle bullet versus a shotgun blast. The rifle bullet is compact and forceful, carrying long distances, whereas the shotgun blast is diffused--with only a short distance of carrying power.

AURAL IMAGE

The next step in achieving the tone quality desired is to establish in the singers' minds a concept of what they should be hearing. This is probably the most difficult task which any voice teacher or choral conductor must undertake.

We listen to our own voices predominantly by way of our Eustachian tubes. This gives us a mistaken notion as to the real sound (timbre) of our voice quality. Persons who have heard their speaking voices played back on a recording are surprised by what they hear because of this false impression created by hearing through the Eustachian tubes. The same phenomenon is true of the singing voice. We must adjust our hearing of our own voices as to what is realistically the sound which we produce and then apply the principles of correct sensation of voice production to the process of singing. Figure 1 shows how this false impression of the actual sound of our voices is heard when speaking or singing.

The reader may ask at this point, "How do I establish a correct aural image of my voice?" The answer is

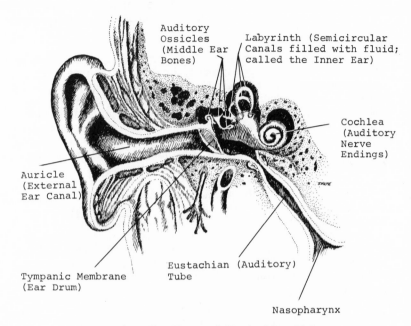

Fig. 1: The Ear and Eustachian Tube
Illustration by Stephanie Wiltse

that the correct aural image is achieved through a clearly
produced vowel sound and experienced through the physical-
aural sensations of the resonance cavities in the head.

> [W]e must hear the pitch mentally to be able to
> sing it.... What we phonate is merely an imitation
> of what we hear. 9

In other words, the singer's mind must direct the vocal musculature to form both the desired vocal pitch and the character of the sound as well, i.e., loud, soft, firm, gentle, etc.,
before the sound is produced by the vibrator.   Likewise, an
actor must envision (subconsciously, at least) the manner of
speaking a given line before delivering it. 10   The singer
must also

> ... [s]imultaneously imagine both pitch and the tone
> color of what he is "speaking" on the vocal pitches

in order to give adequate expression (characteriza-
tion) to the musical and vocal efforts. [11]

Harry Robert Wilson states the concept in similar
fashion:

A singer should have an aural conception of the
tone he desires to produce. [12]

One of the most important concepts for every singer
(tyro or advanced) to keep in mind constantly is

Every vowel has its particular size and shape on
every pitch, and consequently, tonal focus is the
result of proper vowel production. [13]

One final quote to emphasize the importance of the
aural image:

... [D]epending upon the aural image which the
singer has of his own voice, that person might
well darken or lighten his vocal production to imitate the vocal timbre he desires. [14]

In the final analysis of the singing process then, vocalists must gain control of their voices through a clear understanding of the sensations which are known to produce a
good tone quality; this also in relation to the room in which
the sound is emitted, i.e., listening and sensing simultaneously as to what is good tone production.   A reliable tape
recorder can aid significantly in achieving this understanding.

BREATHING AND POSTURE

Much has been written on the subject of "breath support" or
breath management.   The familiar but erroneous statement
"breathe from the diaphragm" has given many singers a false
impression of the process of inhalation and exhalation during
the act of singing.

The anatomical diaphragm is a muscular membranous
partition separating the abdominal and chest cavities (see
Fig. 2).   It is shaped like an inverted bowl, and its function
is to act as a pump which draws air into the lungs.   During
inspiration it pulls down and flattens out against the organs
in the abdominal region, thus pulling air (oxygen) into the

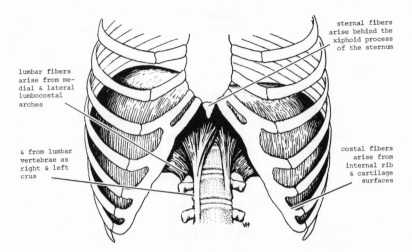

lumbar fibers
arise from me-
dial & lateral
lumbocostal
arches

& from lumbar
vertebrae as
right & left
crus

sternal fibers
arise behind the
xiphoid process
of the sternum

costal fibers
arise from
internal rib
& cartilage
surfaces

Fig. 2: The Diaphragm
Illustration by James J. Van Hare, M.D.

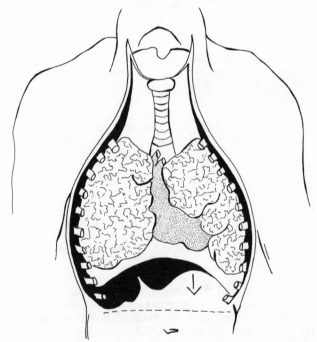

Fig. 3: The Lungs and Diaphragm
Illustration by Nancy Vander Linde Corey

lungs (see Fig. 3). It functions automatically except in very
high altitudes, where special muscular effort is needed to
draw the diaphragm downward in order to pull the thinner
air into the lungs. That is why physical activity is so difficult at high altitudes.

However, in normal altitudes from sea level to about
3000 feet, the diaphragm works quite automatically. We
need only to provide an open channel for the air to pass into
the lungs. The air pressure and gravity causes the diaphragm
to function efficiently in normal persons. Consequently, the
"open throat" feeling, which permits silent and efficient
breath inhalation produces the optimal kind of breathing.
This breath sensation is felt just below the rib cage and all
around the body to the lower back muscles as well. If the
singers will stand and place their hands around their waists,
just above the hip bones, they will experience an expansion
all around the abdominal-dorsal area of the body as they take
a silent breath (see Fig. 6).

An analogy is to imagine that there is an innertube
inside the waist and that inhalation fills the tube equally all
around that part of the body, providing the singer has attained proper posture. The following discussion will elaborate on this most important facet of the singing process.

Proper breathing technique begins with good posture.
This leads to the establishment of control over the abdominal
muscles. Proper posture permits the singer to coordinate
effective action of breath management as a unified feeling.
The total singing process is best illustrated by a pyramid:

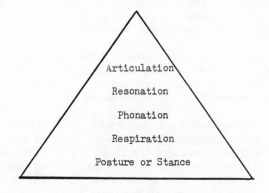

Fig. 4: The Breathing-Posture Pyramid

There are a few basic steps to achieving good posture.
Supported by the spine, the head, chest, and pelvis must be
aligned one under the other. This bearing is achieved by an
erect and straight back, with head and chest held high (but
not tense), and the pelvis ("tail") tucked in. The rib cage
should expand during inhalation, then remain firm and dilated
throughout the musical phrase. The knees should not be
"locked" and one foot should be slightly ahead of the other.
The heel of one foot should be opposite the arch of the other.
(In choral formations, all persons should stand with the same
foot forward--either right or left foot in front.) The only
tension present should be felt in the posterior thighs. The
entire body must be firm but not tense.

When this posture is achieved, all that needs to be
added is the conscious feeling of the "open throat"--a slight
yawning feeling. This sensation is best achieved by consciously inhaling with the silent breath.[15] There should be
little or no audible sound during the inhalation process. As
a result, the diaphragm will flatten out against the abdominal
organs, and the sensation of breath pressure will be felt just
below the rib cage. This action, combined with the correct
posture, will create the feeling of expansion around the waist.
Again, it should be emphasized that this feeling of expansion
should be as though an innertube were inside the body around
the waist area, and that inhalation fills the "innertube" equally
all around the abdominal-dorsal region. The imaginary focal
point of the breath may be described as being in the small
of the back, just above the belt line. Do not permit the rib
cage to collapse during the act of singing. Rather, maintain
the "expanded-innertube feeling" as the chief means of support of the tone. The firmness of the abdominal muscles
will produce the feeling of expansion all around the waistline,
pushing against the lower back muscles.

Some persons have chronic lower back aches and pains.
This could be caused by sway-back posture, which in turn in-
duces strain on the lower back muscles. An exercise which
might help to alleviate this condition is as follows:

> Lie on your back (preferably on a carpeted floor)
> with heels, calves, buttocks, back of shoulders
> and head touching the floor. Then "dig" the heels
> into the floor so that the "small" of the back touches
> the floor. (The main object is to flatten the entire
> lower back against the floor.) The result will be
> a feeling of tension across the abdomen and straight-
> ening the lower back muscles. Hold this position

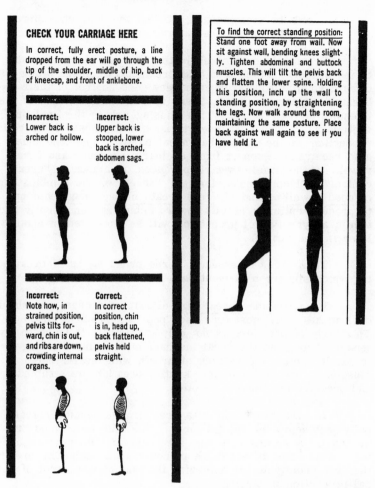

CHECK YOUR CARRIAGE HERE

In correct, fully erect posture, a line dropped from the ear will go through the tip of the shoulder, middle of hip, back of kneecap, and front of anklebone.

Incorrect:
Lower back is arched or hollow.

Incorrect:
Upper back is stooped, lower back is arched, abdomen sags.

Incorrect:
Note how, in strained position, pelvis tilts forward, chin is out, and ribs are down, crowding internal organs.

Correct:
In correct position, chin is in, head up, back flattened, pelvis held straight.

To find the correct standing position: Stand one foot away from wall. Now sit against wall, bending knees slightly. Tighten abdominal and buttock muscles. This will tilt the pelvis back and flatten the lower spine. Holding this position, inch up the wall to standing position, by straightening the legs. Now walk around the room, maintaining the same posture. Place back against wall again to see if you have held it.

Fig. 5: Correct and Incorrect Posture

(Reproduced by permission of the copyright owner, The Schering Corporation)

for several seconds before relaxing. Relax and try again several times. Repeated exercising in this manner should reinforce the feeling of correct posture and eventually the abdominal and back muscles

will be strengthened, so that the correct posture
will become more natural in a standing position.

Frequently overlooked is the fact that there is more
to the support of tone than just breath management.   Singers
often develop adequate or even very good control of their
breathing apparatus.   Yet, there is something missing in the
intensity of their tones.   This missing link in the final production of a "supported tone" is lack of firmness of the vowel
production in the buccalpharyngeal cavity.   The tone must
also receive its support from a clearly produced and firm
vowel.   If the vowel is weakly produced, no amount of "breath
control" will compensate for it.   Therefore, the combination
of good vowelling and efficient breath management team up
to produce optimum results toward achieving consistently good
tone quality.   (Vowel production will be presented in depth
later in this chapter.)

There are, in essence, three broad styles of breathing which singers tend to utilize:

1.   Clavicular breathing--allowing the chest and shoul-
ders to heave as most tyro and "pop" singers tend to do.
This style of breathing is not only inefficient, it leads to
tension throughout the vocal mechanism, causing the singer
to partly control the release of breath with the laryngeal
muscles.   The result of this kind of breathing is strained
and uncontrolled vocal production.

2.   Diaphragmatic area breathing--expanding principally just below the frontal ribs.   This may be termed "rib
or costal" breathing with only the thoracic (rib) cage expanding.   This mode of breathing is better than clavicular breathing, but inadequate for achieving the maximum control of vocal production in singing.

3.   Abdominal area breathing--expanding the abdominal region, which exerts pressure against the lower back
muscles and abdominal organs.   This style of breath management is realized through the posture described above and
the silent breath inhalation.   Finally, this outward expansion
all around the waist should be maintained throughout each
singing phrase.

As mentioned above, the singer(s) can check to determine whether or not this expansion is evident, i. e., place
the hands on the waist just above the pelvis or belt line with

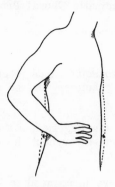

Side View

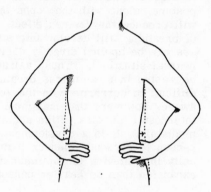

Front View

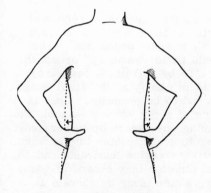

Back View

Fig. 6: Lower Breathing Posture
Illustrations by Stephanie Wiltse

the thumbs in the back.   Then, "breathe into your hands"
(see Fig. 6).

> It will be noticed that expansion takes place from
> the "backbone to the belly button," as the saying
> goes.16

There should be expansion against the fingers and thumbs,
the outward pressure remaining firm throughout the entire
phrase of a song.

Under normal conditions there is no need to engage
in a great number of breathing exercises.   Rather, proper
posture, along with the "open throat" feeling during inhalation
will produce the desired effect.   Consistent use of this method
of breathing will develop into subconscious habit.   This process can be applied directly during the act of singing (the rehearsal situation).   Thus, valuable rehearsal time need not
be wasted in meaningless breathing exercises, which may be
difficult to correlate with the actual singing process.   Be
aware, however, that maximum control of the abdominal and
intercostal muscles in the act of singing may not occur immediately.   It is a developmental process which varies from
person to person.   Slender individuals often have more difficulty in achieving the optimum effects of abdominal breath
expansion than do heavier persons.

APPROACHING VOCAL PEDAGOGY
THROUGH DICTION

Some choral directors take excessive amounts of rehearsal
time to vocalize their ensembles.   Their intent is to teach
their singers how to improve their vocal production.   The
real purpose of vocalises should be to "warm up" or get the
mind and body ready to sing.   To be certain, a few carefully selected vocalises will aid in clarifying the aural image
--the preferable or correct sound to be produced.   Just as
one should not "rev" the engine of a car when it is cold, the
voices needs comparable warming up--especially in very cold
weather.   Some persons prefer to let an engine idle to warm
up and others drive slowly until the engine lubricants can do
their job.   Likewise, a choral director may choose to warm
up a choral group with a slow, simple song or chorale at
soft or mezzo forte dynamics, rather than employ specific
warm-up exercises.

Creative directors will excerpt sections of the music being studied as warm-up procedures. These choices may include rhythmic problems to be found in a given selection, chord clusters for ear training, or just plain diatonic sequences which emphasize intonation, blend, balance, and so on.

The point being made here is that mindless vocalizing accomplishes nothing. In fact, many gymnastic, staccato vocalises may well reinforce bad habits already present in the singers. Staccato vocalises can be very harmful for average choral singers who have minimal control over their vocal mechanisms. Much tension throughout the body--and especially the vocal muscles--is caused by staccato exercises. The cliché that one must learn to walk before one can run applies here. One must learn how to sing legato before handling or proceeding to the precarious, instant phonation demanded of staccato vocal production.

Vocalises, designed to achieve specific goals in vocal or musical development should be carefully chosen for their correlation with the problems and objectives toward which the director and group are working.

The most logical approach to this matter is to establish that the purest choral tone can be achieved most efficiently through diction--i.e., the concept of vowel purity. Unless the singers' vowels are pure, their tone quality will not be clear and their diction will be muddy. To be sure, good diction in singing or speaking depends upon more than just pure vowels, i.e., consonants must also be "in line" with the vowels, thus producing understandable words on the singing tones. There are at least seven positive results of proper use of the vowel in singing:

1. Natural resonance
2. Improved tone quality
3. Improved diction
4. Improved intonation
5. Improved blend (balanced tone)
6. Improved flexibility--agility
7. Increased range (assists in allowing vocal folds to adjust properly)

Clearly produced vowelling is the basis for good singing tones. Deeply-set vowel production, coordinated with a high, forward feeling of resonance (in the mask of the face), provides the singers with a helpful concept of tone production.

All other pedagogical factors must be applied to the singing
process from this point.   A simple, yet effective clarifica-
tion of vowel sounds can be achieved by use of what may be
termed the Vowel Spectrum (illustrated later in this chapter).

   The claim has been made above that good vowelling
produces improved tone quality, and that extraneous vocalises
are less valuable than a system which can be applied simply
and directly to the music being studied.

> There is no other means by which color, character
> and variety are given to speech or singing than
> through vowel formation.   The singer's tone qual-
> ity (rich, full or sonorous; muddy, thick or dull;
> thin, nasal or "dead") is directly related to the way
> in which the oral pharynx and tongue are shaped.[17]

Furthermore, "one utilizes words (language) as the primary
means of producing sounds which should be intelligible to the
listener."[18]

   It cannot be denied that singing is really an extension
of the speech process.   To be certain, singing is more complicated than speech, but the two processes stem from the
same root.   In singing we must sustain sounds and identify
words on specific pitches over a wider range than is experienced in speaking, i.e.,

> 1.   that note values often change the syllabic em-
> phases of the words, and
>
> 2.   a much wider range of sounds is utilized.
>
> ... the basic process of phonation and character-
> ization of sound remains the same in both idi-
> oms.[19]

   This premise is supported by voice authorities through
the centuries of vocal pedagogical efforts, such as Caccini,
Tosi, Porpora, Vaccai from the old Italian schools of sing-
ing, as well as later pedagogues: E. Herbert-Caesari,
Charles K. Scott, Harry R. Wilson, Mario P. Marafioti,
Lilli Lehman, Douglas Stanley, Luchsinger and Arnold, Ralph
D. Appelman, Husler and Rodd-Marling, Victor Fields, Wil-
liam Vennard, and many others.

THE VOWEL AS THE BASIS OF
VOCAL PRODUCTION

It is axiomatic, then, that pure vowel production can be utilized as the primary tool for improving tone quality among
singers in the voice studio as well as in the "group voice
lesson" of the choral rehearsal.

> The vehicle through which the voice student can
> gain insight into his vocal production is a concise
> understanding of vowel production. [20]

The adjustable cavities of the mouth and throat accen-
tuate or suppress various harmonics (overtones) involved in
the amplification of the sound emitted by the vocal folds (the
generator). The size and shape of the buccalpharyngeal cavity governs both the amplification and the tone quality of the
voice.

Therefore, careful attention to vowel production is
easily adaptable to the basic process of singing. It is not
the final element of singing, but rather the basis upon which
the entire singing technique can be built. Good vowel production is a direct means of communication within the group
dynamic for establishing good tone quality, loud and soft volume, blend, balance and flexibility. If the aural image of
the singer's vowel quality is realistically established, a solid
basis of tone-building will result. In solving tone production
problems, first analyze the vowel to determine whether or
not it is clearly produced, and thus, accurate.

English Orthography and Phonology

Before examining the Vowel Spectrum, it is desirable
to clarify some factors relating to languages, particularly
English, which should be significant to most readers of this
book. First of all, our English orthography frequently bears
little relation to our phonology, and thus it is of vital importance to keep in mind the actual sound which is to be articulated, rather than the precise spelling of the word.

Following are examples of homophones (words that
have the same sound as another word, but differ in spelling
and/or meaning). Note that it is the actual sound which is
important to hear in one's mind--not the spelling of the word.

Homophones and Their Vowel Identifications

ate-eight (AY)
aught-ought (aw)
ball-bawl (aw)
base-bass (AY)
cannon-canon (aah)
chord-cord ("oh") - open
    OH
dane-deign (AY)
draft-draught (aah)
faint-feint (AY)
feat-feet (EE)
gilt-guilt (ih)
grown-groan (OH)
hail-hale (AY)
hie-high (AH + vanishing
    ee)
him-hymn (ih)
isle-aisle (AH + vanishing
    uh)
key-quay (EE)
knead-need (EE)
leach-leech (EE)

lean-lien (EE)
made-maid (AY)
mite-might (AH + vanishing
    ee)
no-know (OH)
nun-none (ah)
pain-payne (AY)
pear-pair (eh)
queue-cue (OO)
reign-rain (AY)
read-reed (EE)
sail-sale (AY)
sew-sow (OH)
tacks-tax (aah)
too-(to)-two (OO)
urn-earn (uhr)
use-ewes (OO)
vale-veil (AY)
ware-wear (eh)
wood-would (uuh)
yew-you (OO)
yolk-yoke (OH)

With recognition of this "quirk" in our English language in mind, we can move directly into the concept of the Vowel Spectrum.

THE VOWEL SPECTRUM

This simplified organization of word-sounds can be termed a Vowel Spectrum since it presents the examples of words associated with many different sounds with which the singer or speaker must cope. The purpose of the Vowel Spectrum is to establish a "stencil" by which the singer can easily gain an aural image of the focal point of the sound to be produced. The International Phonetic Alphabet is an excellent vehicle for teaching accurate pronunciation of languages, and many vocal instructors regard it as an effective teaching aid. However, very few "grass roots" singers who have not studied languages in depth will be able to use it as a tool in singing. Learning the IPA symbols is, in a sense, equivalent to learning another language. Moreover, while the IPA is excellent for speaking, singing requirements are more complex. The additional buccalpharyngeal space needed for singing, in contrast to speaking, and the arbitrary sustaining of sounds determined by note values require the singer to have a <u>subconscious vowel sound identification.</u> There must be a sense of freedom of vowel production in singing. This is necessary for good vocal production. The results achieved by the Vowel Spectrum are essentially the same as those of the IPA when applied to the singing process. However, this simplified vowel sound identification stemming from the language itself, does not require learning another alphabetical set.

It should be emphasized again at this point that

> every vowel has its unique size and shape on every given pitch and dynamic level (however subtle the change may be for notes that are a half or whole step apart); that the most reliable clue to the shape of a given sound (not necessarily size ...) is gained through the concept of speech. [21]

Further support of this claim is made by the following vocal authorities:

> Actually, every vibrator adjustment includes an appropriate resonator adjustment. And the vowel is the chief factor whereby this dual adjustment, this coupling system, is secured. [22]

> If the cavity is right, the sound will be right....
> The perfect cavity makes the perfect vowel. [23]

> So many people have developed faulty speech habits that their natural singing voices, if they had any, have been affected. [24]

> Voice is speech, and is produced by the mouth [buccalpharyngeal cavity], not by the vocal cords.
> The vocal cords produce only <u>sounds</u> [really "puffs"], which are transformed into <u>vowels</u> and <u>consonants</u> by a phonetic process taking place in the mouth, and giving origin to the voice. [25]

> ... [M]ost of the failures in the singing profession are due to the ignorance of the important role played by the speaking voice in relation to the art of singing. [26]

<u>The speech track determines the strength or weakness</u>

<u>of the tone</u>. If the pronunciation (diction) is weak and flabby, the tone also will be weak in speaking or in singing. Conversely, if the speech or singing track is firm and precise, the tone will also be firm--regardless of whether the volume is soft or loud. As a matter of fact, the softer one sings, the more concentration is required to produce a firm and focused vowel sound so as to avoid "dead-fish" (unsupported) tones. Note that when whispering one must enunciate in exaggerated fashion with greater use of the lips, so as to be understood. Soft singing is analogous to soft speaking or whispering.

When the vowel is correctly formed for a particular pitch and dynamic level, the vocal mechanism will tend to make the proper adjustment.

THE SHAPE OF THE BUCCALPHARYNGEAL CAVITY

This cavity includes the total space inside the mouth which governs amplification of the sound vibrations produced by the vocal folds. It consists of the pharyngeal area just above the larynx, the oral pharynx, soft palate, nasal (naso-)pharynx, hard palate, and the tongue. The position of the tongue in relation to any given vowel greatly influences tone quality. If it is drawn back in the mouth (humped up as in a full yawn), the nasal pharynx cavity will be closed off and the "ring" of the tone will be lost. Conversely, if the soft palate is "collapsed," the tone will have too much nasal-hard palate focus, thus becoming thin, reedy, and/or harsh.

The illustrations on pages 81-85 showing the shape of the buccalpharyngeal cavity are not anatomically exact, but they graphically illustrate the point made above.

A generalization can be made that the mind will direct the correct mouth position or formation for a given vocal pitch, if the individual hears the teacher produces the desired tone quality. That is the reason why every choral director, who sings even reasonably well, can be effective in demonstrating the tone quality preferred. This practice assists the singer in establishing a better aural image of the sound which should be produced, <u>if</u> there is additional guidance as to <u>how</u> to achieve the desired tone quality. Correct vowel formation is the route by which this objective is realized. If the vowel is carefully formed, it shapes the throat cavities properly for amplifying the vocalic vibrations. The vowel is the basic sound of any language:

Dark Area: incorrect "placement"
Light Area: correct "placement"

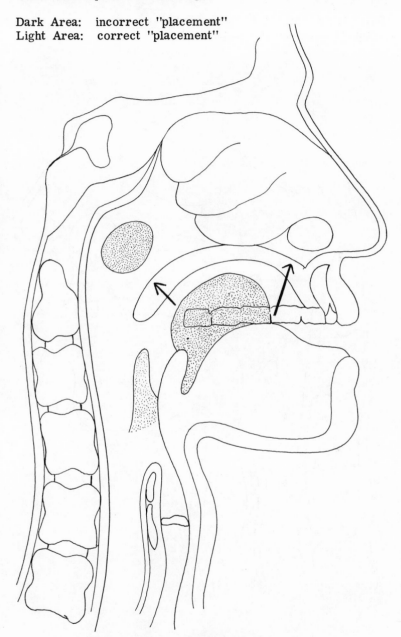

Fig. 7: Focal Points of Resonance--"AH" Vowel
Illustration by Nancy Vander Linde Corey

Dark Area: incorrect "placement"
Light Area: correct "placement"

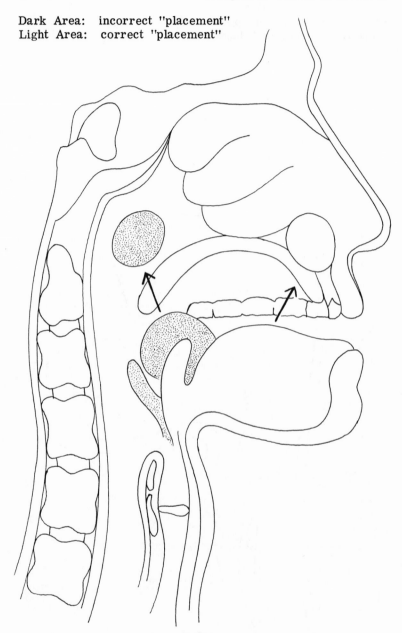

Fig. 8-a: Focal Points of Resonance--"AY" Vowel
Illustration by Nancy Vander Linde Corey

Dark Area: incorrect "placement"
Light Area: correct "placement"

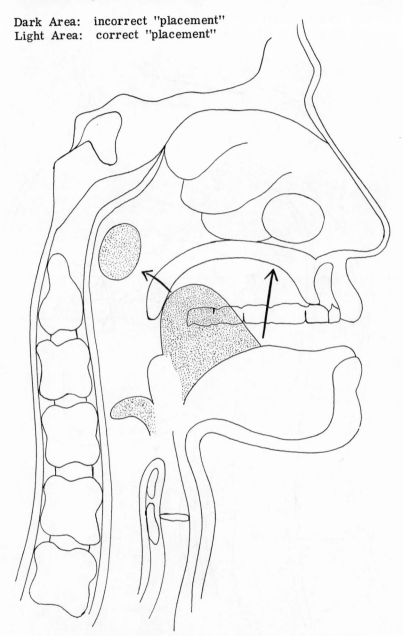

Fig. 8-b: Focal Points of Resonance--"EE" Vowel
Illustration by Nancy Vander Linde Corey

Dark Area: incorrect "placement"
Light Area: correct "placement"

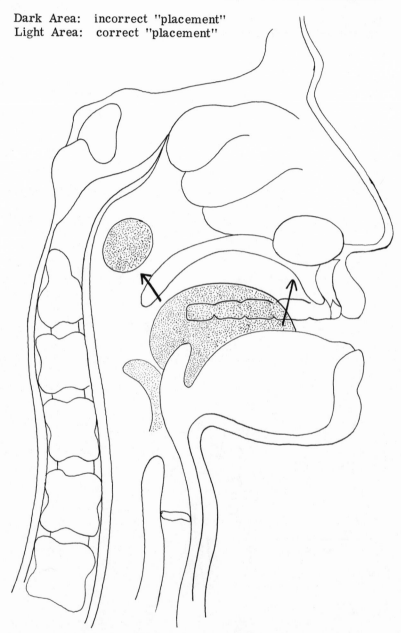

Fig. 9-a: Focal Points of Resonance--"OH" Vowel
Illustration by Nancy Vander Linde Corey

Dark Area: incorrect "placement"
Light Area: correct "placement"

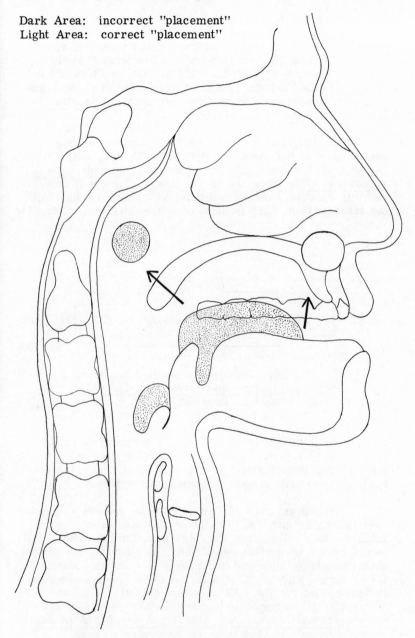

Fig. 9-b: Focal Points of Resonance--"OO" Vowel
Illustration by Nancy Vander Linde Corey

[E]ach fundamental (tone) is associated with a series of overtones. It is the accentuation of certain
brands of these overtones which produces what is
called the "vowel sound. " The term "vowel" is,
then, a special case of "quality" or "timbre" in
which certain groups of harmonies are either ac-
centuated or suppressed by means of shaping the
adjustable cavities. 27

To apply this concept, have the choir members pronounce (speak) the basic vowel sounds EE, AY, AH, OH, OO
in the order prescribed, taking care to sustain the speech
sounds and glide from one to the other.   They will note that
"EE" is relatively small in size, "AY" is larger and "AH"
the largest; then "OH" is smaller again and "OO" is smaller
yet.

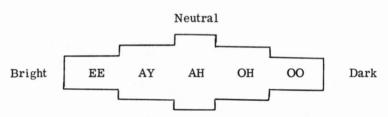

Fig. 10: Vocal Spectrum Relationships
(from Singing--An Extension of Speech,
by Russell A. Hammar (1978), p. 72.)

Next, sing these vowel sounds in unison on a comfortable
pitch (middle register) to apply the speaking sensation to the
singing one, being careful to add just enough buccalpharyngeal space to give proper resonance to the tone.

Careful analysis of these five basic sounds will indicate that "EE" and "OO" are about the same size, but of
different shape; likewise, the "AY" and "OH" vowels.   "AH"
is the center or neutral sound, and the other sounds of the
Vowel Spectrum surround and modify it.   As an illustration,
try to form "EE" or "OO" with the same amount of space
that is needed for the "AH" vowel.   Both the "EE" and "OO"
will be far too large to be accurately formed.   Therefore,
the singer must realize that each vowel has its particular
size and shape for each pitch in the singer's range.

The reason for beginning the vowel sequence with "EE" is that this "forward-placed" vowel tends to maintain a "brighter sound," particularly as the voice ascends to the upper part of its range--assuming, of course, that there is no jaw and/or tongue tension. Some singers produce a "dark," "muddy," or "woofy" sound as they ascend vocally to the upper part of their voice range. Others may not create enough space in the oral cavity to produce a deeply set vowel. Directors should keep this fact in mind as they work on this facet of tone production.

A helpful aid to success in achieving a richer, fuller tone is to have the choir sing a simple homophonic cadence (or other chord progression) very slowly at about mezzo forte dynamic level. As they sing, give directions, such as "yawn into the vowel sound" for those with "collapsed" soft palates, while admonishing those creating too much space to "relax the soft palate slightly." This aids in achieving a more accurate vowel size.

USING THE VOWEL SPECTRUM

Use of the vowel spectrum as a "warm-up" exercise for vocal students and choral groups is especially effective during early stages of learning. Later, when the principle of a clearly defined, deeply-set vowel is mastered, this exercise is not a necessary prerequisite for singing. The clearly defined, deeply-set vowel utilized with a hymn or chorale accomplishes the same objective of attaining depth of tone and still maintaining enough "brightness" of sound to have carrying power.

Beginning in the lower or middle range (about "f" or "g"), the scale is ascended by half-steps, the sequence of the five vowels being completed on each pitch. The singers ascend the scale up to their individual, maximum capacity without strain, while being reminded to form a "high-arch" or slight yawn of the soft palate. At the same time the singers should be reminded to "speak" the vowel sound clearly.

It is generally recommended that warm-up efforts should begin in the lower or middle vocal ranges of the singers rather than at either extreme level. Also, by vocalizing in a comfortable range, unskilled singers can concentrate more fully upon the relationship which the vowel formation has to vocal production.

THE VOWEL SPECTRUM

PRINCIPAL VOWELS

Basic Italian	i	e	a	o	u
Basic English	EE	AY	AH	OH	OO
Examples:	see	say	sight (AH-ee)	so	soon
	dream	fail	father	hold	too, ruler
	seize, grieve	save	star, heart	mow, sew	rude
	believe	late	on, odd	goal	you (ee-OO)
	reach	they, pray	ice (AH-ee)	soul	blew, blue
	real	praise	thou (AH-oo)	omit, obey	rebuke (ee-OO)

VOWEL DERIVATIONS

	ih	eh	aah	aw	uuh	uhr ʡ
Examples:	sit, myth, guilt	set, wed, head	sat, hand, and	sought, saw	soot, should	serve, her
	women, weary	guest, yes	shadow	God (some prefer "ah")	could, full	fur, work
	pretty, busy	bury, any	man, can	warm	good, book	learn, term
	fill, live	said	had, glad	all, hall	crooked	world, word
	hear, fear	their	rapture	ought, naught	startled	over, bird
	kingdom	prepared	that	walk, water	put, stood	mercy

SUB-VOWELS (consonants that sustain pitches)

m, n, (ng), l, r (uhr--above), v, z

MODIFIED VOWELS

	aht†	"ah" ŋ	"oh" (open Italian "o")
Examples:	mother, come, one	the, a, sofa	Lord, yore, glory, for
	of, love, suffers	idea, but, cut	morn, mourn, adore
	blood, wonder	cup, circus	oil (oh-ih-l), boy (oh-ee)

†Three forms of the "a" vowel: AH as in father, ah as in mother and "ah" as in the.
ŋReplaces the [ə] and [ʌ] of the IPA.
ʡThis sound replaces the [ɜ] of the IPA.

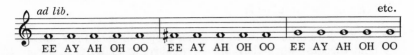

Fig. 12: Vowel Spectrum Vocalized in Unison

A chord progression may be played with this vocal
sequence, if desired, but a cappella unison singing affords
an excellent opportunity for listening to blend and intonation
as well as to tone production. The exercise may also be
sung in harmony so that the choir will receive training in
singing chord progressions. The following is one example
of how such a progression might be adapted to this concept:

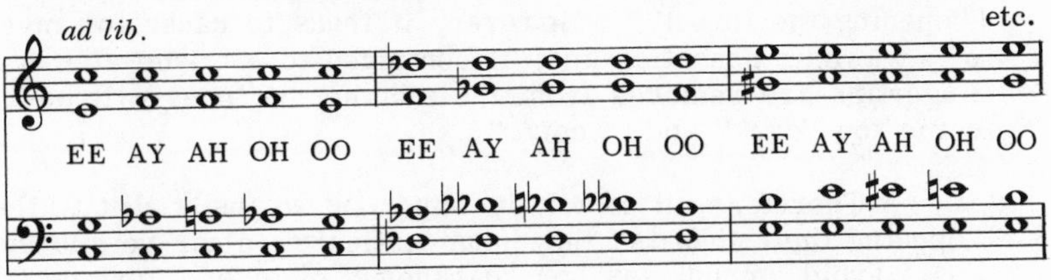

Fig. 13: Vowel Spectrum Vocalized in Harmony

This chordal sequence is particularly useful with
"grass roots" singers in that it can be kept within a comfortable singing range for the voices. However, it can be
extended into higher tessituras when appropriate to the singers' vocal development. Other, more elaborate chromatic
progressions can and should be utilized as well, but the
simple, parallel sequence of notes is a very good basis on
which to begin.

The director should caution the singers to pronounce
the vowel sounds with as much "depth" as possible, insisting
upon clear pronunciation of the vowels. One way of stating
this objective is for the director to say to singers in a clear
and deep tone (as they are singing): "Deep, deep, deep; pronounce it clearly." The slight yawning sensation should also
be stressed while drawing attention to clear vowel pronunciation.

[Opposite:] Fig. 11: Complete Vowel Spectrum (from Singing
--An Extension of Speech, by Russell A. Hammar (1978), p.
69.)

Opening the Mouth (Throat)

It is often difficult to teach people to open their mouths
(and throats) when they sing. According to Wilson, a way to
make singers experience the sensation of the "open throat,"
is as follows:

> Place the first two fingers ... between the teeth
> with the second (or middle) finger on top. 28

This is done while singing a piece of music (preferably homophonic) on which the choir is currently working. (The Vowel
Spectrum also adapts well to his "fingertip therapy.") This
practice is a radical means among singers who produce shallow tones to achieve the feeling of elevating the soft palate
("opening the throat"). However, it tends to cause too much
of a yawning sensation and, if continued to extreme after the
fingertips are removed from the mouth, the tones will become too "dark" and "woofy."

Therefore, it is vitally important to insist that while
"opening their throats" they must articulate clear vowels so
as to avoid "muddiness" or "darkness" of tone. Forming the
vowel accurately aids in keeping the tongue from rising too
far in the back of the mouth, thus eliminating the overly
"dark color" of tone quality so often heard in choirs. "Darkness" should never be confused with depth of tone, since a
tone can be sung deeply and clearly without being "dark in
color." The main purpose of this illustration of two fingers
in the mouth is to stress the importance of making sufficient
room in the buccalpharyngeal cavity, so that sound can be
adequately amplified.

Problems of the Jaw

Many singers have slight jaw tension that is difficult
for the director to notice while standing in front of an ensemble. Therefore, it is a valuable practice if the director
can, from time to time, get a side view of the singers.
Half of the group can face the other half so that the profiles
of the singers can be seen. A subtly lifted chin may be difficult to detect among a large group of singers, whereas it
can be observed more readily on a one-to-one basis in the
vocal studio.

There are at least three types of jaw positions that
are obviously incorrect for singing:

1. Alligator Jaw: the front of the mouth opening far
   too wide in contrast to the soft palate lift. The
   opening of the front of the mouth should correspond to the pharyngeal space created by the soft
   palate.

2. The Jutted Jaw: extreme jaw protrusion forward
   creating a great amount of tension in the tongue
   and in the bony and cartilaginous structure which
   forms the framework of the mouth. (For centuries the Italians have had a phrase which drama-
   tizes the release of jaw tension, "Come un idiota"
   (as an idiot's [jaw]). In other words, the jaw
   should "hang" as though suspended by rubber bands.

3. Turtle Neck: pulling the jaw and head far back
   along the line of posture; the extreme opposite of
   the protruding jaw above. The practice stems
   often from a director's admonition to remedy the
   jutted jaw.

VOWEL DERIVATIONS

The other vowel sounds that are common to our English language are listed in the following order and are labeled "vowel
derivations." This designation is given with the recognition
that these vowel sounds are modifications of the principal
vowel sounds listed above. These are the derivations:

ih	as in	sit
eh	as in	set
aah	as in	sat
aw	as in	sought
uuh	as in	soot
uhr	as in	serve

The above can be considered as derivations of the principal
vowel sounds by the following association. If the singers
will pronounce carefully and slowly all the vowels in a sustained manner, they will note the relationships between them
(see Figure 14 on following page). Note also that the vowel
derivations seem smaller in size than the fundamental vowel
sounds which they modify.

Fig. 14: Vowel Relationships
(from Singing--An Extension of Speech,
by Russell A. Hammar (1978), p. 82)

Furthermore, if the singers pass slowly from left to
right through the "spectrum," they will note that "eh" is mid-
way between "EE" and "AY," "aah" is between "AY" and
"AH," etcetera. These relationships are helpful aids to correct vowel production.

The five principal vowels and the vowel derivations
can be applied effectively to most of our Western languages,
which are the basis for our musical repertoire. The only
Western language which is a little difficult to apply is French,
because of its many subtle, short and nasal sounds.

Relating the Vowel Derivatives

The reader should note that "ih" is formed by a com-
paratively small mouth opening. It is the most "over-formed"
vowel of any of the vowels in the spectrum. It is often mistaken for "eh," particularly as the singer ascends the scale;
"with" is often pronounced as "weth" or "wath." Many tenors, as they sing e, f and g above middle c, emit a blatant,
"wide-open" tone because of a shallow mispronunciation of
the vowel. Accurate pronunciation of "ih," "eh" and "aah"
will invariably cause the tenor voice at this point to adjust
to a lighter "head voice" position. The correct mental image of the vowel, combined with proper depth of tone produces a natural "cover" to the tone. It eliminates the "need"
for vocal teachers to tell their students to "cover" or "darken"
the tone quality so as to make a transition to the upper vocal range. This principle applies to all voices, but the shallow quality is most noticeable in the tenor voice.

When the singers develop the skill to clearly define
each of these sounds as they relate them to words in the
text, they will produce consistently better sound, albeit within
certain limitations of their own "vocal instruments." Moreover, the singers should form the vowel sound and arch their
soft palates simultaneously. The mouth cavity should not

stretch too far to the point of tension or to distortion of the vowel focus. At the same time as they form the correct vowel sound, they will instinctively tend to shape the resonating cavity more carefully to fit the pitch and its characteristic vowel. Again it is emphasized that this approach and description of vowel production is designed especially for the tyro singer, but is frequently of aid to the more advanced singer. The subtle suggestions of vowel shadings can be presented to the more advanced singers, preferably during private vocal lessons where the subtleties can be communicated. Some choir directors elect to give private lessons to promising vocalists as an added stimulus to their interest in the choir. Others arrange private or class lessons on a fee basis.

"Losing" the Vowel

It is interesting and edifying to observe that most singers tend to relinquish the vowel sound which they originally produced when that vowel sound occurs on a note of long duration or on a series of notes. This is especially true when the voice seems to be crossing a "break" or "register." At this point the mind is distracted from concentrating on the vowel sound. The diffusion of vowel focus, then, is largely due to vocal insecurity. Thus, instead of retreating farther from the vowel focus into more diffusion of tone, the singers should be told to concentrate more upon maintaining the vowel sound which they are producing at that point. A clearer conception of the vowel, therefore, will help the singers over the "break," or passaggio (passageway) with greater skill and better tone quality.

Vowel migration is used by some vocal pedagogues as being a necessary concomitant for bridging the passaggio. Other teachers and directors use the term in the negative sense to warn against retreating from the central core or mental concept of the pure vowel. Migrating from the core of the vowel sound is one of the greatest faults of many singers. The purity of the vowel must be maintained throughout an entire phrase, most especially during a melisma.

An illustration of vowel migration that is found in general choral work is the Messiah chorus "For unto Us a Child Is Born." The singers tend to ignore the core of the vowel sound of "born," which is the open Italian "oh" sound (see Vowel Spectrum, p. 88). Even when they begin on an "oh" sound, by the time they have "traveled" the length of the melisma, the vowel has disintegrated to a diffused sound of "uh" or "aw." Rather, it should be emphasized that the "oh" sound should be maintained throughout the entire melisma, as shown in the following example:

Fig. 15:   Losing the Core of the Vowel

Tone quality and flexibility are maintained by clearly defining and sustaining the vowel when singing multiple notes on one vowel sound.

Another typical example of vowel diffusion or migration is found in a passage, such as:

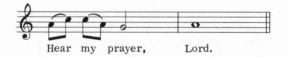

Fig. 16:   Vowel Focus

This is often pronounced as:

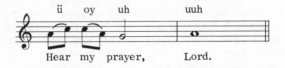

Fig. 17:   Vowel Focus

A clear vowel will eliminate the apparent necessity of overemphasizing diphthongs and consonants. This is not to say that diphthongs and consonants must be neglected. They should be pronounced clearly but, in so doing, vowel pronunciation should not be slighted. Keeping this concept in mind, the choir director should stress the accurate pronunciation of the basic vowel sounds. The illustration previously discussed now becomes:

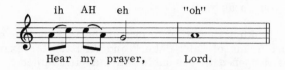

Fig. 18: Correct Vowel Focus

The "oh" sound in "Lord" differs from the pure OH in that the merging "r" sound tends to diffuse the "oh." Thus, the "oh" becomes modified as in the open Italian "oh." (See Vowel Spectrum, p. 88.) If the singer is forming an "aw" for the "or" in "Lord," the addition of the "r" sound results in an unpleasant sound. Again we observe that the best focus for the "or" sound is the open Italian "oh." "Lahrd" or "Luhrd" are mispronunciations of the word. They produce a diffused sound and are certainly bad diction; "r's" should be flipped or rolled.

The central idea is to keep the mind sharply focused upon a definite vowel sound at all times. Any diphthong ending will be automatically applied by the singers. It is the "core" of the vowel sound which is the important factor upon which to concentrate.

The Neglected "ah" Sound

An important consideration is the pronunciation of the "ah" (a short version of AH) as it appears in "the," "us," or "mother." These forms of the "AH" vowel differ basically in their duration. The "ah" in "the" is very short in time value in speech pronunciation. The "ah" in "us" or "mother" is a little less short, but still not as long in duration as the "AH" in "father." Carefully pronounce all three sounds in order: "the," "mother" and "father." They can be characterized by the analogy of the "Three Bears": the

baby "ah, " the mother (medial) "ah" and the father "AH. "
These are examples of the sounds which tend to be neglected
through faulty speech habits. In speaking, only a suggestion
of the "ah" is required to establish the intended sound.   It
is not necessary to sustain the vowel sound in speech as in
singing. In singing, however, its duration depends upon the
time value of notes.   The short "ah" sound, then, is unpleasant when an untrained singer tries to sing it as he would
speak it.   As Gertrude Beckman says, "Sing as you speak
... IF you speak well. "29

Attention should be drawn to the fact that in singing,
the short forms of "ah" ("the, " and "trust, " for example)
must be deepened to resemble "AH" as in "father. " Of
course, one must caution that the pronunciation of "the" and
"father" with the same depth of tone as "AH" would be ludi-
crous.

> There is no such thing as a short vowel in singing:
> that is to say the snappy, tight sound that usually
> comes when we speak such words as "cot, " "eat, "
> "cut. " Singing does away with these almost en-
> tirely. 30

Another example concerning the use of the short vowel
is the singing of "Gloria" from the 12th Mass, attributed to
Mozart: "Glorious is Thy name" (etc.). If a choir sings:

Fig. 19: Short Vowel Formation

as in conversational short sounds, the tone quality and
(rhythm) of the eighth note value "uh" suffers greatly.   This
is likewise true of "Thy" which tends to become "Thuh. " In
these two cases, if the singers will think of an "AH" instead
of "uh, " both rhythm and tone quality will be improved.   For
the best focus of tone, it is suggested that the choir think of
the following vowel sounds in Fig. 20. It should be emphasized that the "oh" in "glorious" is conceived as "oh," but,
in singing, the "r" keeps it from being pronounced as the
"OH" in "go. " This qualification will be discussed in detail
later in this chapter concerning "modified vowels. "

Fig. 20: Short Vowel Pronunciation

The Use of the Short "ah" ("uh") Sound

The short, shallow "uh," as we speak it, however, is valuable in connecting words and also is effective in dramatic fortissimo endings of labials (M, B, P, F and V), linguals (L, N and R), dentals (T and D), sibilants (S and Z) and palatines (C and G) rather than being just a sound to be sustained. The singers should experiment by adding "uh" to each of the above-mentioned consonants with such words as "realm" (r-eh-l-m-uh) and "rob" (r-ah-b-uh) when singing them emphatically on any note. The important fact to remember here is that the "uh" clarifies singing pronunciation when a forceful word-ending is needed. The "uh" must always be pronounced at lightning speed or else it will sound affected. There must be merely a suggestion of its sound, rather than an obvious pronunciation. An example of the "uh" used in this manner is found in the text of the "Bonnie Earl O'Moray," which is sung forte, in a sustained manner (see Fig. 21).

Again, it must be stressed that the "uh" sound should not be overemphasized to the extent that it is out of character with the mood. It must be pronounced as fast as is necessary to establish a link between two consonants, or to finish a word more dramatically, and it must be done with great care lest the singer sound artificial. In this respect it is evident that many consonants are associated with actual sounds and can be sung to specific pitches. As one can see from the above, the "uh" sound is frequently pronounced with b (uh), d (uh), g (uh), j (uh), l (uh), m (uh), n (uh), r (uh), v (uh), w (uh), z (uh) and ng (uh) in dramatic word endings.

THE "SUB-VOWEL"

In addition to the two categories of vowel sounds discussed-- the principal vowel and the derivative vowel--there is a third category of sound. It is identified with singing the liquid consonants. These can be termed "sub-vowels" because they possess distinctive, sonorous characteristics identified with

Fig. 21: The Use of the Short Vowel "uh"

pitch; that is, they can be sung on a "vocal line" just as any
other vowel, except with more difficulty and less resonance.
They are "sub-vowel" in sound but can, and should be, given
pitch recognition in singing. These sub-vowels are "m,"
"n," "ng," "l," "r" (uhr), "v," and "z."

They are listed in order of their "singability." The
humming sound "m" is quite singable; a little less singable
are the "n" and "ng." The sounds "m," "n," and "ng" retain their "native" humming quality when used in the middle

of a word, thus becoming a liaison between vowels. In legato singing, especially, these "sub-vowels" must retain a
vital humming sound. Moreover, they should not be considered as consonants where continuity of tone is so important.
The "m," "n" and "ng" are often used by choral directors
and voice teachers to gain more "forward placement" of the
tone and to emphasize the sensation of "mask resonance,"
which is less noticeable when singing the open vowel sounds.
Vocalises, which utilize "ming," or "mee-may-mah-moh-moo,"
etc., can be useful provided the "m" sound is exploited to
its fullest potential. Merely using the vocalise without specific recognition of its purpose will be of questionable value
to the singers.

       "Amen" becomes AHm (as in humming)--men. A re-
minder to the singers to "hum through" these sounds will
help them identify "m" on a specific pitch. Directors should
be alert to call attention to words ending in "n" and "ng,"
being certain that their singers utilize these liquid consonants
as "sub-vowels." (See Vowel Spectrum for additional examples.) The vowel derivative sound "uhr" (as in "ever") likewise sustains the "r," and as soon as the word ending is
reached, a hard, raspy sound is heard unless the tongue is
rolled or flipped. In any case, the actual "r" sound is quite
difficult to sustain and presents a difficult problem for unskilled singers. When they understand the function of all the
respective sounds as they relate to sustaining vocal pitches,
the singers will have a definite basis for clearer understanding of vowel production as it relates to the singing process.

                        MODIFIED VOWELS

There is another area which will clarify the novices' concept
of singing technique. Some vowel sounds, when combined
with other sounds, tend to lose their initial identities and
their purity when we speak them. Yet, in singing, we must
give these vowel sounds a definite focal point. They are
mainly "oh" and "OO." The "oh" in "forth" or "glorious"
are two examples. Phoneticists often advise pronunciation
of the word "forth" as "fawth" but this produces a sound
which is too broad and diffused when combined with "r."
Singers will be able to focus the sound much more accurately if they think of the open Italian "oh" sound and then
proceed to pronounce the word completely: "foh-rth," flip-
ping or rolling the "r." This is also true when the "oh"
sound is combined with "ee." The singer should think of

"voice" as "voh-eece" rather than as a mixture, "vaw-ce."
The other "modified" vowel sound is the alteration of the
"OO" as in "surely." When sung "sh-ee-OO-uhr-lee" instead
of "sh-uuh-lee," it has a much clearer focus of sound and,
thus, tone.

TREATMENT OF DIPHTHONGS

The combination of two vowel sounds is termed "diphthong."
In speaking, one glides over the two sounds as though they
were one. The requirements of sustaining tones in singing,
however, demand that one of the two sounds be more prominent so as to maintain the focal point of the tone, the other
being a vanishing sound. Failure to focus upon one of the
two vowel sounds results in an indefinite, diffused sound.
This writer refers to the mixing of these sounds in singing
as "vowel migration," i.e., the singers' vowel focus leaves
the core of the sound that should be produced. Diphthongs
interfere with vocal production when they are mixed together.
They also cause the diction in singing to be "muddy." Muddied vowels are the root of all the diction problems of singers. When accurately produced, the clearly-defined vowel
eliminates the need for unusual stress on consonants, which
many choral directors insist upon, to the extent of destroy-
ing the musical line. (This is not to say that consonants do
not require attention and concentration. Rather, the consonant should be cleanly articulated and kept "in line" with the
vowel formation. This will be discussed in more detail later
in the chapter.)

      Ordinarily it is the first of the two sounds which
should be given the longer duration. The second part of
the diphthong should be considered as a consonant or wedded
with a consonant (the vanishing sound). The words "trout"
or "about" provide examples. They are a mixture of the
two vowels "AH" and "OO." If the two vowel sounds are
"mixed," the result is a sound similar to "aw." But since
the intention is not to say "trawt," the word becomes diffused
having no particular definition. This is an example of how
lack of vowel definition weakens tone quality and muddies diction. For this reason it is often difficult to understand the
words which some choirs or individuals sing. The singer,
therefore, must pronounce the word "trout" as "trAH--oot,"
the second part of the diphthong being attached directly to the
consonant "t." The sound of longest duration and most prominence is "AH," the second vowel sound ("oo") considered as
"vanishing" yet clearly articulated.

Reinforcement of this concept can be found in the manner in which the Italians treat multiple vowels. The stronger of two vowel sounds is always given longer duration, even though the weak vowel is also clearly defined, though of shorter duration. When the weaker of the two sounds is adjacent to a consonant, the weaker vowel and the consonant are combined. This results not only in a stronger focus and identification of the sound, but it also provides for clear diction. The following examples, sung on a specific pitch, should be considered:

> "so" is pronounced OH + oo, the "oo" acting as a consonant to finish the word
>
> "say" is pronounced AY + ee, the vanishing "ee" acting as a consonant
>
> "ice" is pronounced AH + eece (vanishing "ee")
>
> "house" is pronounced AH + oose (vanishing "oo")
>
> "boy" is pronounced boh + ee, vanishing "ee" acting as a consonant
>
> "new" is pronounced nee + OO (vanishing "ee" preceding the "OO")

The same principle applies to triphthongs, as in the previous examples of "pure" (pee-OO-uhr) and "surely" (shee-OO-uhr-uhl-ee).

Spelling out the words phonetically demonstrates for the singer the sounds as they appear in the prolonged form used in singing. Unskilled singers especially need to have a graphic means to show them how to improve tone quality and diction in singing.

TREATMENT OF CONSONANTS

In speaking or singing, "consonant" refers to:

> A speech sound characterized in enunciation by constriction of the breath channel (p, g, n, l, s, h, r, w), as distinguished from vowel, which is identified by the resonance form of the vocal cavities; also a letter representing such a sound. [Webster's Collegiate Dictionary, 2nd ed.]

Thus, the consonant is regarded as a constriction of the breath channel.

Wilson regards the use of the consonant in vocal development as being limited,

> and in fact they can be actually detrimental....
> Consonants must not interfere with ... the basic
> resonance, breath action and vowel formations for
> singing. 31

This attitude toward consonants causes many choral directors to neglect them in order to retain the continuity of sound which they desire. Wilson declares,

> No! Consonants must be used to make diction understandable and expressive without distorting the singing tone. 32

Consonants often cause "gymnastics of the soft palate" in that they restrict the flow of breath and tend to leave "holes" in the singing phrase line. The shape of the consonant should resemble the shape of the vowel which it precedes and follows. As has been stated earlier, the consonant must always be "in line" with the vowel; i.e., the singer must make a smooth transition from consonant to vowel and back to consonant, especially in legato singing. The lips must be free of tension when singing hard consonants and softened, as in proper Italian language pronunciation.

Examples of this may be found abundantly in English texts, such as "Thy dwelling place." The tendency of consonants to restrict tone (through losing vowel focus) by constricting the oral pharynx is one of the most prevalent problems in singing, especially in the upper tessitura of the voice.

Advancing a step further, it will be noted that a consonant which is properly related to the vowel will help the singer understand and express diction without distorting the tone. The "hard" consonants (such as b, d, g, j, k, p and t) tend to constrict the throats as they are pronounced. The constriction becomes more exaggerated as the pitch rises. There is great need, therefore, for the singers to relate the consonant to the vowel--to think of the vowel sound they are about to produce while they are forming the consonants which begin and end a word. Achieving this objective requires fewer major adjustments in the buccalpharyngeal cavity during the process of singing, thus assuring smoother vocal production.

There is further corroboration of this concept found in the German language. Most linguistic German scholars suggest retention of the vowel form while pronouncing the consonant "ch" in "ich," "och," or "ach." This tends to keep the throat "open" in the "vowel position." One of the problems among unskilled singers is exaggerated jaw movement, which inhibits vocal production by constricting the throat.

If the above-mentioned principle which the Germans use is generally applied to English consonants, it will tend to keep the mouth and tongue from unnecessary motion (oral gymnastics). The mouth, thereby, does not have to make as many different movements (jawing the words), which tend to interrupt smooth, consistent vocal production.

The Consonant and the Singer's Range

In the lower range of the voice, one can "afford" to have more lip and mouth movement because the soft palate does not need to be raised as high as when the voice is ascending to the upper range. In the upper voice range, therefore, the singer must treat the consonants less percussively than on the lower level, so as to keep the soft palate lifted for singing (the so-called "open throat"). The intensity of the higher tessitura will compensate for the lack of frontal pronunciation of hard consonants as needed for lower tones. Excessive lip and mouth movements, when used in high-tessitura singing, inhibits vocal action. For instance, if singers articulately pronounce "t," "th," "g," or "j" as in "that" or "God," on a high note, the tongue and glottal action of the consonant will tend to constrict the mouth and throat cavities. On the other hand, if singers carefully relate the consonant to the deep-feeling sensation in the throat needed for high tones and treat these consonants less percussively, they are not likely to close their throats when singing high tones. Moreover, as stated previously, the greater intensity of the higher tones compensates for the need to articulate consonants with a great amount of lip action. Again, it should be emphasized that in the singer's lower range, the consonant should be articulated in a "more forward position." Wilson states, "The diction is determined by the manner of pronunciation."[33]

It should also be re-emphasized that muddied vowels require overexaggerated consonants in an effort to achieve

good diction.   Thus, if the vowels are distinctly defined, the
consonants need not be overemphasized for good diction, especially in unaccompanied singing.

SINGING IN THE EXTREMES OF
THE VOCAL RANGE

Singers should be reminded to maintain the high-arch of the
soft palate and to clearly define the vowel, so as to sing high
notes effectively.   The combination thought process of the
raised palate and the pure vowel is an "insurance policy"
against dark or "woofy" tones in the upper range.   If the
singers keep the core of the vowel sound vividly in mind,
they will not lose the focus of sound.   (The use of the "vowel
spectrum," discussed earlier in the chapter, can be especially
helpful in teaching singers how to use their voices in the sustained high tessitura.)   These two basic concepts of vocal
production, combined with the method of breathing described
previously in this chapter, provide skilled as well as unskilled
singers with the means of extending their effective ranges
upward.   It is also important to remind the singers that the
sensation they experience in the mouth is similar to that felt
at the start of a yawn.   This sensation, coupled with clear
vowel pronunciation, greatly aids in maintaining the correct
"voice placement" as the scale is ascended.

The problem of "cover" when singing in the upper
part of the tessitura may raise a question in the reader's
mind, particularly about male voices.   The word "cover"
should realistically be regarded as the effect of certain acous-
tic partials, rather than the cause.   That is, when the soft
palate is arched properly, the tendency toward a blatant tone
is avoided.   Vowel depth avoids the blatant tone, while accurate pronunciation of the vowel eliminates or lessens excessive "darkness" of vowel and "tone color," which may
become heavy in character in the upper voice range when
the term "cover" is in the singers' minds.   A "forward
thrust" (mentally) of the vowel placement (a sneer, if you
will) prevents the vowel (tone) placement from drawing back
into the rear of the buccalpharyngeal cavity.   Again, it should
be stressed that a mental concept (aural image) of the accurate vowel serves the purpose of bridging the passaggio
and singing in the upper vocal range.   According to Friedrich S. Brodnitz,

Covering has to be used with great care because,

in its extreme form, it is hard on voices. Meas-
urements of air volume have shown that the same
note sung by the same singer uses, in covered
voice, up to double the amount of air it uses in
open singing. The reason for this result lies in
the greater tension and thickness of the outer laryngeal muscles as well as of the inner ones, both of
which tense the cords. 34

In other words, the thought-process of "covering"
leads to vocal production that is too heavy. This thick and
often coarse tone quality is analogous to string instrumentalists playing high notes on the thickest string for special effect.

TONE PLACEMENT

Tone placement is a term which is often misused or misunderstood in vocal parlance. It can be clarified, however, in
a few concise sentences.

The concept of being able to aim and place a tone
somewhere in the head or mouth is a misnomer. Rather,
a focused, resonant sound ("well-placed" tone) is the result
of proper vowel formation. Of course, the other factor in-
fluencing tone production--good breath management--is also
important, but true tonal focus emanates from proper "shaping of the horn, " which is the result of correct vowel focus.
It is analogous to putting a nozzle on a water hose. The intensity of the stream of water is dependent upon the size of
the orifice through which the water flows. Likewise, the
volume or carrying power of sound passing through the oral
cavities is governed by the shape and size of the buccalpharyngeal resonators. Thus, the proper adjustment of the resonators results in a more focused ("placed") tone. The
clearly produced vowel provides the correct placement of
tone.

THE PASSAGGIO

The passageway from one "register" to another within the
voice range is a problem which many persons in the vocal
field tend to ignore. They hope that the "break" in the voice
from the lower to the upper range will disappear as the singer
matures. This attitude is fostered by the thought that the

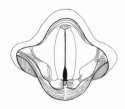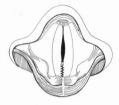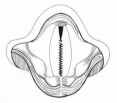

Fig. 22: "Zipper Action" of the Vocal Folds
Illustration by Nancy Vander Linde Corey

voice should function without "registers." That notion is the
ideal, but it rarely occurs in "grass roots" singers--especially
among men. Some singers experience a greater degree of
change than others, which is caused by the fact that they do
not "thin out" the mass of the vocal folds when approaching
the place of change--the passaggio or "break." String players can change to a thinner string as they ascend the scale.
Singers, however, must develop the ability to thin or thicken
the folds with only one "set of strings" as they progress
through a song. Therefore, as one envisages the action of
the vocal folds, one might consider the action of a zipper,
that is, shortening and lengthening of the vocal folds as well
as thinning out their mass. The illustration is an oversim-
plification of the vocalis action described above, but it serves
the purpose of conveying a picture of how the folds must thin
out as well as shorten to attain proper phonation at higher
level pitches.

THE MALE FALSETTO AND THE HEAD VOICE

The route to "ironing out" the break where it occurs in the
singers' ranges is effectively made through intelligent use of
the so-called falsetto. The term "falsetto" was coined by the
Italian masters of the early Bel Canto period, who thought of
it as an unnatural (and, therefore, false) voice. There is
probably no other term in vocal parlance that causes more
controversy than this one. Vennard describes the falsetto
action of the vocal musculature as follows:

> The vocalis muscles fall to the sides of the larynx
> and the vibration takes place almost entirely in the
> ligaments along the edges of the cords.... Such a

vibration can take place at high frequencies, because there is very little mass [of the folds] to be
moved, and the amplitude is small.... The folds
do not offer much resistance to the breath.... 35

This is the reason why the falsetto is so breathy in
many instances, especially in the lower notes of the upper
vocal range and the reason why the tone becomes clearer as
the length of the folds--zipper action--shortens, resulting in
more tension and thus more breath resistance. According
to Brodnitz,

> The falsetto is sung with only the foremost parts
> of the cords left free to vibrate at the margins,
> the rest being damped.... It has less brilliance
> than the head register. It can be used occasionally,
> but its continuous employment gives the voice an
> effeminate character. 36

Proper use of the falsetto is the "prelude" to the development of the "head voice." As the vocal muscles develop
strength in this falsetto position, the "head voice" begins to
emerge. * The "forward focus" of the falsetto position of the
vocal folds produces a stronger tone, while a tone focused
backward in the buccalpharyngeal cavity produces a weak or
breathy tone.

Husler and Rodd-Marling present an interesting view
of the term "falsetto." They state that there are two oppos-
ing views of the falsetto. One is a harmful, false voice;
the other a valuable attribute of the singing voice. Their
description of the phenomenon is that falsetto may be

> [an] extremely thin, breathy tone quality which can-
> not be modified; and which cannot become a transi-
> tion to the full voice ... a collapsed organ.

or

> [a] tone quality possessing greater tension, strength
> and carrying power; one which is modifiable to a
> certain extent and out of which the full voice can
> be developed--i.e., a supported falsetto. 37

---

*For a more comprehensive discussion of the vocal mechanism,
see Russell A. Hammar, Singing--An Extension of Speech
(1978), Chapter II.

Singers should be reminded to think "chest tones" into the falsetto tones.

> The ideal singing is done in a mixture of register characteristics in a voix mixte. Each tone of the compass receives a little tone color of the opposing registers in a mixture that varies from equal parts in the middle of the range to heavier coloring at the extreme ends. 38

The "mixed voice" requires superimposing the heavier production of the "chest voice" upon the lighter falsetto or "head voice" to "blend" the two extremes. One must imagine the result of upper and lower voice timbres being blended together as though listening to one's voice on stereophonic speakers--one speaker being the upper voice (falsetto) quality; the other being the lower voice ("chest"). This process requires a great amount of concentration, patience and determination to accomplish "hearing" in one's mind the two timbres simultaneously. The result of this practice is that the proper aural image of the tone enables the singer to engage the vocal folds a little more thickly while still maintaining their lighter approximation. Most vocal pedagogues work the upper voice down into the lower "register" in studio teaching, so as to make this transition. This practice can be included in the class voice work of the choral rehearsal as well.

The strained chest voice position of the folds often heard as basses sing around their high "c" (middle "c" on the piano) and the tenors around "f" and "f♯" above middle "c" can easily ruin blend and balance in ensemble as well as harm the vocal mechanisms of the singers. Convincing men to use falsetto tones (particularly in the employment of loud dynamics) will achieve blend and still have enough body of tone for balance providing the tone has enough of the higher partials. The men must be convinced that they will be heard; that a well-focused but smaller falsetto tone will have presence and will blend better than the forced chesty tone quality.

This, as stated previously, is achieved by the tone being "focused" forward through the use of the "sneer" (or "snarl"), so that there is "ping" in the tone. It is difficult to convince some men to try this approach to the upper voice because the tone does not seem to have enough body (bulk) to them. A tape recording of "before" and "after" often reveals to them that the falsetto tone is not at all bad. Without a doubt, it sounds stronger and better than it feels. Again, the problem of establishing the correct aural image-sensation for singers emerges. The goal of developing a satisfactory "head voice" tone in male voices is not accomplished in one easy lesson. Good growth occurs in small steps and requires patience. Attaining high levels of development in utilizing the complex vocal instrument requires years of dedication along with intelligent teaching and study. It follows, then, that choral singers need significant time to develop a realistic understanding of their voices.

Voice Classification and Characteristics

The choral director should strive to achieve good balance without ignoring the personal needs of the singers. Therefore, proper voice classification is crucial. Pushing voices to either extreme can permanently harm them, especially in instances in which basses and altos are asked to sing tenor. In either case, young voices of teenagers can be permanently harmed by such abuse. However, it is possible to extend the ranges of singers through intelligent vocal pedagogy. Many so-called baritones are "tenors without a top"--not being able to bridge their passaggi to sing in the upper range.

There are always "borderline voices" which do not appear to have definite characteristics of a given vocal category. When auditioning voices, some may be light, but have limited scope in range; others may be heavy and have a wide range of notes. One of the best means of classifying voices, in addition to timbre and range, is to determine the passaggio of each voice. As stated above, the passaggio of the singing voice is that group of notes on which the voice seems to change in quality, or breaks, or becomes weak and breathy. It is the place in the vocal range in which the musculature makes a major adjustment from the "heavy" mechanism to the "light" mechanism. It is particularly noticeable in untrained voices. Some singers will merely ascend the scale as far as they can go in "chest" or heavy mechanism and then claim that is the end of their range; never realizing that in engaging the falsetto (men and most contraltos) many more notes can be added to their range. Therefore, it is of vital importance to choral directors that they become familiar with the approximate notes involving the passaggio of each vocal category. Following is a means of classifying voices by recognition of the "break."

Beginning with the basses, we can observe that:

1. Low (contra) basses (who are able to sing down to low "e," two octaves below middle "c" on the piano), will experience the passaggio change about "$b\flat$" just below middle "c" to "$d\flat$" (bass II).

2. Bass-baritones: c^1 (middle "c" on the piano) to d^1 (bass II).

3. Lyric baritones: d^1 to e^1 (bass I).

4. Dramatic (Helden) tenor: e^1 to f^1 above middle "c"; also, some voices of lighter quality change on these notes (tenor II).

5. Lyric tenor: f^1 to g^1 (tenor I).

6. Contralto: a^1 to b^1 or c^2 (alto II).

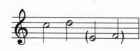

7. Mezzo-soprano: c^2 to d^2, and frequently e^1 to f^1 (alto I).

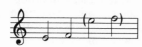

8. Dramatic soprano, e^1 to f^1, and slight adjustment usually at e^2 and f^2 (alto I or soprano II).

9. Lyric and lyric coloratura soprano: e^1 to f^1 (soprano I).

10. Coloratura soprano: f^1 to g^1 (soprano I).

Of special note is that the tenor and soprano passaggi span exactly the same notes. Further analysis reveals that the soprano's passaggio is at the bottom part of her range, while the tenor goes into his "head voice" or falsetto in the upper part of his range. However, e^1 to f^1 leads both sopranos and tenors into their upper vocal ranges. The soprano who has learned to utilize her "chest voice" mechanism can easily sing in the so-called alto range. (Some vocal pedagogues insist that all women have the same passaggi and all are capable of similar ranges; the timbre being the major difference between the voices.) The point to be established here is that the soprano voice is the "flute" of the vocal "orchestra," having less fundamental in the "head voice" tones which she sings. All voices in the upper range have less fundamental, but most of the time the alto and bass vocal tessitura (in choral work especially) spans their "chest voice" range. In contrast, the tenor tessitura often spans his passaggio. Because of the fact that many "should be" tenors have not solved the transition to the head voice or falsetto, there are relatively few men who sing in that section of a choir. Many of these "self-determined baritones" can be "graduated" to the tenor section by detecting their passaggi around e^1 to f^1, and then encouraging them to utilize this falsetto to sing in the tenor range. With care and patience these "in limbo" singers will develop into "legitimate" tenors.

It is important to reiterate that these passaggio ranges may vary with the time of day (early morning versus later in the day or evening) or whether the singer has a cold or an allergy. In these instances the vocal folds are thicker or swollen. The illustrations above should be considered basic indications as to what choral section the singer should be assigned. Occasionally, a singer will demonstrate little or no change in tone quality across the scale of the vocal range. These "natural" singers have instinctively developed the ability to bridge the gap of upper and lower vocal range. In these instances, the assignment to a section becomes one of judging only the singer's vocal timbre. Singers who produce muddy or diffused vowels tend to mask where the passaggio really lies in their vocal range. Therefore, it is especially crucial, when analyzing voice categories, to insist upon clear, accurate vowel production.

INTONATION PROBLEMS

An often overlooked reason for bad intonation in choral groups

is caused by improper vocal production. In Chapter 2 it was
cited that choirs singing with "straight tone" production (devoid of any vibrato at all) often have difficulty with flatting.
This is because many of the natural overtones of the voice
have been eliminated. In choirs composed mostly of untrained
singers, one encounters the "straight tone" production as a
natural concomitant. The result is that there are not enough
high partials in the tones to keep the pitch where it belongs.
Therefore, when a choral group or section flats, it seems
pertinent to analyze vocal production first before attempting
other mechanical adjustments. Modern research has revealed
that our vocal production (speech and singing) is controlled
by higher centers of the brain from which messages are sent
to the recurrent nerve centers. These nerve centers control
phonation, and thus, the link between good intonation and good
vocal production seems obvious: it is the listening-hearing-
sensing activities of the brain which are central in producing
the desired vocal results.

Very likely, weak vowel production will cause flabby,
"dead-fish" tones, completely lacking in vitality. This phenomenon is particularly evident in soft singing, wherein the
singers abandon support of the vocal tones they are producing.
Instead, singers should be reminded that they need to put
more concentrated effort (intensity of tone) into soft singing
than into loud singing; that their concentration upon the firmness of their vowels (pronunciation of words) is more essential for pianissimo than for forte singing.

There are many other factors that can influence intonation, such as physical and emotional fatigue, unfamiliarity
with the music, poor room ventilation (lack of oxygen), and
poor posture. Whatever the conditions that exist in the choral
rehearsal room or concert stage, the intonation problems are
more likely to revolve around inferior tone production. Therefore, it is mandatory for directors of ensembles to alleviate
these causes which may interfere with the production of proper
tone quality. Moreover, the director (vocal instructor) must
act as the singers' collective ears in assisting them to develop keen listening habits concerning intonation. An aid to
this awareness on the part of the singers is the use of a tape
recorder of reasonable quality. Playing back a tape recording
example of the choir's good and bad tone quality and intonation can improve the listening habits as well as the tonal concepts of a choral group. (Of course, correct microphone
placement is crucial to achieving a satisfactory recording of
the group.)

Unaccompanied singing has long been regarded as the best means of improving intonation in choral ensembles. The scales derived from the natural overtone series of the Pythagorean and Meantone tunings provide the best intonation for so-called a cappella singing, i.e., containing those notes within a chord which seem to progress naturally upward or downward in cadential sequences. Most anyone who has studied harmonic progressions of chorales has encountered these notes which gravitate in a natural direction. This phenomenon is dictated by our ears, which have been conditioned to the harmonies of Western music.

The Untempered Scale

An untempered scale is based upon natural overtones. It dates back to Pythagoras and the monochord, which, when stopped (damped) exactly in half, produced the octave; half of the octave produced an interval of a fifth, etc. Consequently, the intervals differed significantly from the later development of the well-tempered scale of the modern piano, the tuning of which is based upon an equal number of "cents" between each half step of the octave. The result of this tuning is to cause the third of the chord to be slightly high and the fifth slightly flat.

The Pythagorean scale, developed about 600 B.C., contains a high third and high leading tone, each creating the feeling of movement upward: the third moving to the fourth tone of the scale and the seventh to the tonic. Pythagoras set up the ratios for the octave (2:1), the fifth (3:2) and the fourth (4:3). According to this scale certain notes of the scale were higher than their enharmonic sharps. For instance, b♭ was higher than a♯, each accidental relating to the neighboring tone from which it derived.

The Just or "natural" scale was developed by Ptolemy about A.D. 150 with lower major thirds and sixths. In this scale the flats were also higher than the enharmonic sharps (i.e., b♭ higher than a♯), but tuning was improved.

The distinctive characteristics regarding the intervals of the Just scale are principally that three fundamental triads are more euphonious than either the Pythagorean or well-tempered tunings. For instance, the triads c-e-g, f-a-c and g-b-d ("natural" triads with a ratio of 4:5:6) were greatly improved in intonation. In unaccompanied singing these I, IV

and V chords had "delicious" intonation, i.e., no feeling of
"dissonance" whatsoever. On the other hand, one disadvantage of using the Just scale was that when chromatic harmony
emerged the chords were noticeably out of tune. For example, the "a" of the C Major scale was out of tune when
the chord d-f♯-a was encountered--as well as other chromatic harmonies relating to the key of C. Another problem
was that a g♯ was lower than an a♭. This phenomenon (problem) also applies to most of the choral music in the repertoire of modern choirs, thus creating even greater confusion
concerning intonation among singers who attempt to employ
the Pythagorean, Just, or Meantone scales. The Meantone
system is similar to the Just intonation. (Meantone tuning
was used extensively around 1500.) Our modern ears have
become so accustomed to the equal (well)-tempered scale that
the perfect intonation of some of the chords in these "natural"
scales is foreign to our ears. However, for reference purposes, choral directors should have some understanding of
the differences among these tunings. In unaccompanied singing, it would be wise to attempt to achieve the intonation
which relates to Pythagorean, Just or Meantone scales, rather
than the Equal Temperament. Quite naturally, the intonation
of the three older scales is best suited to Renaissance music.

The following charts illustrate the differences in pitch
relationships of the various scale systems:

Cycles per second

Temperament	c	d	e	f	g	a	b	c
Pythagorean:	520	585	658	693	780	877	987	1040
Just:	520	585	650	693	780	867	975	1040
Equal:	520	584	655	694	779	874	982	1040

	1	2	3	4	5	6	7	8
	a	b	c♯	d	e	f♯	g	a
Just	440	495	550	586.6	660	733.3+	825	880
(difference)	0	-.6	+4.4	+1.2	-.4	+5.4	+5.7	0
Equal (well)-tempered	440	494.4	554.4	587.8	659.6	739.2	830.7	880
Meantone	440			584	655			880

Fig. 23: Cycles per Second of Tuning Temperaments

It is of interest to note that the Meantone scale is closer to the Equal-tempered scale than the Just, and, therefore, it offers fewer problems of adjustment in tuning.

In Equal Temperament the octave is divided into 1200 cents, each half step having a value of 100 cents. This action affords a means of being absolutely exact for all tunings, so that enharmonic notes (g♯ and a♭, for instance) have exactly the same tunings. The Equal-Tempered scale was brought into practical use by J. S. Bach when he wrote keyboard pieces for the clavier in all keys. Some scholars dispute his adhering strictly to the present rigid equal temperament, believing that it may have been only a close approximation of it. If the reader has ever attempted to do a complete tuning of a modern piano (or harpsichord), he or she can appreciate how keen one's ear must be to detect the slight pitch differences which control intonation. If one attempts to tune by the circle of fifths starting on "a" (440 cps) and does so by using intervals of a perfect fifth up, an octave down, and then again up a fifth, repeating this sequence until the original "a" is reached again, it will be flat in relation to the "d" preceding it. In other words, an expansion of intervals takes place, which the keyboard cannot accommodate in all keys as the circle of fifths is traversed.

To reinforce this point, the following example contrasting the Just and Equal Temperaments illustrates these differences:

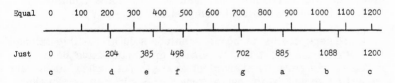

Fig. 24: Comparison of Equal and Just Temperaments

This chart illustrates that equal temperament tuning does not have a single exact interval in terms of the "natural" scale. Consideration of this fact also indicates that, when we discuss choral intonation, we find ourselves in a somewhat ambiguous situation as to judging what we mean by

perfect or even good intonation. We can only make our decisions based upon what our sense of hearing dictates. As
mentioned previously, one remedy is to listen carefully to
factors such as the third of the chord leading to the fourth
or the fourth resolving down to the third (as in a plagal cadence) and the leading tone (7th) moving toward the tonic.
Careful attention to tuning will eventually lead to discrimination concerning harmony that capitalizes upon the natural
overtones of the harmonics derived from the fundamental.

   The ear is the only tuning agent which the voice has;
the vocal "instrument" bearing similar intonation relationship
to stringed instruments, i. e., string intonation also relying
upon the ear to govern playing in tune. It is of importance,
therefore, to note that modern acoustical equipment has made
it possible to measure the intervals actually played by string
players. It was found that accomplished string players (both
in solo and ensemble work) tend toward Pythagorean intervals
rather than Equal Temperament. 39 Similarly, then, the high
third and seventh of the Pythagorean scale suit both strings
and voice needs. Both intervals tend to "pull" upward sound-
wise to the subdominant and tonic, thereby aiding the singers
to avoid flatting. The fact that flats and sharps have slightly
different pitches is of no consequence when the singing does
not need to relate to the well-tempered clavier (modern piano
or organ). As a matter of fact, if all singers of a given
choral group sang the absolute Pythagorean scale, the ensemble would be slightly sharp at the end of a composition.
This is especially noticeable in Renaissance period music in
which intonation problems are exaggerated by the often "open"
harmonic structure. By contrast, in Romantic period music,
the intonation problems are not as likely to be evident because
of the thicker harmonies and doublings of notes common to
nineteenth-century style of composition.

   There seems to be no absolute solution to this intonation dilemma. Most contemporary musicians have been exposed to the equal temperament scale. Yet, when pianos are
permitted to get badly out of tune, it is difficult to develop
any absolute set of true intervalic relationships. Consequently,
when we discuss intonation, we should be cautious as to which
scale we believe we are using and what deviations from the
equal temperament we may employ to suit our own biases.

PHYSICAL VOCAL MALADIES OFTEN OVERLOOKED

Vocal Nodules and Polyps

Unfortunately, a condition of which teachers and students alike are often quite ignorant is nodules on the vocal bands (cords). When we consider that the vocal "instrument" is very small in relation to other organs of the body, it is little wonder why abuse can take place.

The vocal bands themselves are two pearly-white shelves of thin mucous membrane clothing the vocal ligaments, 15 millimeters long (about three-fifths of an inch) in adult males and 10 millimeters long (about two-fifths of an inch) in adult females. [40]

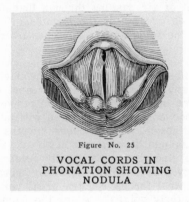

Figure No. 25

VOCAL CORDS IN
PHONATION SHOWING
NODULA

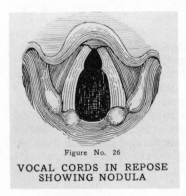

Figure No. 26

VOCAL CORDS IN REPOSE
SHOWING NODULA

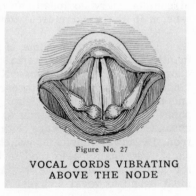

Figure No. 27

VOCAL CORDS VIBRATING
ABOVE THE NODE

Figs. 25, 26, and 27: Vocal Cord Nodules

Is it not amazing the demands we put upon this relatively tiny "instrument"? When the vocal mechanism is
abused through strained singing or playground or grandstand
yelling, nature tends to soothe the irritated area by calcify-
ing (toughening) that particular area of irritation. It is similar to the development of corns or callouses caused by im-
properly fitting shoes which rub the skin. Some physicians
refer to nodes and polyps as benign tumors. Other doctors
claim that nodes originate from obstructed mucous glands,
or "corns on the vocal cords."[41]

Singers may be able to sing quite well above and below the phonating point of the nodules since the vocal bands
can phonate satisfactorily where the "bumps" are absent.
However, when the vocal folds are phonated near or on the
spot of the nodes, a breathy quality is evident, caused by
the great amount of air passing through that area, i.e.,
through the spaces created by the nodules. There is not complete contact of the folds at those pitches over which the nodes
are formed.[42]

Many professional singers fear the development of nodules more than any other affliction. In most cases concert
and opera singers must project their voices over large (loud)
orchestras in huge concert halls, often without the aid of
electronic amplification. Thus, these singers are often prone
to forcing their voices beyond reason so as to be heard.
Wagnerian opera singers are especially vulnerable to these
conditions. Many contemporary solo and choral compositions
with large orchestral forces require great volume, causing
singers to force their voices. Also, the harmonic texture
of contemporary compositions often tends to cause additional
tension in the vocal musculature.

However, even some of the choral music of the Romantic Era can be detrimental to the vocal mechanism of
choral singers. Beethoven's Ninth (choral) Symphony heaps
"insult upon injury" for singers--particularly the sopranos
and tenors. Mahler's "Eighth Symphony" (called the "Symphony of a Thousand") tends to strain the voices as well as
assault the listeners' ears with its volume demands. Songs
from Broadway musicals, which encourage hard and "pushed"
chest-tone quality also tend to be vocally harmful, especially
for high school age singers. Pop and rock singers are the
most prone to vocal nodules.

Generally, sopranos and tenors are more susceptible

to nodule formation because the greater frequency of vibration of the vocal folds in the higher ranges multiplies the harmful effects of disphonia.

Young voices that are employed in singing adult-level choral music can also develop nodules, or at least have their muscular fibers become hardened. Some ambitious elementary school teachers attempt to imitate the more mature high school choral sound as do some high school directors in their attempt to achieve the level of vocal maturity in their ensembles such as that produced by college and professional vocal groups. Boys' choirs in the Anglican Church tradition in the United States and England, plus the Lutheran tradition of Europe (particularly in Germany and Austria), are also among the perpetrators of strained voices. They sing Bach motets, oratorios and other such music which demands mature trebel vocal sounds; this, in an effort to balance the volume of the tenor and bass sounds of the adult males. The result is that the immature vocal muscles of these boys are sometimes ruined by this abuse. However, boys with very strong vocal musculature (muscle tone) are not as noticeably harmed. Some vocal mechanisms can tolerate more abuse than others. (Analogously, the case in sports activity has shown that some children have adverse effects from organized sports, such as Little League baseball and football, whereas, others do not. The young child's muscles are often unable to cope with adult-level strain to which they are subjected in these sports.)

There are also basic physiological conditions which cause some persons to be more susceptible to the development of vocal nodules (or other muscular disorders), such as weak or inflexible muscle tone, a mal-shaped epiglottis, small resonating cavities and the like.

The care of vocal nodules is extremely difficult. Dr. Brodnitz states,

> Voice rest alone does not achieve any cure. Small nodes may disappear after a few weeks of silence, but will reform immediately if speaking or singing is resumed with the same abusive methods that started the vicious circle. [43]

He further claims that surgery is no answer either; that even if the nodules are successfully removed without damage to the vocal bands, new nodules will soon reappear. Furthermore, scar tissue from surgery may leave rough edges on the folds.

Vocal polyps are benign growths which may emerge on any area of the vocal bands.

> They may sit on the cord with a broad base as reddish prominences, or may be attached to the cord by a narrow "neck." They can reach the size of a cherry stone. [44]

Brodnitz goes on to state that chronic irritations, such as prolonged laryngitis, excessive cigarette smoking, and various auditory vocal abuses (such as cheerleading) are contributing factors. However, if the polyps are plainly visible and accessible, surgery, in this instance, is usually successful. Again, remedial efforts must be taken in order to avoid the development of new polyps.

To avoid or remedy the basic cause of these problems, vocal strain must be eliminated through proper pedagogical methods of vocal development. Therefore, it behooves every choral director and voice instructor to be sensitive to the symptoms caused by vocal abuse. This warning implies very strongly that choral directors are obligated to thoroughly understand the vocal mechanism--its limitations as well as its strengths.

SUMMARY

Choral directors are essentially responsible for the vocal development of the individuals in their ensembles. That is to say, they must provide the example by which their singers can be inspired to improve their vocal responses as well as to learn the music. Only in rare instances of professional choral ensembles can singers be almost entirely responsible for the vocal demands of the conductor without pedagogical instruction in the art of singing. The conductor should be knowledgeable about the anatomical components of the vocal mechanism--its limitations as well as its potential. It is one matter to envisage what sounds are desirable for performance of a given musical selection and quite another to lead the singers to better vocal production. Thus, group lessons in the choral rehearsal are essential.

It is imperative that choral directors be able to explain to their charges how to breathe, how to produce good tone quality throughout the compass of their voices, how to help the singers solve problems of the passaggio, and how to achieve better intonation and blend among the voices through improved vocal pedagogy.

NOTES

1. Donald Jay Grout, A History of Western Music, 3rd edition (New York: W.W. Norton, 1980), p. 174.
2. Ibid., p. 293-4.
3. Ibid., p. 455.
4. Reinhard G. Pauly, Music in the Classical Period (Englewood Cliffs, N.J.: Prentice-Hall, 1965), p. 14.
5. Gerald F. Darrow, Four Decades of Choral Training (Metuchen, N.J.: The Scarecrow Press, 1975), p. 2.
6. Ibid., p. 4.
7. E. D. Freud, "Voice Pathology and the Emergence of a New Vocal Style," Archives of Otolaryngology, 62 (1955), p. 51.
8. Darrow, op. cit., p. 119.
9. Victor Fields, Foundations of the Singer's Art (New York: Vantage Press, 1977), p. 90.
10. Russell A. Hammar, Singing--An Extension of Speech (Metuchen, N.J.: The Scarecrow Press, 1978), p. 65.
11. Ibid., p. 66.
12. Harry R. Wilson, Artistic Choral Singing (New York: G. Schirmer, 1959), p. 161.
13. Hammar, op. cit., p. 158.
14. Ibid., p. 174.
15. Ibid., p. 129.
16. R. Cedric Colness, "Tone Quality ... a Pragmatic Approach for High School Choirs," The American Music Teacher, Vol. 17, No. 2, November-December 1967, p. 21.
17. Hammar, op. cit., p. 61.
18. Ibid., p. 61.
19. Ibid., p. 62.
20. Ibid., p. 66.
21. Ibid., p. 62.
22. E. Herbert-Caesari, The Voice of the Mind (London: Robert Hale, 1951), p. 88.
23. Charles K. Scott, The Fundamentals of Singing (New York: Pitman, 1954), p. 218.
24. Wilson, op. cit., p. 62.
25. Mario P. Marafioti, Caruso's Method of Voice Production (1922); reprinted (Austin, Texas: Cadica Enterprises, 1958), p. 69.
26. Ibid., p. 65.

27. Douglas Stanley, Your Voice: Applied Science of Vocal
    Art (New York: Pitman, 1945), p. 69.
28. Wilson, op. cit., p. 161.
29. Gertrude Beckman, Tools for Speaking and Singing (New
    York: G. Schirmer, 1945), p. 84.
30. Scott, op. cit., p. 405.
31. Wilson, op. cit., p. 185.
32. Ibid., p. 185.
33. Ibid., p. 123.
34. Friedrich S. Brodnitz, M.D., Keep Your Voice Healthy,
    (New York: Harper and Brothers, 1953), p. 83.
35. William Vennard, Singing: The Mechanism and the
    Technic (New York: Carl Fischer, 1967, rev. ed.),
    p. 67.
36. Brodnitz, op. cit., p. 82.
37. Paraphrased from Frederick Husler and Yvonne Rodd-
    Marling, Singing: The Physical Nature of the Vocal
    Organ (New York: October House, 1965), p. 59.
38. Brodnitz, op. cit., p. 82.
39. Journal of the Acoustical Society of America (New York:
    American Institute of Physics) "Absolute Pitch" (1955),
    pp. 1180-1185. (No author listed)
40. R. D. Lockhart, G. F. Hamilton, and F. W. Fyfe,
    Anatomy of the Human Body (Philadelphia: J.B. Lip-
    pincott, 1959), p. 538.
41. Brodnitz, op. cit., pp. 158-159.
42. Ibid., p. 159.
43. Ibid., p. 161.
44. Ibid., p. 162.

REVIEW QUESTIONS FOR CHAPTER 4

(1) Compare the vocal textures of Renaissance, Baroque,
Roccoco, Classic, Romantic and Contemporary periods
of music.

(2) Define in detail the schools of choral tone: a) "Straight
tone"; b) "Laissez faire"; c) "Sonorous Blend"; and their
relative advantages and disadvantages.

(3) Define "resonance" and its relevance to choral tone.

(4) Define "volume" and its relevance to choral tone.

(5) What is meant by the term "aural image"?

(6) How do the Eustachian tubes affect an individual's conception of his/her speaking or singing voice?

(7) How does the diaphragm function for inhalation and controlling release of breath in singing?

(8) Cite the proper breathing technique for singing described in this chapter.

(9) Describe the three most commonly used breathing techniques in singing.

(10) Describe how improved vocal pedagogy is achieved through diction and the seven benefits of this concept.

(11) What role does the vowel play in vocal production?

(12) What problems do our English orthography and phonology present in singing?

(13) Construct your own complete Vowel Spectrum, using word examples other than those already listed. Follow the format on page 88.

(14) What is the buccalpharyngeal cavity?

(15) Discuss problems of the jaw in singing.

(16) What is meant by "losing the vowel"?

(17) What problems are incurred by the neglected "uh" sound?

(18) What problems do diphthongs cause in singing?

(19) What problems do consonants cause in singing?

(20) What is meant by the term "cover"?

(21) Define the term "passaggio."

(22) Define the term "falsetto."

(23) Define the term "head voice."

(24) How should the singers (especially males) work to develop the upper range of the voice?

(25) Cite the passaggi of all voices listed on page 110.

(26) What are some effective means of dealing with intonation problems?

(27) Compare untempered and tempered scales and their effect upon unaccompanied choral intonation.

(28) What are vocal nodules?

(29) What are vocal polyps?

● Chapter 5:
MUSICAL DEVELOPMENT OF
THE CHORAL SINGER

This chapter will be concerned with uncomplicated approaches
to sight-singing and with improvement of theoretical perceptions of the music. We shall examine how these skills are developed by using the music being rehearsed, rather than by
introducing extraneous methods and exercises that are supposed to "teach" people how to read music. All too often
choral directors confuse ear training with sight-singing.
Training the ear to follow pitches that are called out by the
director sharpens tonal memory of intervals. It is a prelude
to sight-singing and should not be confused with the actual
process of singing what is in the score.

The principle of using the choristers' musical repertoire
to practice sight-singing supports the notion that individuals
learn what they want or need to know. Therefore, the singers will take the necessary steps to learn the music on which
they are working, providing the music challenges them. Here
is the juncture at which the director must decide whether or
not to allow the singers to learn the music by rote or engage
in helping them really understand the "language" which is necessary to read the printed music page. There are no short-
cuts to sight-reading proficiency. It requires time, repetition and, above all, patience. (We are all prone to desire
immediate results in everything we do.) The director, then,
must continue to assure the singers that "slow and steady
wins the race." Finally, the "deficient" sight-readers must
want to learn to sing at sight--else the attempt by those involved is futile.

THE BASIC PROBLEM OF SIGHT-SINGING:
SELF-RELIANCE

One of the greatest impediments to the development of sight-
singing skills is the fear of attempting to read the score.
We know from our modern methods of teaching foreign

languages that students must first be "immersed" in the
sounds of the language, even before they are asked to look
at the words themselves.   The same is true of reading vocal
music.   Students in junior-senior high schools and colleges,
who have no knowledge of vocal sight-singing, can learn the
rudiments by first becoming involved in the process of try-
ing to sing the music.   Those persons who are deficient in
sight-singing should be located near experienced singers.
These tyro singers will follow the leaders, providing they
are encouraged to sing along as best they can.   It has been
this writer's experience that reasonably alert choristers will
begin to realize relatively soon that

1.   the notes on the page describe the vocal range of
      the song; that notes high on the staff are sung at
      higher pitches than the lower ones;

2.   the notes have time values, indicating how long to
      hold each particular note;

3.   measures mark the general meter of the song;

4.   certain terms (foreign or native) indicate what is
      to be done with the music.

During the early stages of sight-singing experience,
these singers do not need to identify the theoretical terms
which tell them what to do.   They will absorb the terminol-
ogy as they gain confidence and experience in what they are
doing.   For instance, they do not need to know the names
of the notes before they can begin to judge the intervalic
spaces.   That information will come as a result of this "im-
mersion" in the music.   (See Chapter 2 for more detailed
discussion of this educational principle.)

There is no need to "throw" a vast array of terms and
rules at these students before they get the sounds fixed to
some extent in their "mind's ear."   There will be a significant amount of rote learning during the early stages, but
eventually these choristers will begin to understand the language, providing the director utilizes every opportunity to
point out the important elements leading to the understanding
of the music.   These inexperienced choristers will not likely
become as proficient as persons who have had earlier training on instruments and/or in sight-singing; yet, they will
progress at a rather remarkable rate if the choral circumstances are geared to assist them.

The Use of Section Rehearsals

      Section rehearsals, periodically scheduled, provide ex-
cellent opportunities for more concentrated assistance for the
deficient sight-singer. Usually, there are enough skilled
musician-singers in an ensemble to lead the sections in the
special rehearsals. The director should carefully outline the
material to be covered for these assistants and instruct them
as to how to conduct these rehearsals. The sessions should
be tailored to the needs of the personnel in each section. The
singers should be encouraged to ask questions when they are
confused about technical matters. The sensitive section leader
will point out certain details, such as key and meter signa-
tures, tempi and dynamic indications (and other such directions), and certain intervals by name, i. e. , "that's a skip
of a fourth, fifth, sixth. "

      Under these conditions, the tyro singers will not be
under pressure to digest information in technical terms.
Rather, they will gradually learn by doing. However, two
very important facts to be remembered in this context are
that everyone will not progress at the same rate and that
learning theoretical facts about music and developing their
skill will take time and concentration.

The Theory of Sight-Singing and
Its Application

      The ability to sing at sight requires the development
of "tonal memory. " This skill, like all other skills, is
more "natural" or more readily developed in some persons
than in others. Of course, those fortunate persons who have
perfect pitch are our most outstanding sight-singers. Other
persons develop "relative" pitch associations which enable
them to produce reasonably accurate pitches. In many instances, with concentration, they will be able to reproduce
exact pitches for songs with which they are very familiar.

      When individuals have difficulty in matching pitches
it signifies that they have not yet developed their "tonal
awareness. " Some persons have great difficulty learning
to coordinate the vocal musculature with the aural image of
the sound to be produced--both in pitch and tone quality.
(See Chapter 4 on vocal pedagogy.)

      The theory of sight-singing is one matter; exercising

it is another. It is the opinion of this writer, based upon
years of experience in applying his methods, that people can
learn to sight-read without undergoing all of the elementary
theory before actually attempting to sing. Moreover, poor
sight-readers can improve greatly by "doing and doing and
doing." Perhaps many persons reading this material have
memorized a host of theoretical facts and terms about music,
but could not apply them because these facts were learned
out of the context of the music. That knowledge, then, was
rarely, if ever, used. First of all, the choristers should
be encouraged to sing aggressively in rehearsals; to try to
continue singing even if they sing some incorrect intervals.
They should be encouraged again and again to "keep going."
Obviously, they should not be careless, but on the other hand,
the director must assure them not to be embarrassed if they
make some errors.

At times, tyro singers may become hopelessly lost
as they attempt to read the music and will need special attention and help. (If most of the singers are confused, it is
indeed possible that the repertoire chosen is beyond their
corporate capabilities.) As they sing, they should be instructed to mark their mistakes and try to find why they
sang too high or too low, or what were the arithmetical components of the tricky measure.

Once the "non-readers" have gained some experience
in group singing, they can now begin to learn gradually names
of notes and simple theory so as to become more confident
when singing on their own. Roy C. Bennett has written a
most interesting and edifying book for the amateur choral
singer entitled, The Choral Singer's Handbook (see the Bibliography). The last three chapters of this concise paper-
back are devoted to the basic theories of musicianship. Choristers who wish to gain more formal knowledge in an organized manner will find many helpful insights concerning music
theory in this small book. Mr. Bennett writes "from the
other side of the podium." The early chapters of this treatise also give ready hints to choral conductors by way of vividly depicting the role and place of the "grass roots" choral
singer.

It should be remembered that choristers assemble to
sing. Complicated theoretical information can stifle the enthusiasm of these persons who are seeking to experience the
thrill of making music. Therefore, this information should
be introduced in "bits and pieces" as the problems arise.
Long and detailed explanations will usually be a lost cause.

Degrees of Ability to Sing at Sight

Previously, it was mentioned that some persons develop sight-reading skills faster than others. This factor may be discouraging for the slower singers who seem to lag behind. However, with encouragement from the director, they will gain confidence in their ability to read the score.

Ideally, sight-reading of unfamiliar music should be done at every rehearsal. Using the musical repertoire of the singers can and should be used for this purpose. If the idea of Synthesis-Analysis-Synthesis is followed (as described in Chapters 2 and 3), sight-reading experience will take place in the normal rehearsal.

As has been said previously, it is vitally important for directors to recognize that in the average choral organization, very likely there will be readers ranging from those poor sight-singers, who were never encouraged to sing aggressively, to those who read with great facility. Thus, it behooves choral directors to exude confidence in those "inferior" readers, so that they will work to develop further this skill by concentrating upon sight-singing during rehearsals and by being alert as to the instructions given them. The director, then, must be readily able to provide helpful and practical clues and answers for the choristers so as to supply "on the spot" guidance or solutions to problems. The discussion following will provide some examples of how the choristers can develop their skills in sight-reading vocal music.

Interval Detection

Many choral directors believe rhythm to be the most difficult and significant item to tackle when introducing reading to inexperienced singers. However, based upon observations and discussions with "non-readers," this writer has found that interval detection is the primary problem of tyro singers. These persons are concerned first with how far to go up or down to find the correct note(s). Though choral directors are concerned (and rightly so) that meter and rhythmic patterns be established for the skeletal framework of the composition to be introduced, the inexperienced singer is primarily interested in "walking"--taking the first steps toward identifying pitches on the printed page. Only after singers achieve a somewhat common level of intervalic sight-reading

proficiency can rhythmic contours assume a major role in
singing at sight.   This is not to say that chanting tricky
rhythms of a new selection to be introduced is not effective.
To the contrary, it may be of utmost importance at this point,
if rhythmic problems are sufficiently greater than intervalic
ones.

Our central concern here is how to assist the tyro
singers in improving their ability to read a score.   Thus,
while a conductor may introduce a new composition by chanting words and rhythm for the benefit of the whole group, it
should be kept in mind that the tyro singer is probably more
concerned with "getting from here to there." Note values
will tend to fall in line as the meter and rhythm carries the
music along.   Surely, certain rhythmic inaccuracies will need
to be pointed out from time to time.   Once the learning process gets underway, there is no reason why rhythmic and
meter information cannot be taught along with interval detection.   This is another example of the five-lane "highway of
learning" discussed in Chapter 2.

There are some songs familiar to many persons that
may aid in identifying intervals.   These "helps" serve as examples for relating to spatial relationships of the notes.   However, in employing these aids, the director should be careful
about using technical terms.   One might say, "That next note
is five notes away from this one.   This interval is called a
____?   (ask the group); yes, a fifth.   The song 'Twinkle,
Twinkle Little Star' uses that interval.   Just sing 'twinkle,
twinkle' and stop.   That is an interval of a fifth.   We start
counting on the first note on the lines or spaces until we
reach five.   And that is how we determine the name of each
interval.   We have seconds, thirds, fourths, fifths, sixths,
sevenths and octaves (eighths).   Some of these intervals may
occasionally be made slightly larger or smaller by adding
sharps or flats, thus raising or lowering the written pitches.
They are called 'augmented' or 'diminished' intervals.   But
do not be concerned with labels yet.   The time will come
when you can do that without difficulty.   Our main concern
is to be able to connect the 'mind's eye' with the proper
pitches. "

Every director should develop a list of well-known
songs which serve this purpose for his or her group.   One
can also ask the choristers to name songs familiar to them
which also contain the interval(s) being discussed.

Below are some suggestions of familiar songs which a director might use to illustrate intervalic relationships.

Perfect fourth ascending: "Here Comes the Bride"
Perfect fourth descending: "Dona Nobis Pacem";
  "Born Free"
Augmented fourth (tritone) ascending: "Maria" (West Side Story)
Perfect fifth ascending: "Twinkle, Twinkle Little Star"
Perfect fifth descending: "The Star Spangled Banner"
  (first and third notes)
Major sixth ascending: NBC call letters
Major sixth descending: "Nobody Knows the Trouble I've Seen"; "Love Story" Theme
Major seventh ascending: "Bali Hai" (first and third notes)
Octave ascending: "Bali Hai" (first two notes)

The descending augmented fourth (tritone), the descending seventh, minor and major seventh, along with other large and small non-diatonic skips found in serial compositions, have no familiar tunes with which to identify. That is one reason why the illustrations above are limited in value. Thus, it is important in musical pedagogy to go further than merely relying upon these "gimmicks." Instead, the director should call out intervals for the choristers to sing during the warm-up period of the rehearsal, first giving the starting pitch, then specifying the interval(s) to be sung. However, it is important that a direct application of this exercise be made to the music being rehearsed in order to better retain the material being learned.

OTHER AIDS IN SIGHT-SINGING

There are many ways to improve both intervalic and rhythmic perceptions of musical problems.

Finding an Entrance Note from Another Part

When a particular entrance note eludes an individual or an entire section, it works well to cite a note in another part that is either the same (though it may be an octave away) or a phrase line leading to the entering note of the section which is having the problem. See an illustration of this in Figure 28.

№ 39.– CHORUS

"Their sound is gone out into all lands"

Fig. 28: Aid to Note Detection

The director should take difficult passages very slowly
(out of rhythm) emphasizing the entering notes.   Each section
should be asked to sing (quietly) the "cue note(s)" just before
their entrance, and then more aggressively sing their own attack.   Pausing momentarily at each entrance will help the
singers to imprint in their memories the correct aural image
of their entering note.   When more security is gained in these
entrances, the passage should be gradually brought up to
tempo to <u>synthesize</u> the entire problem area.

MASS IN B-MINOR   J. S. Bach

Bass and alto have the same notes.   Tenor and soprano have
the same notes.

Fig. 29:   Aid to Note Detection

In carefully analyzing the score, the director will find
innumerable clues to help singers identify pitches.   A side
benefit of this procedure is to make the choristers aware of
other sections and the interrelationships of the various voice
parts.

Citing Repetitions in Voice Parts

Contrapuntal or fugal entrances contain the same

Bass and alto, tenor and soprano have the same thematic material. Have them sing their parts in unison.

Fig. 30: Aid to Note Detection

material.   Having the entire choir sing each other's parts aids in bringing these similarities to the choristers' attention. Baroque music is particularly noted for these relationships. Examples of this are shown in Figures 29 and 30.

Pointing Out Sequences

Often, there will be phrases that outline the sequential series of notes.   The first note of each sequence of a "run" should be identified for the section.   Then, each note of the strong beat can be pointed out to outline the sequence of the phrase (see Figure 31).

Rhythmic Problems

When measures contain rhythmic complexities, it is advisable to have the choristers write in the main beats, and sometimes the sub-beats (the "and" beats), above the notes in the bar.   The following example (Figure 32) illustrates how a score may be marked to aid singers (and conductor) to identify the correct rhythmic patterns.

Teaching Conducting to Choristers

Teaching choristers to conduct the basic patterns often improves their rhythmic perception.   It helps them identify where the beats of the measure lie and, thus, improves their musicianship.   This is not as formidable a task as it may seem to be when first considering it.   The process also aids the singers in relating more closely to their director's conducting gestures.

There is one outstanding requirement in the procedure to help singers learn the theoretical aspects of music; insist that every member should have a pencil in hand to enter every clue needed to make the score understandable.   Choristers must be encouraged to mark their scores freely.

REVIEW QUESTIONS FOR CHAPTER 5

(1) Interpret the concept which states that individuals learn what they want or need to know.

22945

Fig. 31: Aid to Note Detection

to Elmer Thomas and the Chamber Choir of the
College-Conservatory of Music, University of Cincinnati

Hop out of my way
No. 6 from *Frogs*
for Chorus of Mixed Voices *a cappella*

NORMAN DINERSTEIN

VI
Hop out of my way,
Mr. Toad, and allow me
please to plant bamboo!
CHORA
Translated by Harry Behn*

* Text from *Cricket Songs,* ©1964 by Harry Behn. All rights reserved. Reprinted by permission of Curtis Brown, Ltd.

Fig. 32: Rhythmic Aid

(2) What is the basic problem encountered in sight-singing?

(3) What are the four basic areas of understanding of which the beginning sight-singer should eventually become aware?

(4) When and how should these beginning sight-singers be introduced to theoretical terms and concepts?

(5) How should section rehearsals be utilized to aid in the development of sight-singing?

(6) How does the use of the Synthesis-Analysis-Synthesis concept aid development of sight-singing proficiency?

(7) What are some means of teaching intervals?

(8) Cite some illustrations of your own as to how repetitive or parallel vocal lines can aid in interval detection.

(9) What value will likely accrue from teaching singers to conduct basic patterns?

PART III:

CONSIDERING THE ROLE OF THE CHORAL CONDUCTOR

● Chapter 6:
  THE CONDUCTOR FACES
  THE CHORAL ENSEMBLE

At the first meeting of the choral group, a very few pertinent introductory remarks are appropriate. A general welcome to all persons and a special welcome to new members should create an atmosphere of congeniality. It is also advantageous before the rehearsal to have had music distributed and placed on the chairs along with a syllabus outlining dates, times and place(s) of rehearsals and projected performances. A separate sheet stating rules and regulations of the ensemble is most important for the singers to have outlined for them. Concise statements in the plainest form of English can protect the director from many misunderstandings in the future. In large choirs, name tags for all members, new and old, are very helpful in creating the wanted and needed feeling of congeniality. They should be worn at each succeeding rehearsal.

PROFILE OF SINGERS

Ideally, conductors should not only know the names of their singers, but also have some knowledge of each singer's musical background.

The Profile Form

To facilitate the objective of becoming acquainted with every singer in their choirs, directors should construct an outline of the needed data. In addition to name, address, phone and obvious statistical data, the director might seek information such as the following:

1. Voice category
2. Instrumental study and experiences
3. Vocal study, if pertinent to age of the group
4. Other singing experiences (school and church)

    5. Favorite music sung in the past (specific selec-
         tions or styles of music)
    6. Hobbies

     Information of this kind is helpful to church choir di-
rectors as well as to school educators. Often one discovers
useful instrumentalists nestled among the membership, or
one learns of past experiences which prove helpful in planning
or expediting programs and preparation for them. Most of
all, a profile will aid the director in identifying the membership by name, face, and personality. Below are two examples of forms for the choir director. High school or church
choir questionnaires should be adapted to information pertinent to those situations.

Let's Get Acquainted Form

NAME OF COLLEGE or UNIVERSITY

Year 19____-19____

Semester or Quarter (circle appropriate one): Fall, Win-
ter, Spring, Summer
Class Status (circle): Freshman, Sophomore, Junior,
Senior

(Print)
Name: Miss, Mrs., Mr._____
                        Last   First

Local address:_____
                  Street   Town

_____
   State   Zip   Telephone

I sing: soprano, alto, tenor, bass

Intended Major Department_____

Intended Area of Specialization_____

Reason for joining this organization:

[Continued next page]

Previous Experience in Music (list years)

Private study (vocal and/or instrumental)

Are you willing to become an accompanist?

Indicate your estimate of keyboard sight-reading capability_____
fair-good-excellent

Performing experience (group and/or individual)

Are you playing or planning to play in the Wind Ensemble or Orchestra?

What is your favorite style(s) of music?

List your hobby(ies) or other interests:

For Director's Use Only

Sight Reading (Intervals)_____

(Rhythm)_____

Vocal Quality_____

Voice Classification:

Range_____

Passaggio_____

Comments:

Suggested Audition Form for a Community Chorus

Rehearsal time: Tuesday 7:30-9:45 p.m.
Attendance: Absences permitted for extenuating circumstances only

[Continued on next page]

Name_____

Home Address_____Business Address_____

City_____Zip_____City_____Zip_____

Phone_____   Phone_____

Voice Part_____

Choral Experience

    High School (Number of years)_____College (Number
                                                   of years)_____

    Other (Specify)_____

    _____

Vocal Experience

    Private lessons (Indicate years)_____

    Teachers_____

    _____

    Solo work (describe)_____

    _____

How many years have you lived in this community?_____

Other pertinent information, including instrument(s) in
which you are proficient_____

_____

_____

_____

For Director's Use Only:

Tone quality and blend_____

[Continued on next page]

Intonation_____

Sight reading_____

Agility_____

Remarks_____

_____

AUDITIONING SINGERS

For most choral singers, auditions are a frightening--and
threatening--experience. Rarely do amateur singers perform
up to their potential at auditions. Therefore, the introductory moments are crucial in order to alleviate as much apprehension as possible for the auditionee. Some vocally timid
persons may even refuse to be auditioned; others may not attempt to join an ensemble which requires auditions.

High school students (especially males) are generally
shy about exposing their possible ignorance or deficiencies
in a solo audition. This is understandable since young people, during adolescence, are striving mightily to protect their
egos and to establish their individual identities. The threat
of failure (or at least of being inadequate to a task) is about
the last thing to which they wish to expose themselves. Therefore, the term "interview," instead of audition, may be helpful in alleviating anxiety on the part of the person wanting to
join an established choral organization. The "interview" may
also encourage some "timid souls" to "try out" for ensembles
which they would avoid if the term "audition" were used. In
view of these factors, each director must make plans carefully according to his or her individual situation. (If the pool
of potential singers is large enough, it may be propitious to
have a basic group of non-auditioned singers from which to
draw a more select group, who are willing--even eager--to
try out for it on any terms.)

The Get-acquainted Interview

It is of vital importance before any audition type of
procedure for the director to consult the profile forms of new

singers, such as illustrated earlier in this chapter. This
form, listing the background of experience and training of
each person in the group, can permit the director to choose
somewhat compatible quartets (if that method of audition is
used--see below) according to the experience and background
of each singer. With this information, the audition-interview
can be conducted upon a more efficient and understanding
basis.

Auditioning by Quartets (SATB, SSAA, TTBB, etc.)

Possibly, the least threatening means of accomplishing this task is to arrange for the new singers to sing in
quartets. Choosing a simple song such as a chorale or other
homophonic selection, usually alleviates tension and anxiety.
The objective of the interview is to select the best way possible of determining the potential contribution of each singer.

At the interview, a few introductory remarks by the
director as to what it will entail should suffice, conversing
briefly about their musical tastes and their previous singing
experience. It may be well to use piano accompaniment to
double the parts of the singers on the first selection to be
tried. Then, gradually they can be "weaned" away from the
keyboard support to determine how independent they are as
singers. Also, progressing to more complicated scores (a
reasonably short sample is sufficient) will reveal sight-reading
independence. It is important to have a piano or organ accompanist assisting at the interview, so that the director can
give full attention to the singers, carefully analyzing tone
quality and observing other manifestations of the singers.
Notes should be made on the individual profile sheets in
enough detail to provide a reliable record of each singer.
It is imperative that there be a variety of music available to
allow the quartet to demonstrate its highest potential.

Some choral directors perfer to audition their singers
individually. This person-to-person encounter is valuable in
that more detailed information can be attained. Where time
and psychological conditions permit, this practice may be
preferred. On the other hand, the primary information needed
is the ability of the individual to function in the ensemble situation. Analysis of individual voices can be gleaned from
quartet singing, although determining the total ranges of the
individuals in the quartet is difficult to document because of
lack of the personal one-to-one contact provided by the solo
audition.

SEATING ARRANGEMENTS

There are many opinions concerning the "best" seating plans for choral groups. Obviously, in the final analysis, the arrangement of singers must be determined by the best overall communication both visually and audibly. These decisions must be based upon the physical conditions and acoustics of the room or hall in which the rehearsals and performances take place, the vocal and musical maturity of the singers, the balance (make-up) of the various sections, etc. Each conductor should solve these problems by imaginative experimentation, adapting specific choral personnel formations to suit his or her own purposes. (Several books listed in the Bibliography at the back of this book contain material suggesting a variety of formations for singers.) There are some principles that govern seating or standing arrangements which should be helpful in making these placement decisions. Variations of formations should be tried according to (a) the potentials and limitations of the rehearsal room, (b) groupings on concert risers, or (c) conditions in church choir chancels. Certainly, there can be no prescribed formation for all purposes--even within one choral situation.

Quartet or Scrambled Versus
Section Arrangements

It requires little imagination or experience to realize that quartet or scrambled section arrangements demand vocally and musically mature singers. The chief advantages of this set-up are as follows:

1. Better intonation in homophonic music is achieved because the singers can function in greater harmonic relationship to the other choral parts.

2. Some adherents to this arrangement claim that blending of the voices can be more easily and effectively achieved (providing the singers in a given quartet possess relatively compatible voices).

3. This arrangement tends to improve the independence of the singers because they must rely only upon themselves to produce what is needed for the musical objectives.

These comments also apply to "scrambled" seating in

ensembles in which there are not equal numbers of persons for each section, but the singers are placed in "vocal clusters."

There are, however, some disadvantages to this kind of seating arrangement, such as these:

1.   The director may have difficulty in achieving the spontaneity and flexibility for nuance with each section as compared to communicating with each section as a block.

2.   Initially it may weaken the sections vocally because the voices are scattered instead of grouped together.

3.   Visual communication between conductor and some individuals is made difficult because of size differences, i. e. , taller persons blocking the vision of shorter persons, who may be placed together because of their vocal compatability.

4.   It often prevents symmetry for the ensemble in the eyes of the audience--an important factor to many conductors and persons who attend choral concerts, or where a church choir is in the front of the sanctuary.

Research in the field of acoustics has revealed that vowel formants (overtones, which provide the tone color, volume and intensity for the voice after the initial sound is produced in the larynx) reinforce each other.   Thus, the arrangement of voices close to each other in sections tends to produce a more concentrated tone than if they were separated. John Backus refers to this as "chorus effect."[1]   His illustration refers to violins, but the application to the voice is exactly the same in that stringed instruments have many characteristics in common with the human voice.

> The quality of the sound of two or more instruments playing together is different in respect from that of a single instrument.[2]

Backus continues his discussion by stating that each violin will have a similar, but yet a slightly different sound. Likewise, there are significant timbre differences among voices in that, generally, the tones will not have the same fundamental

frequencies. Consequently, the beats per second which differ among ten violins will produce an entirely different quality than one violin amplified to ten times its original power.[3]

If one applies this principle to choral placement of
sections, it can be realized that the voices do reinforce each
other. As any experienced choral director can testify, one
strong voice in a section (providing it blends reasonably well)
can cause the section to sound geometrically stronger because
the overtones of the surrounding weaker singers are reinforced by the strong voice.

Therefore, to list some of the arguments in favor of
section grouping, one should recognize the points below, especially in average "grass roots" choirs.

1. It affords the most security for singers.

2. It strengthens and reinforces the tone quality of
    a given section.*

3. It permits the conductor to adjust the choral bal-
    ance as needed by cueing a particular section for
    emphasis.

4. It allows for more spontaneity of performance be-
    cause the conductor can communicate with various
    sections to re-interpret the music as the inspira-
    tion of the moment dictates.

5. It encourages each singer to relate his or her
    own performance to those nearby.

6. It permits weaker singers to emulate stronger
    singers next to them. (However, it should be
    mentioned that some directors believe this to be
    a disadvantage and a crutch for weaker singers,
    impeding their vocal and musical development.)

We have seen that there are advantages and disadvantages to both ways of seating. However, some directors utilize both practices: the section system for tackling new and
difficult compositions, then forming quartets or scrambled

---

*One should be careful to avoid putting two strident voices
next to each other because they will reinforce each other's
harsh tone qualities.

seating for intermediate stages of learning the composition
and finally returning to sections again for advanced stages
of learning and the performance.   Others use section placement for learning the music and scrambled or quartet placement for the final stages and the performance.

For recording purposes, some argue that better blend
of voices can be achieved by quartets or scrambling.   Others
claim that proper microphone placement can overcome problems of blend when the section arrangement is used.

In the final analysis, each director must make his or
her own decision on the matter according to experience and
preference.   This decision should stem from experimentation
with the various options.

Outer and Inner Voices Arrangement

The early a cappella tradition espoused the concept
that the best blend, intonation, and balance were to be found
in seating the bass section directly behind the sopranos and
the tenors behind the altos.   This arrangement is based upon
the concept that the outer voices (bass and soprano) are frequently octaves apart, especially at final cadences where intonation is crucial, and tenors and altos most often have the
inner harmonies (third and fifth of a chord).   In this prox-
imity all voices are thought to be placed in the best position
to relate to each other--thus achieving better intonation and
blend.

Like-Voices Together

A contrasting view is one which holds that tenors and
sopranos, basses and altos should be together in section blocks,
because their voices are quite similar, though being an octave apart.   Many choral ensembles that sing mostly or entirely with accompanying forces (piano, organ or orchestra)
find this to be a very satisfactory arrangement for the voices.
With instrumental accompaniment, choral intonation is not
usually as critical a problem as in unaccompanied singing.
For situations in which choral groups must utilize both accompanied and unaccompanied styles of singing, conductors
would do well to experiment with each of the above cited arrangements as well as the quartet or scrambled seating.   In
doing so, they can determine the most effective seating plan
for their particular ensembles.

ATTENDANCE CHECKING

Attitudes concerning attendance vary among choral leaders.
Most directors will agree that, ideally, every member should
attend every rehearsal (and concert), but reality dictates that
illnesses and occasional pre-empting demands will cause singers to miss rehearsals.   The decision that each director
must make is how much tolerance of individual absences
should be allowed.   There is probably nothing more demoralizing to any group of performers than to have chronic absences among the personnel.   Rightfully, members will think,
"If 'so and so' can miss rehearsals, why can't I?"

   Some school directors have a limit of one, two or
three absences per term without grade penalty.   (When extended illness is a factor, the rule is usually not applied.)
Ensembles, which meet during a regular hourly period of the
curriculum, have altogether different attendance problems
than do those which meet before or after scheduled classes.
The latter instances are similar to volunteer church choir
situations, except that in scheduling after school rehearsals,
the students are already in the building or on the campus.

   Naturally, the more prestigious the ensemble, the
greater the desire for singers to become a member of the
group.   Under these circumstances, the director has the
power to eliminate anyone who does not uphold the standards
and rules of the group, since there will be someone equally
as proficient ready to step into the vacated seat.

   Directors who must depend entirely upon the "good
will" of their singers for membership are at the mercy of
the individuals in the group.   Thus, it behooves directors
to make their rehearsals vitally interesting and educational,
so that musical growth and prestige can reach the stage in
which the singers are proud to be a member.

   It has been observed that some conductors, who have
assumed direction of an ensemble where attendance previously
has been lax, have become very strict immediately upon assuming control of the group.   Some have built highly successful ensembles under this policy; others have failed.   Still
others have gradually become more strict by instituting stif-
fer rules of attendance and behavior by degrees, thus avoiding a sudden shock of changed rules for the members.   It is
surely evident that the conductor's personality, musicianship,
and consistency of policies influence attendance.   If the singers

feel that they will miss something of value by being absent, attendance problems will be minimized. However, there is one significant factor which all conductors should recognize: a clearly stated set of rules for attendance, supported by the conductor's attitude of respect for individuals, may well be the basic ingredient upon which to build rapport with a choral group.

Class Credit and Student Attitude

Even though the academic credit awarded for ensemble work in most schools and colleges is very little, the psychological factor of a grade is influential in maintaining good attendance. It can produce a positive (or at least not an overtly negative) influence, if handled carefully. Used as a threat, it has very little clout or value. Moreover, students who join school ensembles usually do so because they enjoy "making music," regardless of grades.* Therefore, conductors should realize that there is a very positive force working for them in that students have elected to sing. Utilizing this desire for self-expression can be a powerful force in developing an outstanding ensemble beyond merely earning the small school credit.

Influence of Grading upon Attendance

As cited above, academic credit for ensemble work in most schools and colleges is so insignificant, directors should not rely upon grades as the means by which they attempt to achieve discipline or consistent attendance among the singers. Pride in the group's accomplishments will outlast dictatorial edict, and thus produce consistently positive attitudes on the part of the singers.

The mechanical means of taking attendance may concern many conductors, whether they function in academia or are directors of volunteer choirs. Most conductors do not wish to be bothered by taking roll, so they assign the duty to a secretary or assistant director. Moreover, many con-

---

*Even more so, people who join community or church choirs participate in them because they have a desire to sing--to fulfill a need for self-expression which, in most cases, they could not accomplish alone ("grass roots" theory).

ductors strongly believe that the less obtrusive the attendance taking, the better for all concerned.

Yet, some directors feel that it is important for them to take attendance personally at the beginning of the rehearsal period. Unless the group is unusually large, it helps them become adquainted with new members of the group and it establishes and retains a personal contact that may be worth the time and effort.

One interesting way of taking attendance is to make a large chart with members' names and all of the scheduled rehearsals and concert dates. The singers then check off their names as they enter. This chart also helps to acquaint the members with each other. If a member is late to rehearsal he or she marks "L" in the square for the day instead of an "X." The chart can be set up on an easel in the path of entry. Although this system is generally efficient, it has three distinct disadvantages:

1. Occasionally, there will be a long line of persons to check in, thereby causing delay in starting the rehearsal on time.

2. If the rehearsal is changed to another location, the chart and easel must be brought along.

3. Cheating: some students may have others check their names when they are absent.

GRADING SYSTEMS

Evaluations in Educational Situations

Perhaps one of the most difficult and controversial items of ensemble administration is that of grading students for their participation. Few ensemble situations offer the opportunity to grade students in a truly objective manner. Usually attendance (or lack of it) is the major factor in determining grades. Yet, there are other factors, such as attitude, vocal progress and musical development which should be considered as well as attendance.

Attitude

In large choral ensembles, personal contact with students

is so vague that accurate assessment of this factor is almost impossible, unless the student displays a noticeably negative or positive attitude, or is especially outstanding vocally and musically. A singer may be very subtle in his or her antagonistic attitude, and the director may not be aware of this undercutting of his or her effort. One or a few negative-acting persons can erode the rapport between the conductor and the group. If conditions are generally favorable, peer pressure may counteract the opposition. If peer pressure fails, and the director notices the bad attitude, the director should seek a private conference with the "offender." In any event, it is rare when a reprimand in front of the entire ensemble is an effective answer to this problem. As mentioned in Chapter 4, a "gripe/suggestion box" for singers to anonymously vent their frustrations may be an answer to this problem.

Vocal Progress of Individuals

The overall vocal progress of a choral group over a given period can be assessed quite readily, especially with the aid of a tape recorder to play back the group's performance. Yet, it is exceedingly difficult to determine the progress which individuals make during that period of time, unless the director arranges to have individual tests. This would be an almost impossible task to assume for anyone directing a large ensemble, and it is rarely, if ever, done to this writer's knowledge.

Musical Development of Individuals

In some instances this progress can be assessed by quartet testing, providing the director has the time to arrange for this activity. Yet, this may be a rather inaccurate way to determine progress in sight-singing or whatever else is being measured because there may not have been any objective means of establishing the singer's level of development at the beginning of the term--unless each singer is auditioned on a regular basis and careful records kept.

One Solution to the Grading of Ensembles

There is a solution to this grading problem, but it is also not a perfect one--that of "Honor System Grading."

This approach to grading the work of the various members of a large ensemble may well work better on the college-university level than in lower age groups.

The Honor System invites the ensemble members to grade themselves on their assessment of the items listed for analysis with the proviso that the director retains the option to challenge any item. Below is a sample form for Honor System grading.

NAME OF ENSEMBLE_____(Please Print)

NAME_____

No. of absences from rehearsals during the term_____
(Check with attendance taken for accuracy)

HONOR SYSTEM GRADING CRITERIA
for College Ensembles
Fall Winter Spring Summer Term 19___

The following criteria have been established by your colleagues as the most objective manner in which to evaluate each ensemble member's contribution to the group as reflected by his/her individual growth. Each of the following four items is equal in importance in determining your grade. After determining your grade in each area, I, II, III and IV, by an A, B, C, D, F (using minuses where necessary), average them and state your final grade, signing your name to the sheet. You may wish to assign A=4, B=2, C=1, D and F=0. Then divide the total by 4 to receive the correct average, taking into consideration any minuses or pluses. The director reserves the right to challenge the grades where there may be a discrepancy of attendance or contribution.

You are urged to make constructive suggestions about your ensemble experience this term. Please use the reverse side of the paper for your comments. You may wish to suggest names of composers whose music you have sung in the past as well as certain styles of music which interest you (i.e., Renaissance, Baroque, Classic, Impressionistic and Contemporary periods--but

---

[Continued on next page]

be specific about Rock or Folk information). Would you
like to work on a major-length choral piece during one
term?

    Please return this sheet to your director before
the end of the term. IF YOU DO NOT RETURN THE
SHEET, THERE WILL BE NO CHOICE OTHER THAN TO
RECORD NC (No Credit).

I.   Participation: This may be defined as your attitude
toward the group effort and toward the music being
rehearsed, as well as concentration during rehearsals and your contribution to the group effort.
Letter Grade ____

II.   Attendance: Since the group's success and progress
depends on everyone being present at rehearsals,
this is an important factor in evaluating one's contribution (group responsibility). Letter Grade ____

III.   Preparation: Evaluate your individual work outside
of rehearsal to "shore up" weak spots to fulfill
your responsibility to the group and to the music
under preparation. If you are a poor sight-reader,
you would need to work outside of class. (Probably 90% of the singers need to work on their music outside of class.) Letter Grade ____

IV.   Progress: Did you use the ensemble situation as
an opportunity to employ the pedagogy of the director toward improvement in musicianship, technique,
and tone production? Do you have any suggestions
as to how the learning situation can be improved?
Letter Grade ____

    Average (Letter Grade) ____

    Signed_____

Use of the "Honor Grading System"

    At the end of the term, the students are given the
grade form above and instructed to follow the directions on

the sheet. It is assumed that everyone is capable of receiving an "A" for each category.

I. Participation: The student's attitude toward the total efforts of the group, concentration during rehearsals, and assessment of his or her contribution to the work of the ensemble.

II. Attendance: Along with the honor grading sheet the students receive a slip from the ensemble secretary indicating the number of absences they have had during the term. All absences are noted; if over three, each absence drops the grade point average one half (1/2) point, unless valid reasons for being absent are documented in writing (preferably ahead of time) in consultation with the director. A whole point is deducted for each missed performance unless the reason is clearly beyond the control of the student.

III. Preparation: Students are usually very candid about whether or not they have worked on the music outside of rehearsals. Very few students indicate that they do not need additional study beyond the regular rehearsals. Most students feel they should have spent more time outside of class studying their parts.

IV. Progress: This item underscores the students' responsibility to try to learn as much as possible from the association with the instructor and their peers. It also places the teacher in a position of responsibility for making the rehearsals a rewarding experience in learning for the choristers. The students can usually judge their own progress better than can the director. They will note progress, or lack of it, quite honestly, citing whether they have improved their vocal production and/or whether they have gained some proficiency in musicianship.

PERSONAL RELATIONSHIPS WITH SINGERS

Conductors must be very careful about their personal relationships with the members of their ensembles.

Be Friendly, but Keep an "Arm's Length" Away

There is always the possibility that an innocent comment

or even a vague physical gesture can engender envy or resentment by one or more other members of an ensemble.
This is why conductors must develop the ability to be friendly
--yet remain "an arm's length" from all of their singers.
There are frequently those members who want special attention and/or privileges from the director.   Beware of being
alone with a student for any length of time in the choral library or robe room.   If possible, leave the door open when
working with only one student.

Perhaps there is no way in which a director can get
to know sixty or seventy or more people very well as a result of only the distant contact established at rehearsals.
However, social events often aid in accomplishing the objective of becoming acquainted with each other: singers with
other singers; singers with the director.   The morale of a
large group of singers can become very fragile if there is
not some strong motivating force such as the prestige of a
fine ensemble or a social relationship--and in most cases,
both.   However, if the singing experience is satisfying for
the singers, socializing is of secondary importance to maintaining good morale.   Significant music, well rehearsed and
performed, is often sufficient to accomplish the desired goals.

This is not to imply that relationships other than singing may not be valuable catalysts in building and maintaining
morale in choral groups.   Traveling to festivals, contests
and touring are certainly factors which can enhance the feelings of unity within a group, and, unquestionably, this has
a significant and positive effect upon the singing efforts of
the ensemble.   Most persons reading this treatise will have
experienced (as singers or conductors) the effectiveness of
this kind of activity.   The main problem of touring or a special trip is "keeping the lid on" during the ride to the event.
Young, inexperienced singers are prone to be overly stimulated and boisterous en route.   It is often difficult to convince them to save their energy for the performance.   Only
experience will educate them to the need for conserving their
energies.

Some words of caution are important to be inserted
at this point.   As cited previously, it is paramount that a
conductor's close personal relationships with one or more
individuals in a choir be very carefully handled.   Frequently,
there are persons who will resent what appears to them to
be favoritism by the director to a few within the group.   The
tour bus can present problems if the conductor does not try
to mingle with all of the personnel during a given trip.

The choice of soloists should always be handled as fairly as possible by auditioning those who wish to apply. If too many persons apply to audition for a given solo, a lottery can be established, the "losers" getting their opportunity another time.

A further cause of resentment by students is inconsistency in enforcing the rules of the organization. Any exceptions to the rules must be clearly explained in a printed statement of the organizational procedures or verbally explained at the time of the incident.

PERSONALITY CHARACTERISTICS OF THE CONDUCTOR

Be Your Own Person

Of primary importance for the aspiring conductor is to be honestly unpretentious. He or she should not attempt to be a rubber stamp of an admired conductor of the past or present. However, any effective techniques and ideas demonstrated by another conductor certainly can be assimilated into one's own technique, developing a style which is consonant with one's own personal and physical characteristics. An admonition to all aspiring conductors should be that no matter what else you have in mind, always try to "look like the music." All conductors should work diligently to achieve a level of physical coordination that will permit their conducting gestures to be so automatic that their individual personal qualities will shine through the motions while reflecting the intrinsic values of the music itself.

The Place of Humor in the Rehearsal

One of the most important elements in any rehearsal situation is the use of humor. Again, the personality of the director is paramount in guiding and controlling this component of working with people. A sense of humor really revolves around a director's being able to laugh at oneself or with others but, of course, never at someone else or the group. In the ensemble, rehearsal humor must arise spontaneously-- never be calculated, always having the objective of enjoying a mistake or situation which can happen to almost anyone. Sarcasm can rarely be construed as humor.

Conductors who can find humor in their own mistakes,

or capitalize in a positive way upon the humor evidenced in
another's mistakes, usually find that it is a welcome ingredient in the rehearsal.   It often relieves subtle--or even major
--tensions or frustrations among the singers.   When everyone
can laugh with no embarrassment to any individual, a very
positive force toward good morale emerges.   This writer
has had the good fortune to have at least one or more persons in each of his choral groups who were punsters or catalysts for humor.   A good laugh at any time during the rehearsal period will enhance the feelings of camaraderie in
an ensemble.   Of course, silliness throughout the rehearsal
cannot be condoned.   The conductor must remain in control
of the rehearsal situation by appreciating the humorous element, and then capitalizing upon the momentum caused by the
joke, wisecrack, or obvious blunder, such as a person or
section "cracking" on a high note with a good laugh by everyone; then quickly returning to the situation or problem at
hand.

THE IMPORTANCE OF AN AFFIRMATIVE ATTITUDE

Controlling the Ensemble Forces

        Tyro conductors are rightfully concerned about their
total control of an ensemble.   As student assistants, they
may have had discipline problems because of peer rivalries.
That experience may still be vivid for them.   It is often difficult for students to control their peers when put in charge
during the instructor's absence.   Therefore, it is vitally important for any young director to be firm, but not antagonistic.   It should be assumed that the "new" personality in
charge (whether a new teacher or student conductor) is musically prepared to lead the group.   The young or new conductor must convey a sense of confidence in the group as
well as in himself or herself; i. e., transmit the attitude
that, "of course," the group can accomplish the goals of
the rehearsal!   Confidence must be reflected in all mannerisms: facial, body, vocal and vocabulary.   Authority derives
itself from a total command based upon musicianship, interpretative sensitivity, preparation for the rehearsal, and respect for the singers--not dictatorial edicts.

A Working Partnership

        Achieving a working partnership may well be the fun-

damental concept upon which rapport between conductor and
the ensemble is built.   The most desirable goal in the professional relationship between conductor and ensemble is that
they are all working together toward a common goal.   At all
costs, the director should avoid conveying an attitude that the
ensemble is working for him or her.   Rather, a sense of
sharing the work load must be established.   Since the conductor should know the music so well as to have complete
command of the technical aspects involved, an atmosphere
of the director's superiority quite naturally exists.   This is
as it should be, but the conductor must not exploit this air
of superiority to the detriment of the singers.   He or she
must remain "human."   The comments below in the form of
analogies will best demonstrate the point.

The Pick and Shovel Versus the
Fingernail File

When a choral group is struggling to learn a musical
selection which is difficult for them, the director must "get
down" to their level and work equally hard with them.   He
or she must never imply that the singers are stupid, just
because they cannot do what seems to be so simple for the
director, who should be a better musician--as well as having studied (mastered) the complexities of the score before
distributing the music.   Analogously, the director must roll
up the sleeves, grasp the "pick," and "chop away" at the laborious task of learning the music.   (See Chapters 2 and 3
for concepts of learning and Chapter 4 for practical vocal
techniques.)   Eventually, the "debris" can be "shoveled" away
when most major problems are solved and the finer techniques (the "fingernail file" finishing touches) can be applied.
There is nothing more frustrating to a group of singers than
to see the conductor exhibiting a finished conducting technique
while they are struggling to find notes and rhythmic patterns.
They are in no position to pay attention to refined details of
conducting at this point.

Specifically, what are some examples of the "pick and
shovel" technique?   First of all, the director should know
that, in order to achieve results in a minimal amount of
time, certain physical movements may have to be exaggerated.
The list of suggestions below comprise only a basic indication
of how to use imagination and spontaneity to act out the solutions to the technical and interpretative problems lying dormant on the printed page.

1. The director may need to "dance" (exhibit) the
    particular body movement which conveys the rhyth-
    mic patterns desired as the ensemble sings.

2. The director may need to clap while the group is
    singing, so as to clarify rhythm, or to regain en-
    semble unity. (The group also should clap rhythm.)

3. The director may need to sway back and forth to
    convey a legato feeling.

4. An occasional stomping of the foot is an example
    of a dramatic gesture which exaggerates an "ac-
    cented" rest or a breath before a strong attack.

These illustrations indicate the kind of dramatic gestures which may be required to save time and to demonstrate
certain vocal actions to be taken by the singers. When the
singers are concentrating heavily on reading notes and rhythm,
the conductor's gestures must, somehow, "get over" the musical scores into their consciousness. Stopping an ensemble
to "lecture" them as to what to do at a given point merely
wastes time and causes boredom and confusion among the
singers. However, if the director, at the moment of required action, attracts the singers' attention through an effective command or body movement, much time and frustration can be avoided. If the volume is not too great, or if
there is a rest, a verbal command of one or two words will
indicate the correct reaction desired from the singers in the
early stages of learning the music.

The refined "fingernail file" technique should be the
style of conducting used only during the later "polishing" rehearsals and in the performance. A note of caution here is
that the conductor must learn to discern when to use either
the crude "pick and shovel" technique and when to "graduate"
to the use of the "fingernail file." Fewer things are more
grotesque than attending a concert in which the conductor
"gets in the way" of the music with gross physical gestures.

The conclusion to be made here is that the conductor
should look like the music in a blunt manner in the early
stages of work, and then in a more subtle, refined manner
during the final stages of preparation and in the performance.

Redundant Gestures

One of the most dangerous pitfalls for any director is to develop a single mannerism, that seems comfortable and effective, and to use it for every style and gesture in conducting a musical score. A conducting gesture may be effective for one interpretation of a musical passage, but completely contradictory to the meaning of another passage.

Lawrence Marsh, Assistant Professor of Conducting and Music Education at the University of Michigan, has stated humorously his view of conductors based upon his experiences adjudicating choral festivals. He modestly adds, "Don't be alarmed if you glimpse yourself in one or more of these fictitious characters. I've seen myself more often than I would like!"4 These are Marsh's characterizations*:

> First there's Norman Kneedipper. He assumes the singer's posture with all the expansiveness and energy which that implies, only to lose the support and evenness of line by becoming weak in the knees on each strong beat.
> Then we have Peter Palmer, who habitually conducts with his palms facing the choir in a kind of "stifle" gesture. He is particularly consistent in this when the music requires a soft dynamic. Even though he realizes that soft singing demands more energy, and asks for that verbally, his choir never sings a very exciting sound, and tends to lose pitch in the lower dynamic range.
> Billy Bigswinger uses one large-sized gesture for all dynamic levels. He wonders why there is so little contrast in his choir's performance.
> His good friend, Sharon Shusher, attempts to solve the problem by occasionally bringing her pointer finger to her lips, often emitting a sound much like a leaky steam pipe, with results similar to those of Peter [Palmer].
> Then there's Connie Cuemeister who points sharply at the section that is to enter as though demanding that they sing. She wonders why the tone is brittle and lacking in warmth.
> Harry Hollowchest, although a fine singer himself, somehow loses his posture when assuming his

---

*Used here with the permission of Lawrence Marsh.

conducting stance. He often reaches too far out toward his choir, causing his rib cage to collapse. Harry is dismayed when his choir faithfully imitates him.

Now we come to Michael Metronome. Mike never varies from the tempo, no matter what the stylistic demands of the piece are. More importantly, this Sousa devotee believes that a bar line is always followed by a down beat. The sharp vertical motion of his gesture causes his choir to sing with fine rhythmic precision but without any sense of forward motion or phrase direction.

Mike's opposite is Roberta Rubato. She milks each phrase for its last ounce of sentimental beauty. This self-admitted romantic conducts all styles with a liquid, imprecise motion, causing every piece to sound like bad Brahms with the added feature of consistently unintelligible text.

Gary Grabber releases his choir at phrase endings with an abrupt gesture as though attempting to catch flies in mid-flight. His choir often experiences difficulty with final consonants.

Mona Mouther, tries to solve this and other diction problems by consistently mouthing the words. She has rendered her hands virtually useless, since her choir always watches her lips.

Freddie Forkfinger, who conducts with his fingers wide-spread, wonders why his choir can't seem to eliminate the breathiness from their tone.

Derrick Driver has quite a different problem. He conducts as though he's being screentested for the lead in "Rocky III." The clinched fist and tight biceps create a big choral sound. Yet, he questions why his singers often complain of throat pain.

Then there is Orville Overcontrol, who also exudes considerable tension, but confines his gestures to a tight central area. His singers have yet to explore the entire potential of their instruments.

Lastly, please meet Linda Limpfish whose conducting arm resembles a wet dishrag. She wrings her hands in discouragement over her choir's lifeless sound. [5]

Marsh further cautions the conductor never to move merely out of habit. Any conducting gesture which expresses the correct mood of the music is good, but the most important factor to remember is that conducting is a study in con-

trasts. That is, various moods and musical expressions require a variety of gestures to convey what the music has to
say. Any one gesture that is used throughout a musical selection becomes redundant and meaningless. Fortunate, indeed, are those conductors--experienced as well as tyros--
who have access to videotape machines to visually record
their rehearsal gestures for self-analysis.

CHOICE AND PREPARATION OF MUSIC

Repertoire and Program Building

One of the most difficult tasks for any director is
proper choice of repertoire. When choices must be made
before a particular ensemble has been assembled, the director must have many options in mind. This dilemma is
lessened considerably in situations in which there is little
attrition from year to year or from term to term.

The musical repertoire should represent a variety of
textures, moods, volume, styles, and musical periods which
the particular ensemble can "digest." Directors should also
realize, however, that they cannot please everyone all the
time by their choices; yet, the music must appeal generally
to the majority of the group. Also, the manner in which the
selections are introduced, has a definite effect upon first im-
pressions which the group may form. As emphasized in
Chapter 2, the singers wish to know immediately how the
whole piece basically sounds, even in the early, cruder stages
of exposure to it. That is why the Gestalt concept of the
whole is a valuable aid in establishing a positive attitude
about the music at hand, and why it is crucial that the selections be within the grasp of the ensemble's ability to master. In the final analysis it is the director who must be responsible for introducing and rehearsing the music in a challenging and interesting fashion. Even suitable music under
the direction of an inept conductor will likely present morale
problems for the singers.

INTRODUCING NEW MUSIC

Synthesis-Analysis-Synthesis

In Chapters 2 and 3 the concept of S-A-S was introduced. In this chapter we will explore the practical application of this idea. First of all, it is important to recognize

that S-A-S is the means by which the singers can grasp and
maintain a basic understanding whole--the profile of the music.

   The first synthesis to be made is to sing through the
entire piece of music. The level of difficulty of the composition chosen must be somewhere near the group's ability to
sing without breaking down completely and often. However,
there may be occasional times in which the group stops singing or must be stopped because of the complexity of the musical or vocal demands. It may be necessary at this juncture
to employ some analysis in order to continue singing the
piece. However, at this point the director must not feel that
the whole problem must be solved, at all costs, by spending
a great deal of time on the particular problem. Rather,
there should be just enough insight gained to enable the ensemble to continue its first synthesis, because the objective
is to give a first complete reading. The singers want to
"taste the whole" before working on the parts.

   The first analysis should be made by working on the
most obvious problems encountered by the ensemble. If the
director studies the score thoroughly in advance of the rehearsal, many of the major problems can be anticipated and
noted. However, during the first synthesis the director should
have a pencil at hand (preferably red) to circle problem
places in the music which may not have been anticipated.
As many of the major impediments as possible should be
"attacked" at this first analysis attempt. Moreover, it is
of extreme importance for the director to recognize that
most of these major problems cannot be solved immediately;
that the five avenues (paths) of musical growth must take
place on the road to mastering the music being rehearsed;
that gradually, insight will accrue and that finally the skill
to perform will emerge. Some progress should be made in
perfecting the performance of the music, but complete solutions should never be expected in this early stage of rehearsing the piece.

   The next step is synthesis again, i.e., synthesizing
what progress has been made toward mastering the whole
piece (or movement of a larger work). This action permits
the singers to gain a clearer insight into their concept of
the whole.

   The entire cycle of S-A-S should be repeated at each
rehearsal, gradually refining each problem until the final

synthesis produces the desired perfection.   The director
strives to lower the "peaks" of the musical problems each
rehearsal so that, as time progresses, the peaks are eliminated.   By the tenth week there should be only minor peaks
(problems) with which to deal.   In other words, the progression through the music should have no major obstacles, and
the total synthesis produces a thorough understanding of the
composition.

The most difficult places (highest peaks) should be an-
alyzed and rehearsed first; then return to the whole, if time
permits.   In each successive rehearsal the greatest problem
areas should be rehearsed until the whole of the composition
is "traversed" and perfected, the peaks being lowered.   The
director should never attempt to perfect the greatest problem
areas in one rehearsal.   The peaks should be gradually perfected as they "level-off" to the next successively difficult
problem area.

The cyclical process of returning from the analysis to
the synthesis is the means by which the context of the whole
selection is kept in mind for the singers.

The first synthesis of S-A-S need not be repeated at
each new rehearsal.   When the ensemble has a reasonably secure concept of how the composition should sound, the director can begin the analysis process immediately upon rehearsing it, then synthesizing again to gain a deeper insight
into the whole.   However, at each rehearsal some section of
the music should be brought to fruition, so as to achieve a
degree of satisfaction for the labor having been put into the
refining of the musical intent.

PACING OF THE REHEARSAL

Some Special Tips on Analysis Rehearsing

1.   Have a definite rehearsal plan in mind.   A syllabus
     for the span of rehearsals should be distributed to
     each chorister, showing a specific sequence of the
     music to be worked on for each rehearsal period.
     Plan in advance the time bracket for each selection
     or segment to be rehearsed.

2.   Insist that every singer have a pencil to mark spe-
     cific points of emphasis.   Repeat instructions, if
     necessary.

3. Move quickly from one problem area to the next. Long pauses between decisions lead to boredom and restlessness.

4. Be flexible: change the order of selections, style or pace of the rehearsal to accommodate as needed unanticipated problems or events, such as poor attendance caused by emergencies or lethargy among the singers.

5. Give instructions explicitly. Call out page and bar number (when available); hum pitch, and then begin with proper verbal and/or conducting preparatory beat.

6. Rhythmic problems should be chanted on a selected vowel with speech intonation to clarify them.

7. Polyphonic or fugal passages may be sung by sopranos with tenors and altos with basses singing each other's parts, or everyone singing the thematic material together.

8. Use the piano only when necessary so that the singers will develop independence in sight singing.

9. Call attention to the note(s) in other parts which lead to a difficult one for a given section to find. Sometimes a phrase or motif is sung by another voice part a few beats or bars before the next voice part enters. Ask the section having trouble to sing or think the notes of the previous entering section with them, so as to be ready for their own entrance (see pages 132-37 for further discussion).

10. Instruct the choristers to number the beats and/or sub-beats of bars having difficult or tricky rhythm. In instances of syncopation the singers should number the even beats and, in addition, indicate the sub-beats.

11. Have choristers circle places in the music which may require more concentration and additional individual work outside of rehearsal.

12. Instruct the singers to mark intervalic skips (a

3rd, 4th, 5th, 6th, etc.) to clarify spatial relationships among the notes, thus enhancing their
musicianship.

13.   Have the singers recall intervals of familiar songs
      which illustrate the skips, such as "My Bonnie
      (Lies over the Ocean)" for a skip of a 6th, and
      "Maria" from West Side Story for a tritone inter-
      val. See page 131 for a more complete list.

14.   Encourage choristers to establish their own hiero-
      glyphics for clarifying the musical intent.

15.   Keep your remarks to a minimum. Short sen-
      tences or phrase commands (sometimes called
      out over the group's singing) saves much time;
      don't stop to make comments.

16.   Try to establish and maintain a quiet, but reas-
      suring manner in the tone of voice used in giving
      instructions. A constantly loud and ebullient voice
      elicits excitement and uneasiness among the chor-
      isters, whereas the calm voice reassures them.
      (This is not to say, however, that the director
      should be unenthusiastic.)

17.   Insist upon good sitting or standing posture at all
      rehearsals. The choristers may need to be re-
      minded often to maintain proper posture.

18.   Rehearse difficult passages slowly, so as to give
      the group the opportunity to think while they are
      rehearsing.

19.   Be bold--not timid in "attacking" the music in re-
      hearsal. Do not be fearful that the choristers
      will make gross individual or collective mistakes.
      They need to be encouraged to read music aggres-
      sively at the risk of committing errors. This
      positive attitude toward rehearsing music will im-
      prove musicianship. The ensemble should be in-
      volved with determining what is wrong, if at all
      possible.

20.   Drill only when absolutely necessary. Try to
      solve problems by gaining insight into them rather
      than depending upon rote learning (drills). Use

the "pick and shovel" technique where needed and
the "fingernail file" when appropriate.

21. Constantly keep your long and short goals in mind.

22. When working with only one section for more than
     a few seconds, try to keep the attention of the
     other sections by including them in the process,
     such as humming their parts while the lone sec-
     tion sings; having the entire group sing the pas-
     sage together; having the troubled section or whole
     group sing by numbers or solfège syllables; hav-
     ing all sections chant tricky rhythmic material.

23. Develop a definite technique of vocal pedagogy that
     can be utilized with the actual music being sung:
     solve vocal problems where they occur in the
     music--not by assuming that intangible warm-up
     vocalises will do the job for you.

24. Constantly remind the sections to listen to each
     other for blend, intonation and balance.

25. Don't waste time singing portions of the music
     already mastered or easy to sing. Periodic re-
     view can be accomplished by following syntheses.

26. Frequently instruct the singers to locate their
     pitches without the aid of the piano or pitch pipe
     when repeating phrases in diatonic music. This
     develops their listening ability and aids in main-
     taining concentration by the choristers.

27. Silent-imagery singing of selected phrases is an-
     other valuable means of achieving a high level of
     concentration. First, have the group establish its
     pitch and then "sing" the given passage silently for
     a few notes. Next, instruct them to sing aloud
     on command.

28. Always explain why you are asking that a section
     or phrase of the music be repeated. The choris-
     ters deserve to know why it should be repeated.

29. Always try to synthesize a composition (or move-
     ment from a longer work) after the analysis proc-
     ess has been worked on so that the difficult pas-

sage(s) can be integrated with the whole. Occasionally one runs out of time or misjudges the
complexity of the musical problem(s) to be solved;
thus, the synthesis must be done at the next rehearsal.

30. Record as many rehearsals as possible to study
further what went undetected in the session and to
analyze your own technique.

These are only a few of the practices which may be
helpful in working on the analysis level of a rehearsal.   The
points are cited here to illustrate the kinds of circumstances
which occur during a rehearsal.   Experience, and even mistakes which the conductor makes from time to time, may un-
cover other such exigencies that will enable him or her to
become more efficient in perfecting the performance of the
score.

Vertical Versus Horizontal Pacing

Previously we have discussed readiness to learn, motivation in learning, and the avenues of musical growth involved in the choral experience.   It is also important to recognize the factor of pacing, best described by Louis Thorpe
as "... the intelligent distribution of work and rest periods
in the mastery of new materials or problems on the part of
the learner."[6] Thorpe states that pacing must be tailored
to the maturation level of the individual pupil and that it must
be considered as being both vertical and horizontal.

By vertical pacing is meant presenting to the learner
increasingly difficult or complex tasks to perform
as he develops, i.e., as he becomes more mature
(manifests greater insight) regarding the type of
tasks involved. [7]

Horizontal pacing is described by Thorpe as

... selecting the psychologically optimum distribution periods of work (practice) and rest in connec-
tion with the mastery of either skills or conceptual
materials. [8]

This concept can be adapted to the learning situation
in the choral rehearsal.   It concerns itself with the amount

of time available for rehearsal and the choice of music suitable to the maturation level of the learners.   The wise director will select repertoire for his or her ensemble which
will challenge them--yet be within the general grasp of the
group.   Thus, the whole of each composition is likely to be
perceived without undue trauma.   The following graph in Figure 33 provides some insight into a formula for dealing with
the overall procedure of rehearsal pacing.   The concept deals
with the difficulty of the music in relation to the rehearsal
span as follows:

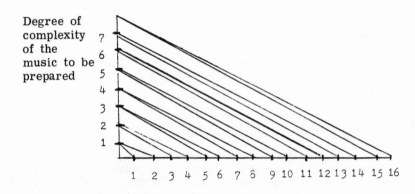

Number of rehearsals available

Fig. 33: Vertical and Horizontal Pacing Graph

     This graph indicates for the conductor that music
must be selected which is suitable for the ensemble in relation to the rehearsal time frame.   The question to be asked
is, "How many hours of rehearsal are available to bring the
music up to satisfactory performance level, given the achievement level of the group?" If all or most of the music is so
easy or trite that the group will become bored singing it, or
if there are too few selections to provide variety and challenge, the director has erred considerably.   Conversely, if
the selections are too difficult and/or numerous, the group
may become discouraged, demoralized, or even resentful.
Therefore, thoughtful analysis of the limitations, needs and
potential of a given ensemble must be applied to the choice
of music and how the rehearsals are to be conducted.

Rehearsal Sequence

There can be no fixed formula for establishing the
ideal rehearsal sequence. However, certain principles are
noted here for the director to follow in planning each rehearsal.

1.   Careful thought should be given to the proper
      warm-up of the voices. That is, complicated
      vocal gymnastics, which are beyond the profi-
      ciency level of the ensemble members, can only
      lead to exacerbating the vocal problems of the
      singers. It is frequently effective to use a chorale
      (or hymn in church choir situations) as a warm-up.
      The homophonic nature of the music can be used
      to concentrate upon intonation, blend, balance and
      many other facets of choral-vocal pedagogy. (See
      Chapter 4 for vocal pedagogy.)

2.   Alternate difficult music with easier pieces when-
      ever possible. Also alternate softer music with
      louder selections.

3.   The most vocally demanding and complex music
      should be rehearsed when the ensemble is warmed
      up, but still fresh in energy--about one-third of
      the time into the rehearsal period.

4.   To maintain interest keep in mind variety of mu-
      sical textures as well as musical styles. There
      is enough good music available to provide this
      variety, if enough time is spent researching cata-
      logues and requesting music on approval. (As
      mentioned previously, some publishers will send
      single review copies.)

5.   Close the rehearsal with a composition which the
      group will likely enjoy. This will tend to send
      them out of the room singing phrases of the mu-
      sic, or at least give them a sense of accomplish-
      ment for their efforts.

DRILLING

Reference has been made earlier in this chapter that drilling
music should be done only as a last resort. That is not to

suggest that repetition is not a necessary component of any
rehearsal.   It is mindless drilling that produces dubious results in the musical growth of the choristers.   Moreover,
drilling for its own sake can be a great source of boredom
for the singers.

However, it may be necessary to repeat carefully a
difficult rhythmic or intervalic motif several times in order
to discriminate and gain insight into the problem. This action
is reinforcement of the "five-lane highway" of learning cited
in Chapter 2.

Instead of thoughtless drilling of musical problems, it
is surely better to employ some intellect to their solution.
In confronting intervalic problems, the director should develop a repertoire of familiar songs which use the same skips
as those being confronted in the problem area of the composition.   Most choristers can "negotiate" intervals of a minor
or major second on up to a perfect fourth.   However, beginning with intervalic skips of a perfect fourth and an augmented
fourth (tritone) on up to the octave, the singers are apt to
encounter significant difficulty.   Therefore, it behooves each
director to research a series of songs familiar to the group.
Grade school children on up to adult community chorus personnel require different songs which are familiar to them.
That is why a complete list published here would not suit all
of the needs of each age level in illustrating intervals.   Chapter 5 cites some examples of aids which can assist choristers to identify problem intervals.

MEMORIZING

The process of memorization of music is a somewhat controversial subject.   To some degree the memorization of scores
is a combination of innate ability, early training in the skill,
the amount of rehearsal time available and the complexity of
the score and text.   Thus, no generalization can be made as
to the best method of memorization for either the conductor
or the choristers.

Memorizing by the Conductor

Conductors who bury their noses in the score cannot
expect concentrated attention from their singers.   Thus, preparation of the score by thorough study is paramount for every

director. Some persons "digest" printed material more readily than others. Therefore, directors should function within
their own proclivities and limitations to achieve as much independence from the score as they can. Some aids in memorization of scores are worth citing:

1. Analyze the score thoroughly as to form (A-B-A,
   etcetera).

2. Study the text carefully, relating the syntax of the
   words to the rhythm of the music.

3. Make associations of
   a) text and music related to the musical form;
   b) words with other words;
   c) words with music.

Memorization by the Ensemble

Some conductors who find memorization an easy task
will, no doubt, expect their choristers to memorize their music. This, of course, is an ideal situation. Yet, a director
who has many choirs and a large repertoire to be prepared,
and who possibly is not a "quick study," will likely be unable
to find the time to memorize great amounts of music. The
question then surfaces: if directors don't memorize their music, can they expect memorization from the singers? The
answer may well be yes, within reason. It is not too much
to expect that simpler homophonic songs be memorized by
singers. In performing long, complex works, particularly
with large instrumental forces, the score, though learned
well, will be difficult to memorize totally. In such instances,
the singers and conductor should use the score for referral
purposes only; that is, to refresh the memory. The eyes of
the choristers should be mostly on the conductor--not buried
in the score. In contrast, choral sheet music of four to
eight pages in length certainly should be memorized by the
choral groups and the conductor, particularly in situations in
which adequate rehearsal time is available.

As cited earlier, the factors of adequate rehearsal
time and the experience of the group are important ingredients for memorization. This writer has found that proficient sight readers usually memorized more slowly than those
who rely largely upon rote learning to master their parts.
The latter usually commit the score to memory during the
rehearsal process because of their lack of reading proficiency.

There are two distinct methods of memorization:

1.   The "whole method," which is more effective with
meaningful material and quick learners; that is, gradually ab-
sorbing the entire song in general sequence.   Isolated parts
may need special attention, but the whole composition is not
broken down into parts.   It should be emphasized, however,
that this method is more effective with easy material than
with complex scores.

2.   The "part method" of learning concentrates upon
repetition of phrase by phrase: first with the music; then
without reference to the score; next, checking to see where
mistakes or omissions were made; and finally repeating the
phrase without the aid of the score.   After a few phrases
are rehearsed in this fashion, synthesizing a page or section
should be done to recover some semblance of the whole again.
It is wise to set limited goals of a few pages or a short section of the composition to be memorized at each rehearsal.

3.   "Farming out" the music to each chorister with
instructions to have them individually (or in small, ad hoc
groups) memorize it out of class.   In situations in which
there is much competition for membership in a particular
ensemble, this method is very efficient, because little rehearsal time needs to be spent on memorization.

There are some psychological factors that motivate
individuals to memorize their music:

1.   We tend to concentrate best upon ideas and concepts that interest us.   Therefore, the choice of music is
crucial to this process.   The choristers will concentrate
more readily upon music that they enjoy and find challenging.

2.   Memorization requires training.   Many singers
actually know their music by memory, but are reluctant to
divorce themselves from looking at the score.   Persistent
effort and training in this endeavor is necessary to encourage choristers to develop their independence of the score.

3.   The group dynamic can aid in the memorization
process in that usually not everyone will forget the same
phrases, thus carrying each other through the selection.

4.   The director should maintain an optimistic attitude throughout the memorization process.

5.   The S-A-S process, described earlier in this chapter, should be applied to memorization technique.   Generally, it is best to memorize the music and text simultaneously, although it is sometimes effective to isolate the words from the music after the notes have been sufficiently mastered. However, always return to the "whole" after working on the parts.

6.   If possible, "overmemorize" the music, i. e., keep working on the score until it is so secure that the words and music become subconscious.   (This may well be impossible, however, in situations having limited rehearsal time available.)

MAKING MISTAKES

Conductor's Errors

Conductors have a phobia about making mistakes in front of their ensembles, often feeling that people will think less of them if they are not always perfect.   This is not to minimize their need to be articulate, proficient leaders.   Yet, the notion of their being "human" needs to be put into perspective.

As cited earlier in this book, when mistakes are made, conductors must acknowledge their errors so as to maintain the respect of their ensemble members.   It is imperative that the conductor be well enough prepared so that his or her conduct is not one of continual apologies.   Redundant errors should not be tolerated by either the director or the singers.

Admitting mistakes establishes a climate in which the choristers feel that the director is "human" also; they can thus more readily accept the leader's role as one of pointing out errors as the score is being learned.

The director should be equipped with a colored pencil to circle or "X" the places that should be studied further before the next rehearsal.

Singers' Errors

Choristers are frequently reluctant to try to sing music

at sight, lest they become embarrassed by their mistakes.
Since one of the conductor's roles in rehearsal is to correct
mistakes, the members are frequently reticent to read the
score aggressively in the early stages of rehearsal for fear
of being criticized. Therefore, as emphasized earlier in
this chapter, the conductor must avoid, at all costs, the attitude that the group or any individuals in it are dull or stupid. Corrections and criticisms need to be handled in a
very positive manner, encouraging the ensemble members to
"explore."

The important factor is to stop at the point of a gross
error (during the analysis part of the rehearsal) and determine the cause. This is the time when music education principles of teaching theory or vocal pedagogy can be most effective. Here, also, is the place at which the director's
musicianship or knowledge of vocal pedagogy is "on the line."

INTERPRETATIVE FACTORS

Interpretation, beyond adhering to the technical demands of
the score, is one of the most neglected areas in musical endeavor. Many competent conductors are able to develop their
ensembles into exceptionally proficient technical performers.
However, this feat in itself does not lead to a truly sensitive
reading of the score. It is the subtle, intrinsic meanings in
the music and text which must be sought. The musical notation is merely an abstraction which is meaningless until it
is given sound. That sound should reflect more than singing
fortes and pianissimos at the correct places, or "negotiating"
all the notes correctly, or having fine attacks and releases,
or even delivering beautiful diction and tone. These achievements are all prerequisites to giving the performance a meaningful interpretation of the score. This is the juncture at
which artistry emerges. Artistic singing, be it solo or choral,
must be the final objective of every ensemble and its conductor.

How can artistic singing be accomplished? It is,
first of all, achieved by careful, respectful analysis of what
one believes the composer has meant to say in assembling
the notes and directions in the score. This writer has occasionally asked contemporary composers to interpret their
scores for him. Their response usually has been a thoughtful, "What does it mean to you?" The score can have many
different meanings to various individuals. Yet, this is not

license to violate the composer's basic intentions. We must
function within the framework of the composer's essential
message, even though we may need to adjust the tempi and
dynamics according to certain conditions, such as room acoustics, the most effective tempi for the particular ensemble,
the size of the group in terms of dynamics, and body of tone
for proper vocal texture.

It is laudable for the conductor to have a thorough
understanding of musical practices among the various periods of music history. In recent years, musicologists have
helped us achieve a deeper understanding of our musical heritage. Yet, this knowledge gives us only broad guidelines
for breathing life into the abstract musical score. It is mandatory, then, for every conductor to interpret the score beyond the technical aspects. For instance, the director's preoccupation with keeping the group together will often lead to
unexpressive interpretation of a legato composition. (This
subject and several other important facets of interpretation
will be discussed more thoroughly in Chapter 8.)

Another concern of this writer is that many directors
who have an excellent background in musicology hold to certain statements as though they were inviolable letters of the
law. One familiar notion concerns Johann Sebastian Bach.
It is common knowledge that Bach almost constantly pled with
his town council and ecclesiastical superiors to supply him
with more and better singers and instrumentalists. He is
known to have stated that seventeen singers were the minimum number that he needed to sing his music. Therefore,
some musicologists state that choral groups should perform
the music of Bach (and, for that matter, all Baroque period
music) with no more than twenty singers; that any larger
choir violates the texture of his music. Though it is true
that the contrapuntal lines of Baroque music must be cleanly
and crisply sung, this writer maintains that larger choral
groups can sing the complex lines equally as clearly as
smaller ensembles, providing all members are musically
proficient. In other words, if four sopranos can sing their
part with clarity, why not add four or eight more? The addition of equally capable voices will provide better blend and
balance because the security of greater numbers permits them
to sing more lyrically. With fewer voices, there is a tendency to sing with vocal production that is too heavy for "negotiating" the rapid passages with needed flexibility. The
overall texture of the music need not be lugubrious just because more voices are employed. Here again is the acid

test of the conductor's ability to be an effective musical and vocal pedagogue. Chapter 8 will discuss in detail some specific interpretative considerations in choral singing.

CONCERT PROTOCOL

The stage deportment of choristers in performance is crucial to the successful presentation of the music. We must always remember that many people "hear" performances first through their eyes. Slovenly posture, lack of attention to the motions of the conductor by the singers (face lost in the music or looking out at the audience) will significantly mar the overall performance of the ensemble. Therefore, it is important for directors to educate their choristers in proper protocol.

Backstage Deportment

While awaiting their entrance, the ensemble should be reserved and quiet in preparation for their performance. The director should be certain that everyone is lined up properly in order to make a dignified entrance on to the stage risers. When the singers enter, the first row should lead in, followed by the fourth, third and second. This should be carefully rehearsed at the "dress" rehearsal. (Some directors prefer to file in with the fourth row first; then the third, second and first following in sequence.)

On Stage Deportment

Assuming that the singers have now entered the stage and have good posture and a bearing of intensity and interest in their concert performance, they are ready for the conductor to enter. There must be no conversing.

The choristers should have pleasant expressions on their faces to transmit their enjoyment of being on the threshold of a stimulating evening of music. They should stand with dignity, all assuming the same posture. If music is used, everyone should carry the folder in the same hand and be ready to raise it and open it at the same time. Military rigidity is surely not necessary, but all movements should be graceful and proper.

The conductor, upon entering, should walk briskly,

but not hurriedly, acknowledging the applause (if any) with a conservative, dignified bow, turn toward the singers and "deflect" the audience's acknowledgment toward them. After the applause has subsided, the director should then mount the podium or step to the station for conducting and indicate with arms (and facial expression) that the singers should prepare for their first attack. If music is used the folders then should be brought to the correct singing position. All eyes should be on the conductor as the introduction is played or the preparatory beat is given for an unaccompanied attack. Pitches for a cappella selections should be given as unobtrusively as possible by pitch pipe or by someone with perfect pitch humming the key note. Then, the ensemble members should hum their parts of the beginning chord very softly. (Sounding out the pitches on the piano for each section is obtuse.) On the other hand, if the choir members are trained to imagine their pitches from the pitch pipe, or a single soft organ tone or chord or from the hummed note of someone with perfect pitch, the demeanor will be much more "professional."

From that juncture on, complete concentration upon the performance of the music is imperative for both the conductor and singers to establish absolute unity. The dynamic conductor will inspire the ensemble to become so engrossed in the music that they will be relieved of any anxieties which they may have entertained.

Stage Management

Any moving of the piano or instrumental forces should be carefully planned. It is preferable to engage non-singers to act as stage managers. Where this is impossible, certain members of the chorus should quickly step down to effect the necessary physical changes. Plans for this movement should be made well in advance of the concert and the stage work should be done with great efficiency. (Audiences become fidgety when there are random and inefficient movements between selections.)

Applause is usually expressed by the audience after each selection. The conductor should then step down from the podium and acknowledge the applause, next having the soloists, if any, bow, after which he or she should turn to the ensemble and acknowledge them.

At the Close of the Program

     If the ensemble has chairs instead of choral risers,
it is best to have them sit immediately as the applause begins.   Then, have them stand to acknowledge the response
from the audience after soloists have made their bows.   The
chorus should have its special moment of acclaim.

     Before the choristers exit, there is an important item
of protocol to be observed.   The conductor should exit and
then quickly return for additional bows of acknowledgment for
all the performers.   When the applause has subsided and the
conductor has again left the stage, there should be a prear-
ranged cue for the first person to lead the group off the stage.
Usually the first row should exit, followed by each successive
row.   Again, dignity is the important ingredient for proper
protocol in recessing of the choristers.

NOTES

1.   John Backus, The Acoustical Foundations of Music (New
        York: W.W. Norton, 1969), p. 105.
2.   Ibid., p. 105.
3.   Ibid., p. 105.
4.   Lawrence Marsh, ACADAM, Newsletter of the American
        Choral Directors Association of Michigan, May 1979
        (Vol. VII, No. 6), Thomas Hardie, ed., p. 2. (Used
        by permission.)
5.   Ibid., p. 2.
6.   Louis P. Thorpe "Learning Theory and Music Teaching,"
        Basic Concepts of Music Education (Published by the
        National Society for the Study of Education, Chicago,
        1958, Nelson B. Henry, ed.), p. 173.
7.   Ibid., p. 173.
8.   Ibid., p. 174.

REVIEW QUESTIONS FOR CHAPTER 6

(1)   What use does the "profile form" have for the director?

(2)   What are the advantages and/or disadvantages of
        a) the get-acquainted interview?
        b) auditioning by quartets?
        c) solo auditions?

(3)   What are the advantages and disadvantages of
        a) quartet or scrambled seating assignments?
        b) complete sections?

(4) What is the basic value of arranging tenors to sit behind altos?

(5) Why do some choral directors prefer to have sopranos seated in front of tenors and basses behind the altos?

(6) Cite the psychological and practical concerns involved in attendance checking.

(7) What influence does grading have upon attendance and vice versa?

(8) Cite some methods of grading ensemble singers.

(9) What are some cautions about which every director should be aware in personal relationships with singers?

(10) List technical and personality characteristics which should make up the profile of the conductor.

(11) What effect does choice of repertoire have in the motivation of the ensemble?

(12) How is the S-A-S concept utilized in the introduction and continued rehearsal of musical scores?

(13) List the concerns in the pacing of rehearsals.

(14) Describe vertical pacing of the rehearsal.

(15) Describe horizontal pacing of the rehearsal.

(16) What are some principles to keep in mind when planning the rehearsal sequence?

(17) What role does drilling play in rehearsals?

(18) What are the advantages of memorization by
a) ensemble members?
b) conductor?

(19) What should be the attitude regarding making mistakes on the part of the ensemble members and conductor?

(20) Describe artistic singing.

(21) List the important concerns of concert protocol.

Chapter 7

SOME TECHNICAL CONSIDERATIONS
FOR THE CONDUCTOR

In Chapter 6 some important philosophical and psychological
aspects of the conductor's demeanor were discussed. We now
come to some of the technical considerations that are necessary composites to efficient rehearsal technique.

BEGINNING THE REHEARSAL ON TIME

Some conductors are hesitant to begin the rehearsal until
most or all of the ensemble members are present.   Although
it is true that attempting to rehearse a partial, unbalanced
group is demoralizing to most everyone concerned, it is even
more important to establish in the minds of every member of
the group that the director is absolutely serious about utilizing every moment of the precious (limited) rehearsal time
allotted to the group.   (Occasionally, bad weather or a traffic
jam may cause many members of a church choir or community chorus to be late, but that should be only an isolated
circumstance.) The successful conductor will develop measures to cope with habitual late-comers. It must be established with the choristers at the outset that rehearsals will
begin at the appointed times.   Thus, if there are singers
who are habitually tardy, a private discussion with them as
to their sincerity and desire to contribute fully to the group
is in order. This can be accomplished with a firm, but
friendly attitude. If there are singers who must arrive late
or leave early for what the conductor considers to be valid
reasons, this should be explained to the entire group.   To
neglect this matter is to invite resentment from those who
are punctual. This situation must be handled with extreme
care and clarity, so that resentment does not develop among
those who are required to be prompt.

PHYSICAL AND PSYCHOLOGICAL CONDITION
OF THE SINGERS

Actually, it would seem that there is no ideal time for a

choral rehearsal. The very early morning rehearsal often
finds sleepy, sluggish singers. The early afternoon rehearsal has to take into account the after lunch "let down." Late
afternoon finds energies waning, with evening rehearsals finding energies lessened.

Any time a conductor comes before a group of singers, he or she must be able to awaken or refurbish the energies (concentration) of the choristers. There must be imaginative disciplines to suit each ensemble, being cognizant
of the conditions resulting from the time of day in which the
rehearsal is scheduled. These efforts might include some
"wake-up" procedures, such as yoga-type isometric exercises:

1. Stretching the arms high above the head;

2. Touching the toes (or grasping the ankles for the
    less agile);

3. Clasping hands behind the head and then pushing
    back against the hands; then releasing the pres-
    sure and pulling the chin down into the chest to
    stretch the neck muscles;

4. Turning the head from side to side, then forward
    and back to alleviate tensions and relieve fatigue;

5. Having everyone yawn together while inhaling deeply
    to replenish the oxygen in the blood.

Another measure might be to include certain warm-up
vocalises or selections from the group's repertoire at enig-
matic tempi.

Be certain that the room is well-ventilated. Stale air
will surely affect the physical well-being of everyone.

Atmospheric Conditions

All people are affected more or less mentally and
physically by atmospheric conditions. Cloudy, overcast skies
with low barometric pressure can cause people to be lethargic, uneasy, or fidgety. The singers will be more apt to
converse among themselves during the rehearsal, or at least
have more difficulty in concentrating on the music. This
condition is even more obvious with younger children and

adolescents, who will sometimes sound like magpies. Therefore, it is important to realize that it may not be possible
to accomplish as much as had been planned at a rehearsal
during which the atmospheric conditions are heavy. The director must be especially patient, calm, and reassuring under such conditions. A sense of humor and the ability to
keep the rehearsal attitude relaxed may prevent some severe
problems.

Regardless of the weather (barometric pressure) or
other distracting circumstances, there should never be instant chatter at every pause in the singing. However, singers should feel free to raise a hand to ask questions about
the music if their points are valid. Often, it is important
for a singer to have the problem solved at that particular
moment, rather than to wait to see the director at the end
of the rehearsal. Perhaps, when a problem which a singer
has observed has escaped the notice of the conductor, it would
be well to discuss it at that point. A climate of "we are in
this together" is a healthier one than that of the conductor
being the task master. A director eventually learns to dif-
ferentiate between persons who are alert with helpful suggestions and those who fuss over unimportant matters.

PEDAGOGICAL USES OF REPERTOIRE

Warm-up and Improvement of Tone Quality and Musicianship

We must constantly seek to refine our methods of
working against time, since time is at a premium in almost
every choral situation. That is why utilizing the actual music being studied as pedagogical material is so all-important
in building satisfactory choral groups. The use of chorales,
hymns, and excerpts of materials from current repertoire
has been cited previously as appropriate for warm-up material. The following examples will illustrate just a few ways
in which warm-up, vocal progress, and theoretical knowledge
can be found in the music at hand, rather than the use of
intangible vocalises which may have little correlation to the
problems encountered in the music. Of prime importance
is the need to stress vowel purity in preparing the singers
mentally and physically for singing. The example in Figure
34 illustrates how emphasis upon clearly produced vowels
can be used both as warm-up and as pedagogical procedure.

JESUS DEAREST MASTER

Fig. 34:   Use of Chorale as Warm-up Exercise

Teaching Legato Singing

Sustaining vowels, subvowels (see Vowel Spectrum, page 88) and careful use of consonants can be achieved using the following steps:

1.   The vowels should be pure and deeply set to achieve a rich tone quality and good diction.

2.   Long vowels and softened (but clean) consonants will engender a smooth legato line.   Legato singing is analogous to a clothesline.   The line extends from point to point; the clothing hanging on the line represent the vowels; the clothespins represent the consonants.   The clothesline is continuous, yet, the clothing and clothespins do not interfere with the continuity of the line.

3.   The consonants should be "in line" with the vowel. Plosives should be softened and should not constrict the oral pharynx.

4.   Utilize m's, n's and l's (sub-vowels) to attain legato singing (see Vowel Spectrum).

5.   Silent breath inhalation (open throat) leads to breath and vowel support of the tone without "holes" (breaks) between the notes.   The objective should be to produce smooth, uninterrupted phrase lines.

Other benefits accruing from the use of chorales in warm-up procedures are opportunities to train the choristers in 1) listening for blend and balance; 2) precise attacks and releases; 3) dynamic and tempo changes; 4) responding sensitively to the conductor's physical gestures.

When working toward flexibility in the voices, the conductor should insist upon the following:

1.   Producing a light, crisp vocal texture achieved by a "forward projection" of the vowel, highly arched behind the upper front teeth.   This should be accompanied by a slight yawning sensation (elevating the soft palate).

2.   Maintaining pure vowels throughout an entire melisma.   Have each person write the basic vowel

sound at the beginning of each measure throughout
the entire melisma.

3.   Silent breaths during inhalation;

4.   Keeping the feeling of open throat at phrase end-
     ings, particularly when fast breaths must be taken,
     i. e., don't collapse the palate on consonants (again
     meaning the consonant should be "in line" with the
     vowel);

5.   Rhythmic pulse, including sub-beats.

When needing to work on syncopation, chant the rhythms
on neutral vowels and tones, using the actual music.   Have
the singers mark the major and sub-beats with their pencils.
Apply the text to the music so that the syntax of the word-
rhythms fits the musical rhythms.

In all of these situations above, stop where the problems exist and have the sections recognize the intervalic relationships, such as fourths, tritones, fifths, sixths, and
other augmented intervals as well as rhythmic problems.

With intelligent application and practice, both the conductor and choristers will develop facility in utilizing the music to achieve the necessary pedagogical objectives.

BODY POSTURE AND MOVEMENTS OF
THE CONDUCTOR

The caricatures presented in Chapter 6 by Lawrence Marsh
(pages 163-64) highlight some of the peculiar mannerisms we
conductors are prone to embrace in leading our singers.   An
ensemble will invariably reflect all of the conductor's strengths
and weaknesses.   Thus, the musical ideas must be effectively
"acted out" through body and facial expressions:

1.   The conductor must first feel the mood before it
     can be conveyed to the singers.

2.   "Singing mentally" will convey to the group that
     the conductor is experiencing the total expression
     with them.   (This is not to imply that the direc-
     tor must sing with the ensemble, except possibly
     in special instances during early rehearsal stages
     to cue them in.)

3. The director's every action and expression must convey the exact mood, quality, and quantity of the musical intent.

4. The intensity required for pianissimo passages must clearly show in the conductor's facial expressions and movements.

Conducting Posture and Gestures

The conductor must assume a strong, but not stiff (rigid), posture. A conductor's tenseness is immediately transferred to the singers' vocal mechanism, thus inhibiting their vocal production. For instance, a tense fist gesture will tend to cause the singers to respond with vocal tension (strain). Arm movements must freely express the exact mood of the song, keeping in mind that directors must do the following:

1. Convey the mood of the music (body, hands and face) in a coordinated whole. The conductor is the dramatist through whom the musical expression is made.

2. Be flexible and flowing for legato (not floppy).

3. Be crisp and exact for staccato work.

4. Be articulate and firm (again not tense) for marcato passages.

5. Keep all arm movements basically within a relatively small radius (perpendicularly and horizontally), so that accents can be made effectively when needing to move outside the normal scope of gestures for contrast. The focal point of each beat should relate to the center of the body as much as possible.

6. Keep elbows from "flailing" outward. They should be close to the body unless special accents are needed.

7. Conduct only the necessary rhythm. Indicating too many sub-beats destroys the horizontal movement (drive) of the vocal line. Allow the momentum

of the music to carry through the unimportant beats. These sub-beats can be indicated with subtle wrist gestures, when it is necessary to reinforce rhythmic values.

8. Be economical with all gestures, carefully studying how to conserve energy and avoid "getting in the way" of the music. The conductor should, in a real sense, be an "invisible object" between the audience and ensemble. His or her motions should always be consonant (yet subtle) with the musical performance. (Ray Still, first oboist of the Chicago Symphony Orchestra states, "[M]ost conductors are not clever enough to know that fifty percent of the time they are "getting in the way."[1])

9. Develop the skill of making all gestures automatic, subtly revealing the nature of the musical expression. Loud and soft attacks and releases should be exactly in keeping with the mood of the music. The goal should be to "look like the music."

10. Attempt to avoid redundancy in conducting gestures. What is effective for one style or mood of music may be entirely out of place in another. Conducting is a study in contrasts.

11. Exude facial expressions of confidence in the ensemble to reinforce their self-assurance.

FACIAL EXPRESSIONS

We have mentioned above the need for the conductor to "look like" the music, implying that facial expressions--i. e., being an actor--are part of the role of dramatizing the musical intent. Specifically, the facial expressions should convey confidence in the group's ability to adequately meet the requirements of the music. Over and above that expression, some appropriate moods to be conveyed (acted out) are joy and happiness, nostalgia, pain or sorrow, pleasantness, pleasure, humor (smiling expression), anger, pathos, and introspection.

To sum up the total responsibility, the conductor must inspire the choristers to reflect the proper mood. For example, nothing is more uninspiring to the audience than to see sober or sad expressions on the singers' faces as they perform joyous or humorous songs.

BATON OR HANDS

The use of the baton is a rather personal matter, especially with choral conductors. While most instrumental conductors rely upon the baton to be effective leaders of their forces, many choral directors feel that the vocal medium is too personal to rely upon a stick, which "comes between" the leader and the choristers or is too rigid for expressive singing.

In contrast to this view, it should be recognized that a baton tends to minimize body movements and keeps the arms from flailing unnecessarily. Long, thick batons are usually unnecessary for conducting choral ensembles. They can be cut off to about eight or twelve inches and sanded down to an attractive shape, and being light, they will become a comfortable extension of the hand. With a light baton, the last three fingers can be extended outward to enhance expression (along with the free hand), allowing for the needed personal contact with the singers.

The baton should be "seated" in the center of the palm and held in place with the index finger and the thumb. The manner in which the baton is grasped, i.e., by the entire hand or just two or three fingers, can convey moods from firmness and strength to gentleness and soft singing.

As stated in Chapter 1, the use of the baton also tends to discipline the conductor to convey the beats more precisely and effectively for the singers, thereby providing a focal point for visual contact for them, especially when singers are using scores. However, it is possible for choristers to learn to sing very articulately without the use of the baton. It is just more difficult to achieve adequate precision without it for most conductors.

Another factor for choral conductors to consider in regard to the use of a baton is the size of the group and the distance between the conductor and the choir. The singers can see the conducting beats at a distance more clearly than the hand--especially during early stages of learning the music.

In almost all instances when conductors are doing works involving both choral and instrumental forces, a baton is recommended. In these situations the conductor is usually a relatively long distance from the singers.

It behooves every neophyte conductor to learn to use a baton--to become comfortable with it, so as to be able to use it when it is deemed necessary. The use of a videotape machine can be very effective in revealing exactly how the conductor looks. Even experienced directors can benefit by this kind of review.

THE PREPARATORY BEAT

Although most beginning conducting courses stress the need for a preparatory beat that reveals the mood and tempo of the phrase to be performed, it is still very easy to lapse into the bad habit of imprecise preparation for attacks. One may conceive mentally of the mood and tempo of the coming musical phrase and still not physically convey it clearly enough for the singers through the preparatory beat. These motions preceding the attack serve to indicate breath inhalation for the singers, as well as mental preparation. It is often a valuable exercise for both conductor and singers to practice silent breath inhalation along with the preparatory beat(s): preparatory beat, silent breath, attack.

It is especially important that the preparatory beat always characterize the ictus (precise focal point of the stroke) to indicate proper tempo of the music. The often-termed "up-beat" also should indicate the dynamic level of the music. For example, in 4/4 time the preparatory beat is inscribed as follows for the attack (ictus):

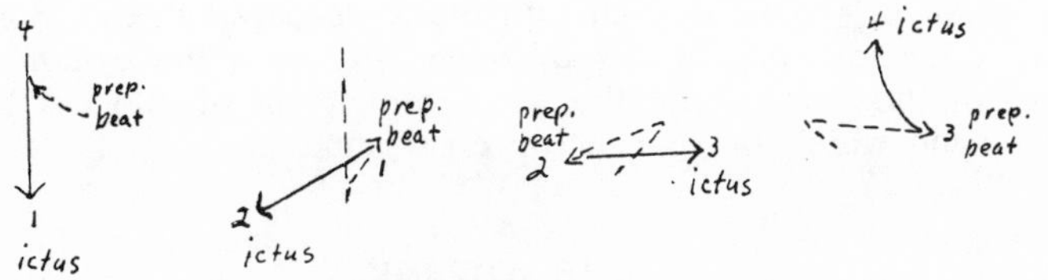

Fig. 35: Preparatory Beat

Piano and pianissimo attacks are usually the most difficult to articulate in the preparatory beat because the motion(s) must be small and extremely precise. Insist that all eyes be on the conductor so as to have total concentration for the attack.

The soft or legato attack may be made more exact by
the use of a baton for reasons noted previously. It sharpens
the focal point of the beat and minimizes an excess of arm
movement, which tends to elicit attacks that are too loud.

THE ICTUS

The ictus is the precise instance at which the rhythmic pulse
is confirmed. It is most often blurred when conducting soft
and legato passages. When a great amount of "warm" expression is needed for a given passage, the director's beat is
likely to lose the precise point of the ictus. Another example of the difficulty in demonstrating the ictus for the ensemble is found in conducting chorales, when it is a relatively
simple matter to beat time in a stodgy fashion. However,
much care and concentration is required to produce a beautiful chorale phrase (one that has intensity of tone and horizontal movement) while establishing and maintaining the synchronization of the voice parts. There must be a smooth--yet pre-
cise--movement from ictus to ictus (beat to beat). The use
of the wrist to indicate the ictus within the smooth character
of sustained notes will establish the needed emphasis for conveying the precise beats to be sung. There are many subtle
uses of this wrist action which can be determined by the admonition, "look like the music." Sir Adrian Boult, the famed
British conductor, always referred to this action as the
"click." The beginning conductor should analyze whether his
or her arm, wrist, and hand are conveying the ictus properly.

The "click" of the wrist is effective in controlling both
the pulse of the main beat and the syncopated beat. Some
arm movement may be used, depending upon the dynamic
level of the music, but the wrist movement should be the
area upon which the conductor concentrates.

THE ATTACK

The attack should follow through in the same mood and tempo
as the preparatory beat, although the size of this gesture
should be a bit larger. The ictus (point of attack) of the
first few beats must be sharply defined, so as to establish
a secure beginning for the song, yet avoid being stodgy. The
problem here again is to be able to keep the definition of the
beat when singing soft, legato passages. The beat must convey the mood and still be clearly perceived by the choristers.

Therefore, tyro conductors should practice all styles and moods of attacks in front of the mirror to observe the contrasting character of movements required. With enough practice, these gestures will become comfortable and automatic so that they are consonant with the nature of the score's musical intent.

There is a significant difference between a vocal and an instrumental attack because singers must deal with consonants and sub-vowels before the actual sound is produced. Therefore, the consonant must be articulated a fraction of a second before the sound is to occur on the ictus. This to be done simultaneously by every singer. The pronunciation of the consonant cannot be directed; it must be anticipated in the rhythm of the forthcoming musical pulse. Some choral directors stress anticipation of the consonant preceding the vowel. This may be confusing or awkward for the choristers. This writer has found through experimentation that if the singers are trained to phonate the vowel exactly on the beat the consonant will fall in line automatically. It is this preciseness of the preparatory beat, setting the correct tempo, which permits the choristers subsconsciously to feel the ictus strongly enough to produce the consonant just that fraction of a second before the actual phonation of the vowel sound.

THE ANACRUSIS

One of the most neglected areas of both choral and instrumental work is the anacrusis, the unstressed beats preceding a strong downbeat. It involves both technique and interpretation in concept. The anacrusis usually occurs on the one or two pick-up notes preceding the down beat of the following measure and is frequently found in three-quarter or three-eight time. The emphasis of the natural accent of the rhythm distorts the important word emphases and gives a stodgy "vertical" effect to the phrase line. A large skip upward tends to emphasize itself rhythmically, as in Figure 36, Handel's "And the Glory of the Lord" (Messiah).

The anacrusis diminishes the effect of the emphases occurring in the wrong places in regard to the text. Therefore, the conductor must de-emphasize the strong accent of the third beat and stress the "down-beat." In effect, the second and third beats are almost inconsequential in the illustration of Figure 36. The motion of the music should suffice to carry the horizontal movement of the music and avoid pedantic singing.

A. *Incorrect*

and all flesh— shall see it to - geth-er

B. *Preferred*

and all flesh— shall see it to - geth-er

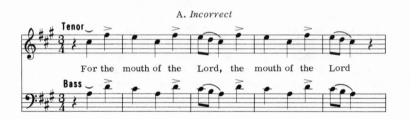

A. *Incorrect*

For the mouth of the Lord, the mouth of the Lord

B. *Preferred*

For the mouth of the Lord, the mouth of the Lord

Fig. 36:   The Anacrusis

If the beats marked > are accented (see examples "A" of incorrect way) the musical pulse becomes extremely stodgy. The down beats on "flesh" and "see" and "geth" (of "together") should receive the emphatic beats rather than the notes marked >. Therefore, the (accented third) beats should not be given strong pulses. In a sense, there is an implication of the waltz feeling--a pulse of one beat to the bar, the second and third beats being very small and only slightly indicated.

The point of this discussion again underscores the need for the director to conduct only the important beats, indicating very subtly the sub-beats, so as to assure the flow of the musical line.

THE RELEASE

Cut-offs often cause problems for tyro conductors. When the ensemble is holding a long note that has no definite pulsation (usually at the end of a composition or a section), the inexperienced conductor is confronted with the problem of indicating a unified release, regardless of the dynamic level. A cut-off devoid of a warning from the hands or arms will likely cause a ragged release. The other problem to be considered is whether the hand goes up or down, or sideways to indicate the termination of sound.

First of all, the facial expression of the conductor, conveying anticipation of the pending release, such as raising the eyebrows, can signal the preparation for the end.

Secondly, the upward movement of one or both arms can indicate simultaneously with the facial expression the rhythm or signal of the release.

Following are some suggestions as to kinds of basic releases which should become natural in feeling to the conductor.

1. In dramatic forte or fortissimo releases, the arm movements can effectively stop the singing by
    a) a "guillotine" perpendicular drop with sharp ictus using one or both arms;
    b) a sideways "slash" of the arm or both arms, again with a sudden stop (a weaker gesture than the perpendicular cut-off);

  c) a diagonal "slash" with the right arm (also not
  as strong as the perpendicular motion).

2. In softer, mezzo-piano, piano or pianissimo releases, the same basic movements can be made,
  except that they inscribe a more delicate and
  shorter movement.

  The upward release is a very weak gesture, and
should be used with caution, since it conveys a signal similar to the preparatory beat.

  The left hand can be used effectively for quick releases for one or more voices if the momentum of the music
carries on in the other parts. The left hand can indicate a
release, while the right hand and the conductor's attention is
given to the on-going forces. These motions require discipline and should be practiced faithfully to "school" the left
hand to work independently of the right hand. The left hand
should rarely beat time in the same fashion as the right hand.
Occasionally, the left hand can assume the same pattern as
the right hand, but this should be done only to reinforce the
beat in certain instances. Otherwise, both hands and arms
inscribing the same patterns for most or all of a composition
becomes redundant and boring, and also robs the left hand
and arm of their expressive potential.

  Again, it should be stressed that the inexperienced
conductor should practice cut-offs in front of a mirror, carefully scrutinizing all movements to be certain that they are
effective gestures.

CONVEYING MUSICAL IDEAS AND MEANINGS

So far, this chapter has dealt with concepts of technical considerations. These techniques are the natural bridge to the
discussion of interpretative concerns, discussed in Chapter 9.

What Happens Between the Beats

  After the conductor completes a successful gesture
for the ictus of a beat, the concern is to get to the next ictus. Yet, the intensity and expression of the arms and hands
between the beats is frequently overlooked, particularly in

sustained passages.   This psychological and physical phenomenon is one which significantly affects the continued energy of the choral tone.   Instrumentalists will usually continue sustaining a tone, even if the conductor does little to
maintain the intensity of arm movements between the beats.
However, choristers, almost invariably, will permit their
tones to become weak and/or unsustained, unless the strong
arm of the conductor "supports" their vocal production.   It
is crucial, therefore, that the choral conductor maintain the
energy and intensity of tone produced by the singers during
the movement of the arms from beat to beat, most especially
in legato passages.

   The important point to be made here is that, after
the ictus is established, the conductor's "arm and hand energy" should continue through the transition to each succeeding beat, thus avoiding a diminishing of the tonal intensity in
the voices.   Any abandonment of this intensity will cause the
singers to sing in a weak or a stodgy, metronomic manner.
Achieving true legato singing will be discussed further in
Chapter 8.

NOTE

1.   Charles Blackman, Behind the Baton (New York: Charos
     Enterprises, 1964), p. 205.

REVIEW QUESTIONS FOR CHAPTER 7

(1)   Why is punctuality in beginning rehearsals so important
      to efficiency and good morale of the ensemble?

(2)   Why is it important for the conductor to be aware of the
      physical condition of his/her singers?

(3)   What are some means of relaxing singers before they
      begin to rehearse?

(4)   What effect does atmospheric condition have upon sing-
      ers?

(5)   What are various means of
      a) "warming up" the ensemble?
      b) improving tone quality?
      c) improving musicianship?

(6) Why is mastering legato singing important in choral development?

(7) Cite the important elements of the conductor's body posture and movements and their effects upon the singers.

(8) List the posture points and gestures which the director should maintain for optimum results in conducting a choral group.

(9) What facial expressions are important for the conductor to express?

(10) What are the advantages and disadvantages of using a baton or just hands when conducting choral and/or instrumental groups?

(11) What is the specific (critical) role of the preparatory beat in conducting?

(12) What is the significant difference between a choral and an instrumental attack?

(13) What is the ictus?

(14) Define the anacrusis and cite its importance in interpretation of musical motifs.

(15) Discuss the problems of the release of choral tone and the various kinds of release gestures.

(16) Describe the psychological and physical concerns of what happens between the beats.

- Chapter 8:
  SOME INTERPRETATIVE CONSIDERATIONS
  FOR THE CONDUCTOR

It bears repeating to state that mastering the technical demands of the music is only a "means to the end" for revealing the intrinsic qualities that often seem to lie dormant in
the music. It is rather tempting for conductors to feel that
the correct notes, rhythm, tempo, and dynamics comprise
interpretation. This notion is the safest way to avoid the
problems of keeping the ensemble together throughout the entire composition. The strict metronomic and vertical beat,
with a strong ictus, provides the singers with a sense of
great security. However, the real challenge begins when the
conductor seeks a truly fine legato line in the phrase; or
when a very gradual crescendo or diminuendo is sought; or
when interpreting strophic songs having different word emphases in the several stanzas; or in seeking rubato and tenuto; or with "giving life" to long notes. This chapter is
devoted to a discussion of the achievement of the intrinsic
values to be found in musical composition through the conductor's leadership and total mannerisms. In order to serve
faithfully the needs of each period of music, the choral director's understanding of the various styles should lead to
the development of the effective conducting techniques that
are needed to express the subtle, intrinsic musical values
awaiting re-creation.

VOCAL TEXTURE RELATING TO
HISTORICAL PERIODS

It is of basic importance for the conductor to have a thorough
understanding of music history and the general styles of the
various eras of music, so that the musical performance accurately represents the period in which it was written. This
is not to suggest, however, that the choral director should
not rely upon innate instincts in interpreting the music. For
instance, room acoustics will have a strong influence upon
tempi and dynamics. A "dry" room (lacking in reverberation)

can accommodate faster tempi than a resonant one. It is
easier to attain a satisfactory forte of fortissimo in a resonant room, whereas pianissimo sounds tend to be lost in a
"dry" room. It is important to recognize that soft singing
requires a tremendous amount of intensity of tone in order
for the tone quality to retain its vitality. These and many
other acoustical factors must always be considered by the
director in analyzing the performance of the group.

Renaissance Music (1450-1600)

There is a basic difference in tonal texture among the
various musical eras and a significant difference between each
succeeding historical period of music. As cited in Chapter
1, Renaissance period music contains open harmonies, which
are usually the result of independent vocal lines. Therefore,
the vocal texture must be lyrical (not dramatic) and free to
flow along. Moreover, the feeling of strict bar-line emphases
were not established before the late Renaissance, and thus the
vocal lines, in their relative autonomy, created their own
parameters. Achieving this freedom of movement among the
voice parts, while still maintaining ensemble unity, requires
exceptionally thorough study of the score by the conductor.
Sensitive renditions of this music are difficult to achieve.
For this reason the music of this period is often performed
ineffectively.

There are conductors who prefer tone production of
Renaissance music to be devoid of any vibrato so that the
transparency of the voices will allow the respective vocal
lines to be clearly defined. However, it must be recognized
that this "straight tone" vocal production, as cited in Chapter
4, tends to put a strain on the vocal musculature because the
laryngeal muscles must be held in a rather fixed (tense) position, especially for those persons having vibrato.

Dry-room acoustics will absorb some of the vibrato
among the voices, if the vibrati are not too large and powerful. Clear vowel production will aid greatly in controlling
excessive vibrato among singers whose voices do not blend
well, thus achieving greater unity of sound. Choral ensembles that are entirely comprised of rich, resonant voices will
need to envision a much more lyrical concept of tone than
they would for music of the Romantic period. It is the opinion of this writer from years of experimentation that, when
vocalists with vibrant voices are taught to sing with a lyrical

concept, their voices will blend well in Renaissance music. This eliminates the need for insisting upon a sterile tone to achieve blend and the proper light vocal texture.

Baroque Music (1600-1750)

The early Baroque music, in a sense, has one foot still in the Renaissance and the other in the avant-garde of the "new" era. Such early Baroque composers as William Byrd (England), Giovanni Gabrieli (Italy), Orlando Gibbons (England), Claudio Monteverdi (Italy), Heinrich Schütz (Germany), Jean-Baptiste Lully (France), and Henry Purcell (England) were among the dominant ones whose compositions still retained strong Renaissance influences. Yet, these composers struck out for themselves to build a new era of musical expression. In view of this, the conductor who performs the works of this early Baroque era must keep in mind the characteristics of both the Renaissance and middle Baroque periods. Therefore, the reserved Renaissance texture of the music must be amalgamated with a new and expanding freedom of harmonic structure, voice leadings, and vocal virtuosity. This period witnessed the emergence of the soloist in contrast to the choral forces. The cantata began to emerge as a means of expressing religious (theological) doctrine. It required such entities as an evangelist (tenor) who usually expounded the scriptures to unify the choruses, solos, and duets which were based upon the cantata libretti. Therefore, any conductor who assumes the assignment of performing these early Baroque works must carefully study the relationships among the vocal forces along with the inclusion of more instrumental work to fulfill the composers' ideas. A study of the composers' biographies and the historical practices of that period are certainly basic requisites to understanding how to interpret their works.

The Middle Baroque era of the entire seventeenth century is again one which straddled early practices with innovative ideas. Most of the outstanding composers of this middle period continued to develop their skills into the Late Baroque style, which fulfilled the ornate conceptions of highly complex music. Today, no one disputes the superior craftsmanship of Johann Sebastian Bach (1685-1750). Few composers of this era were able to conceive of counterpoint in such a dazzling--and yet deeply religious--manner as did Bach. Because of this complexity, the performing forces in Bach's time were frequently unable to cope with his musical genius.

Only he, at the organ, could seem to do real justice to his music. Other great names of choral composers of this period include Georg Phillip Telemann (Germany), Antonio Vivaldi (Italy), Dominico Scarlatti (Italy) and George Frideric Handel (Germany-England).

Each of these cited composers had his own style within the Baroque influence. For instance, both Handel and Bach require lyrical, flexible tone production, but Handel's compositions are generally less ornate than those of J. S. Bach. Handel openly admitted that he wrote more for public consumption than did Bach, whose total emersion in the church overshadowed any "commercial" inclinations he may have entertained. Bach really did wish to be more universally accepted, but his dedication to orthodox Lutheranism prevented him from composing for the sake of public acclaim. Therefore, the deeply religious orientation of Bach's music should cause every conductor who chooses to prepare and perform one of this great master's cantatas, motets or major works to carefully examine the text as it relates to the music, with all of the implications that embrace the composer's religious convictions and theological concepts. Through this process the director will discover that there are deep, intrinsic meanings which need careful attention--even beyond the sometimes almost insurmountable problems of "negotiating" the notes and embellishments of this incredible man's music.

We are sometimes led to believe that Baroque music is "objective" and devoid of emotion and feeling; that it needs very little expression. "Such a theory flouts both nature and evidence. "[1]

> The precautions necessary to ensure that the performer, in yeilding to his flow of expressive feeling, shall not violate the style, are of immense importance and difficulty. But they are perfectly concrete precautions, largely of a technical variety, and even though the best interpreter cannot guess them, they can be taught, particularly if the teaching is by ear. [2]

Pursuing this concept further, the conductor should develop the ability to listen imaginatively for the basic sound, the texture, and the "flow" of the music beyond the mere mastering of notes and rhythm.

As to mood and tempi, Baroque music indications are

of limited assistance to the conductor. Presto or adagio of
that era does not indicate our modern concepts of these
tempi. In all cases, the musical intent must be sought carefully to determine the most effective tempo of the selection.
Again, we are reminded that room acoustics affect tempo and
texture of sound.

In regard to rhythm, Baroque notation is deliberately
imprecise. In some contexts, notes written with even values
should be performed unevenly; in others, uneven values must
be performed evenly. (Understanding these practices goes
far beyond the parameters of this book, being almost a complete study in itself.) In the majority of instances, however,
notes written as dotted figures may be double, triple or quad-
ruple dotted for desired effect; this according to the desired
interpretation of the music. [3]

The correct accentuation, although dependent upon bar
lines, is to be found in the natural peaks and stresses of the
harmonies and phrases as they reach their apex. Mechanical
accents of the bar lines should give way to the natural accents of the texts and musical flow (horizontal drive of the
musical line).

Concerning dynamics, there are scholars who maintain that mezzo-fortes did not exist in Baroque music. Though
it is true that complete sections or phrases of this music are
indicated to be either forte or piano, the interpreter must use
good judgement in balancing the parts so that the important
contrapuntal lines can be distinguished. The word of caution
seems to be that utmost extremes of loud and soft must be
avoided generally; one should seek a fair balance first by using moderate fortes and piano dynamics, which are usually
"terraced" in the writing.

Another issue to which the choral director must pay
attention is that of the crescendo and diminuendo in Baroque
music. Again, the caution of moderation is in order. The
development of the harmonies and the "terracing" of the voices usually builds a crescendo without consciously working
to achieve it. Likewise, this applies to the diminuendo.
Therefore, be skeptical of editors' markings of long crescendos and diminuendos, lest the effect be overdone.

Ritards should be very carefully considered in the context of the musical intent. While the music should never "run
off the end of the page," neither should a ritardando become

a huge, massive allargando, such as is found in music of
the Romantic period. It is also the custom for Baroque music to avoid long fermatas. This mark for chorales indicates
only that the last note of a phrase should not be chopped off
prematurely. It is also believed that the fermata indicated
that the slight hold gave the congregation a chance to catch
up with the organist during the singing of chorales in the
Lutheran service. The tyro conductor should practice indicating controlled, and often quick, releases, with the next
attack being precise so as to signal the re-entry of the singers.

        In regard to tone quality, the bombastic, huge choral
tone of the Romantic period is completely out of place since
the Baroque vocal texture must have transparency. The texture will differ noticeably from the Renaissance music. This,
of course, is the result of different harmonic qualities between these two eras. There is very little place for pesante
singing in Baroque music, although the term is used in some
orchestral compositions of that period.

        The often highly ornamented style of Baroque music
demands that its dynamics be light enough to "negotiate" the
notes with great flexibility and clarity, in order to maintain
the transparency of the complex vocal lines. Then, the resulting harmonies will also be more clearly defined. Achieving these results will require years of study, discipline, and
experimentation for the conductor.

The Classical Period (1750-1830)

        The music of this era was dominated by such compos-
ers as Franz Joseph Haydn, Wolfgang A. Mozart (Austria),
Carl Philipp Emanuel Bach (Germany), Giovanni Pergolesi
(Italy), and Christoph Gluck (Germany-Italy). Not to be neglected is Johann Christian Bach, called the London Bach because he settled there. His musical style was similar to
that of Mozart. This period was known as "the Enlightenment" of humanity. People revolted against supernatural religion and the Church. [4] It was also a cosmopolitan age when
national differences began to disappear in favor of the common humanity of all. It was a time when rulers began to
assume the responsibility for social reform and they also became patrons of the arts, many of them achieving the status
of accomplished musicians. This era witnessed the rise of
a growing middle class abounding in increased learning.

C. P. E. Bach, second son of Sebastian, has been termed
the founder of the Classical style of music. Lutheran church
music declined in influence during this period, giving way to
more concerted oratorios which were not well-suited to church
services. Operatic style repertoire began to emerge as a
dominant form of musical expression.

This music revolted, in a sense, against the ornate
characteristics of the Baroque. Yet, one can still note the
influence of the earlier period on this later one, when counterpoint was employed in the Classical period compositions.
Therefore, we observe that the logic of the Baroque independent voice writing greatly influenced the technique of these
Classical era composers. As we conductors approach and
study the Classic era compositions, we should keep vividly
in mind the need for very precise, "clean" vocal production
so as to do justice to these compositions. Any histrionic
vocal production, such as that expressed in the excessive
Romantic style, is strictly out of place in this delicate, "lace-
cuff" music. To be certain, there are Romantic period elements in the music of the Classical era. Yet, the delicate
elegance of the last half of the eighteenth-century and the
early nineteenth-century society requires careful reflection
by the conductor so that the music performed from this period will reveal the proper texture and meaning.

The musical texture of the Classical period is more
linear than the Baroque. The florid writing of the earlier
period succumbed to more simplified melodies. The use of
the continuo still remained in church music, but the parts of
the middle range (the harmony) generally were transcribed
for the keyboard. Thus, figured bass fell into disuse. Although orchestras still remained relatively small, the choral
forces became noticeably larger during the Classical era.
However, small choirs remained the norm in churches because of spatial limitations. More care was also given to
provide exact notation for all performers, although full scores
for the singers came later. It was not until the latter part
of the nineteenth century that full scores were provided for
singers. Previously, each vocal part had its one line printed
and during rests, small cue notes were indicated to assist
the singer in entering again.

In interpreting the music of this period, we find that
tempi generally seemed to increase over that of the Baroque.
However, this might only be the effect that the simpler musical style has upon the performer and listener. Where once

eighth, sixteenth, and thirty-second notes abounded in Baroque music, the quarter note now became the standard measurement for melodies. Also, there was a noticeable growth toward more use of the rubato, even though the practice was known to have existed previously. The main characteristic of the Classical rubato is that when the melody slowed down slightly, the accompaniment kept a steady tempo. Achieving this end with choral groups requires extensive training and skill for both conductor and singers, but is a very effective interpretative element in musical expression.

In approaching the study of scores of the Classical period, one should carefully study its basic structure, noting that the more simplified lines accommodate themselves to lovely, delicate phrasing. The counterpoint of this period is usually less complex than the Baroque, and thus, more easily mastered. Moreover, as in the Baroque period, exaggerated, heavy singing is completely out of context. One can conclude that this music should always be approached with the "lace-cuff" delicacy mentioned earlier.

The Romantic Period (1820-1900)

Ludwig van Beethoven (Germany-Austria) was the most significant example of a composer to evolve from Classicist to Romanticist. He inherited the musical forms of Haydn and Mozart, but he developed them into highly articulated expression of the Romantic era style. A study of his symphonies reveals that he was a strict classicist during his early years, gradually developing into an ultra-Romanticist as exemplified by the famous Ninth (Choral) Symphony. Although Beethoven wrote many choral and vocal works, it is the opinion of this writer that he lacked an understanding of the limitations or the capabilities of the human voice. Nevertheless, his influence upon the choral field has been noteworthy.

Other renowned choral composers typified by this era were Franz Schubert (Austria), Hector Berlioz (France), Felix Mendelssohn (Germany), Giuseppe Verdi (Italy), Anton Bruckner (Austria), and Johannes Brahms (Germany). A study of the compositions written by these men reveals both their association with and their respect for the Classical and Baroque heritage in musical composition. Yet, they forged ahead to build a new era of musical spirit, which reaches back into the past and forward into the future with no immediate bounds. Grout tells us,

... Romanticism cherishes freedom, movement, passion and endless pursuit of the unattainable. [5]

It is during this expansive era that the "grass roots" of vocal expression began to emerge with the German "Sing-kreis" and the "Glee" in England. As these forces grew, Romantic era composers began to write for the "common man" and, thus, many of the more popular choral pieces were written. Folk songs were also arranged and these homophonic, strophic songs became the staple of the modern choral movement.

In-depth study of this music provides the choral director with a much easier task of preparing it for performance than the Baroque, since its simpler melodic lines suit the level of many community and beginning choruses. The rich harmonies avoid many of the intonation problems found in the music of earlier periods. However, it is not intended to imply here that all Romantic period music is simple and homophonic. On the contrary, the era encompasses some of the most complex writing to be explored by any excellent choral group. Operatic repertoire dominated the scene and large works were written for huge choruses of singers and instrumentalists. The nineteenth-century composer became obsessed with tonal volume. The German operatic composer Richard Wagner stated in 1869, "Tone sustained with equal power is the basis for all expression." [6]

What is to be established here is that this period opened up a vast expansion of choral expression, which, more than 100 years later, is still dominant. The great masses, oratorios, cantatas, operas, folk songs and lieder have given us an almost inexhaustible heritage of beautiful melodies and rich harmonies. These characteristics exploit the potentials found in the human vocal apparatus. In many instances, the music carries itself with little or no assistance from the conductor. Yet, it behooves choral directors to be careful not to allow their performances of this music to become sentimental, rather than romantic, in character. The freedom of expression given to this music must still retain a certain discipline of form and style promulgated by the earlier periods of music from which it sprang. While extremes of tonal color and dynamics are sought, they should always be within the bounds of good taste.

The Twentieth Century

Our early "modern era" has proven to be no different
from previous periods in reverting to earlier musical styles.
In fact, even this late in the twentieth century, a significant
amount of our choral music coming off the presses is predominantly Romantic and Neo-classic in character. The reason for this may be that the vocal mechanism lends itself to
this style of music more readily than any other period. The
fact that singers have no valves to push, or keyboard to finger,
surely causes them to feel more secure with warm, rich harmonies which are based upon a tonal center. Few singers
today can cope with serial compositions, which contain "awkward" intervals, and thus are extremely difficult for the mind
to "hear." The instrumentalist can basically manipulate an
instrument to "negotiate" odd intervals, but the singer must
have an accurate aural image of the interval before establishing the pitch. There is no fingering of the vocal instrument.

Thus, the music of such American neo-classicists as
Charles Griffes, Douglas Moore, Randall Thompson, Howard
Hanson, Aaron Copland, and Samuel Barber have bridged the
gap from Romanticism (and Impressionism) to the more avant-
garde music of such men as Paul Hindemith and Ernst Krenek (Germany-America), Arnold Schoenberg and Anton Webern
(Germany), and Krzysztof Penderecki (Poland).

Our truly contemporary music is usually too difficult
for choral groups other than professional and advanced college-
university choral ensembles to perform. Church choirs that
are capable of performing complex contemporary music are
few and far between. It requires courage and perseverance
to attempt the truly contemporary music of the twentieth century. The public, at large, is still unwilling to accept this
"dissonant," "unmelodic" style of music. Aleatory (chance)
music strives to be free of overemphasizing control in music, such as serial (twelve-tone) technique imposes upon composers. Music composed to be sung with a prerecorded tape
is another twentieth-century innovation. Usually choristers
are intrigued by the challenge to syncronize their performance with that of the tape, unless the composition is so complex that it demoralizes them.

Music of the avant-garde has created, out of necessity for expressing and directing its "off-beat" ideas, a vast
set of new symbols. In the frontispiece of the composition,
the composer often charts the symbols used and states their
meanings for the performers.

Readers of this book may find that they have a long way to go toward understanding the language and embracing the performance of twentieth-century avant-garde music. First of all, one must have a great deal of time to pursue this difficult musical expression. Secondly, the ensemble preparing this music must consist of above average to excellent sight-singers to cope with the notation, although, with enough time, an average group can learn much of the material by rote.

Perhaps the next decade will witness more progress in the acceptance of avant-garde musical expression. It behooves those of us in the music profession to keep an open mind to try to understand and then master these new techniques, so that the progression of musical development will continue on course.

Having discussed some historical views and customs of music, we shall next consider some specific ideas concerning interpretation. The items to be discussed below all rely upon the ability of the conductor to vividly (but with good taste) dramatize the intent of the music. The hands, arms, body, and face must all act in consonance to convey mood, expression (such as dynamic level), tempi, meter, and rhythm. It calls for a psychology of the "strong arm" of confidence upon which the choristers rely. The "grass roots" singer, especially, needs the security of articulate strength in the conductor--both physically and psychologically.

LEGATO

This writer has observed that attaining a true sense of legato is one of the most neglected areas of choral (and also solo) singing. It often seems that the phrase line is either too stodgy or too sloppy. The singers want to know where the ictus of the beat is, despite the desire for a smooth phrase line. Therefore, the responsibility for achieving a controlled legato line begins with the conductor.

A vivid way to "act-out" the sense of legato for singers is to imagine that the director's arms and hands are under water--as in treading water while swimming. The resistance of the water provides a smooth flow of the arm and hand movements, yet the ictus (beat) can be properly indicated without difficulty with the wrist and hands or baton. The traditional conducting patterns should be practiced in this manner until the feeling of treading water becomes a natural set of movements. In a sense, this action is isometric, because some muscles must work against others to provide the slow resistance movement of arms and hands. It is important also to keep in mind that the size of the beat should indicate proper dynamics for the legato because the arms and hands will function differently for larger (louder) legato dynamics than for the smaller (softer) dynamic passages.

The legato tone must remain alive and vital from note to note with no "holes" between the notes (words). Therefore, especially careful attention to diction is necessary to achieve the true legato. The hard consonants must be softened so as not to interfere with the smooth flow of the music. The "sub-vowels" (m, n, ng, etc.; see Chapter 4, Vowel Spectrum), more commonly known as liquid consonants, should be exploited in order to sustain the tones throughout each legato phrase.

One of the most neglected aspects of legato singing is maintaining the core of the vowel sound through the entire length of the note and into the consonant or "sub-vowel." This transition from vowel to consonant to vowel must be carefully and smoothly articulated. Otherwise, the intensity and flow of sound will be interrupted.

Another important factor in achieving true legato phrasing is the "support" of the breath. Proper breath management is crucial in keeping the tone from dying away. (See section on breath management in Chapter 4.)

Long notes must not become static or fade away. The legato line depends upon the tone remaining vital, especially when singing softly. These sustained tones should always maintain a sense of horizontal movement, even during a decrescendo. Therefore, it is important that the conductor's arms, hands--the entire body, for that matter--convey the entensity needed throughout the entire phrase.

It is very important to emphasize here that what happens between the beats is equally as important as what happens on the beats.

STACCATO

The main concern for the conductor in attaining a satisfactory

staccato feeling is that of synchronization.   If the director's
beats are small and precisely in the correct rhythm, the
singers will have strong visual direction for singing short
notes.   However, in addition to an articulate staccato beat,
the conductor must be aware of other factors which may interfere with the choristers' ability to produce the tone and
then release it in the proper rhythm.   These are important
considerations:

1.   Consonants must be pronounced so quickly that
     phonation of the voice takes place precisely on
     the beat or sub-beat.   This requires concentra-
     tion with quick movements of the tongue and lips.

2.   Proper breath management is needed to maintain
     the vitality of tone and proper intonation.   Poor
     intonation is one of the major problems emerging
     from staccato singing.   Therefore, the conductor
     should caution the singers to support the short
     tones by concentrating upon clear vowel produc-
     tion and proper breath management (see Chapter
     4).

Usually, staccato passages are not loud, so the director's motions can be small and kept in front of the body.
However, when staccato singing requires a fuller tone, the
arm movements must become larger--yet never so large as
to disturb the rhythmic pulse of the music.   It is imperative
that singers be required to look over the tops of their music, if scores are used, so as to give full attention to the
leader.   This is of vital importance to the achievement of
synchronized staccato singing.   Choristers who memorize
their music should have less trouble in keeping together, because their full attention can be focused on the conductor.

MARCATO

In a sense the style of the marcato beat is an amalgamation
of the legato and staccato movements.   Usually, the marcato
calls for louder singing than either legato or staccato.   The
marcato mood requires the ictus to be very strong, and the
notes of longer duration.   Therefore, the intensity (not tension) of the arm and hand should remain statically strong
throughout the length of the note after the ictus is articulated.
Then, the movement to the next beat should be lightning fast,
repeating the gesture successively from beat to beat.

Probably more arm or body movement is acceptable for marcato, although one should be careful to avoid grotesque motions.

CRESCENDO AND DIMINUENDO

Untrained singers--and even some trained choristers--have
difficulty in executing poco à poco crescendos and diminuendos. They know that they should increase or decrease the
volume of a given passage, but often they will suddenly become too loud or too soft. The crescendo and diminuendo
are difficult for most singers to accomplish gradually. Consequently, much time and discipline is required to achieve
this objective. The extremely gradual crescendo and diminuendo is most frequently found in homophonic music, where
it is most effective. (Contrapuntal music accomplishes its
gradual crescendos and diminuendos by adding or subtracting
voice parts.) One method of accomplishing this objective is
to require the singers to mark each measure or appropriate
measures:

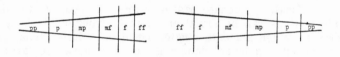

Fig. 37: Crescendo and Diminuendo

        This method assumes that the choristers are very fa-
miliar with the dynamic levels suited to the size and maturity of their ensemble sound. The main word of caution here
is that, upon reaching the climax of volume, the voices are
not forced. In order to achieve a very gradual crescendo
and diminuendo, the singers will be obliged to curb their im-
pulse to increase or decrease their dynamic levels too quickly,
thereby building up certain vocal tensions. There is a kind
of inhibited feeling for them as they attempt to avoid moving
too rapidly through the successive dynamic levels. The prolonged crescendo can produce a forced tone quality when the
singers finally reach the apex of the crescendo. On the way
to the decrescendo, the choristers are prone to forget about
vowel and breath support. Therefore, in working with this
problem, the conductor should continually remind the singers

that they should maintain good vocal production, as well as good posture.

PHRASING

There is no excuse for poor phrasing. Careful analysis of text and music provides ample cues for breathing and carrying over of one phrase into another where it is effective to do so.

Strophic Songs

Songs which have several stanzas are particularly prone to bad phrasing. When studying the meaning of the words of a strophic song, one should realize that the text usually takes precedence over the music. In the singing of hymns, almost invariably people will breathe at the end of a musical phrase, even if a word has to be split to do so. Actually, hymns are religious poetry, so punctuation (including breaths) should be observed at the same places one would breathe if the text were being spoken, rather than sung. In deciding upon the carry-over of certain phrases, one must be very careful to observe the places to breathe, which are usually marked by commas in the text. Occasionally, awkward rhythms will be encountered and then the "snatch" breath technique will have to be applied. This method of choral breathing requires the singers to take quick breaths (preferably between words) each at different places so that there is a continuing phrase line without noticeable breaks. The choristers must learn to relate closely to each other to sense when they can catch a quick breath. Incidentally, this exercise in concentration tends to improve the feeling of communication among the singers in their sections or quartets.

Contrapuntal Music

Independent vocal lines require a great amount of attention as to breathing and phrasing. If the music is well-adapted to the text, the punctuation usually dictates the proper breathing places. However, translations often present problems because the text may not always correspond with the music. This condition introduces some of the same problems as those encountered in strophic songs, so the choristers' scores should be marked carefully for proper phrasing.

Much rehearsal time can be saved if this is done during section rehearsals under the guidance of the leader, who has gone over the markings with the director. Advance planning for these contingencies will contribute significantly to the efficiency of the rehearsal.

It is essential, although often difficult, to bring to the awareness of singers that specific breathing places in the music are significant elements in interpreting phrases properly, even when a breath is seemingly not needed for the singing process. The conductor must be ever mindful that the music provides another dimension for expressing the meaning of the text. Therefore, the director's overall conducting technique must be so clear and secure that the choristers will respond sensitively to the nuances of the phrasing.

RUBATO AND TENUTO

The rubato, or rhythmic flexibility within a phrase or a measure (literally meaning robbed time), must be dealt with thoughtfully. It must be subtle--never interfering with the flow of the phrase line. Yet, it must arrest the attention of the listeners that a special emphasis is being made. Previously, Mozart's comment was cited that (in piano music) the right hand should slow down slightly, but that the left hand should maintain the original tempo. The accompanying voices in choral singing can accomplish this, although it is most difficult to do.

When the rubato occurs in accompanied choral works, the piano, organ or instruments should maintain the basic tempo ("bending" only slightly to the voices), while the chorus deviates from it. This condition requires that the conductor be able to indicate the accompanying tempo with the left hand and arm while the right hand designates the rubato for the singers. Advanced conducting skill is required for the conductor to develop clear signals for both instrumentalists and singers.

In unaccompanied singing the sense of the rubato usually occurs in all voices, particularly in homophonic music. The use of the rubato in chorales is especially effective when done with good taste.

The rubato in vocal music is shaped and governed by word emphases. A note or group of notes may be given a sense of rubato by special attention to a word or a group of words in a phrase. Thereby, the note is stressed by the manner in which the word is pronounced. If the music and text are compatible, there will be common areas of emphasis. The music should allow "sitting" on certain notes (words) within the natural accent of the word rhythms. The director should try to discover in the text the subtle and special points of stress which set a particular phrase apart from the others. Care should be taken to keep all rubato emphases in good taste, never permitting this form of interpretation to destroy the "sense of progression" which every musical work should have.

The term "tenuto" is often misunderstood. In musical terms, it means literally to give the full value to the note. Frequently, it occurs on the last note of a phrase, and no problem is encountered. Where no breath is required following a tenuto, there is little problem in dealing with it. However, if one takes a breath, the note will be robbed of its full value. In singing chorales, one very frequently encounters this problem where the fermata actually indicates only that a tenuto is to be observed. In these instances, the flow of the music is in danger of being broken. (This will be discussed below under FERMATA.)

The conductor's main concern in handling the tenuto is to indicate the release with the left hand, while the right hand continues to maintain the established meter, simultaneously indicating the breath (upbeat) for the next attack. These movements must be made absolutely clear to the choristers. Otherwise, ragged releases and attacks will occur.

One other point to underscore in the use of the tenuto is that during its observance the conductor's beat (arm) must remain firm, so that the intensity (support) of the tone does not diminish--even during a decrescendo. The singers, very likely, will allow the tone to lose vitality if the intensity of arm and hand movements is not maintained by the director.

THE FERMATA

The fermata has been used for four centuries, according to Elson's Music Dictionary. [7]

Its length varies with the character of the music. When found over a long note, it is not necessary

to double the value of that note, but when found
over a sixteenth it may more than double in value.
Its length can be varied by the words lunga (long),
piccola (little), G. P. (grosse [grand] pause), and
other signs.   Over a double bar it usually signifies
the end of the composition. [8]

The key sentence in this description is that the "length
[of the fermata] varies with the character of the music." In
the Baroque and Classical eras, the fermata was used with
great discretion.   With the excesses of the Romantic period,
the use of the fermata was extended in duration, thus developing huge climaxes in the music.

For contemporary use, the fermata has two definite
characteristics: the moving and the stopped.   The moving
gesture is indicated by the hand(s) and arm(s) to keep the
feeling of the music going, whereas the stopped gesture signals ritards or stops the rhythm.   However, in the use of
the stopped gesture, the arm(s) and hand(s) should indicate
whether there is to be a crescendo or decrescendo, or at
least a maintenance of the volume established.

The fermata at the ends of chorale phrases is often
misconstrued as a hold of one or more extra beats.   This
is incorrect.   In Baroque times, the fermata really meant
to punctuate the end of a phrase or composition (or movement of an extended work).   In the chorale of this period,
the fermata was used more as a tenuto than as a hold.   Some
interpreters of the chorale give the fermata note its full value
and add a rest for the breath.   Technically, this adds an extra beat to the measure.   However, the extra beat may also
be construed as a pause in the rhythm of the music.   Other
conductors attempt to give almost the full time value to the
note, then quickly indicate a breath for the next attack; this,
in an effort to keep the flow of the chorale phrase going
without interruption.

The example in Figure 38 illustrates the discussion
concerning the use of the fermata in singing a chorale.

The release on "wander" (bar 2) needs no special cut-
off because the word has no final consonant.   The fourth beat
of the bar "flows" smoothly by indicating the breath on the
up-beat after the ictus.   On the repeat phrase, the word
"ponder," and "excelling" very likely should be carried over
without a breath for textual reasons.

Chorale from <u>The Passion According to</u>
<u>St. Matthew</u>   J. S. Bach

Fig. 38: Chorale Illustration of Fermata

The half-note fermati on "again," "pain," "confess"
and "righteousness" should be released on the fourth beat,
but with a slight "stretching" of that motion, in effect, giving only a quarter note value to the half note.

The last note of the chorale (on the word "dwelling")
should have a slightly elongated fourth beat, and then the release. It should not be held for any appreciable length of
time over its quarter beat. Also, any ritardando of the last
phrase should be minimal and the tempo should be about
MM 69-72.

In the use of the fermata for Romantic and Contemporary music literature, the custom is to lengthen the time
value of the note. It usually implies the termination of the
musical pulse. Thus, it is a fully stopped gesture. In conveying the correct usage of this type of fermata, there should
be no definite indication of a beat. For instance, there may
be subtle indication of each beat of a long-held whole note in
4/4 time until after the fourth beat; then the rhythm is stopped with a steady, slow movement until the release. This
writer has found that some movement of the arm(s) and hand(s)
is necessary to maintain the volume of a loud passage or to
indicate more crescendo. The conductor should never beat
full sized beats through the long-held fermata. This action
will violate the arrested feeling which the stopped fermata is
supposed to indicate.

HORIZONTAL MOVEMENT OF THE MUSIC

There is no factor more important in the performance of music than attaining and maintaining the horizontal (on-going)
feeling of the musical phrase. Even staccato and marcato
passages should cause the performers and listeners to feel
the sense of horizontal movement of the music. In view of
this point, the reader should reflect upon the topics discussed
previously in this chapter concerning legato, staccato, marcato, crescendo, diminuendo, phrasing, rubato, tenuto and
fermata. Proper use of these concepts will assist greatly
in achieving the objective for musical renditions to "go somewhere" and "say something significant."

It seems that stodgy pedantic performances of music
abound everywhere in the choral world. The technical obstacles may be very well mastered, but the intrinsic subtleties of the music are frequently overlooked. That is why
special emphasis is made here regarding the great need for
sensitivity to the "horizontal drive" lying inherent in all mu-
sic--regardless of its style and mood. Achieving the proper
"flow" of the music requires this blending of sensitivity and
solid technique. This is the juncture at which one can sep-

arate a technically good performance from the artistic one.
This writer would rather hear a performance with a few technical blemishes in which the intrinsic values of the music are
expressed, than one which is technically perfect, yet ignores
subtle nuances. No words can describe exactly what should
be done, since each piece of music requires interpretation
to bring forth the special emphases lying inherent in the abstract language of the score. Vocalists have the special advantage of words which are wedded to musical notation, providing additional clues to interpretation of the music. We
should exploit this opportunity through our careful study of the
subtle meanings and emphases that the text provides in its
influence upon the musical notation.

Finally, concerning horizontal movement, it is most
important to conduct only the important musical pulses (beats).
The late Dimitri Mitropolous, brilliant former conductor of
the New York Philharmonic Orchestra, once told a group of
aspiring young conductors to indicate only the largest pulsations in any given phrase in order to avoid pedantic emphases
which are subordinate to the "on-going" movement of the music. This is not an easy assignment for any conductor.
There is a much more secure feeling for performers to have
every minor--as well as major--beat indicated for the group,
so that they can "stay together." However, this "meter-beat
conducting" restricts the "flow" of the music.

BLEND AND BALANCE

Previously, we have made references to blend and balance
as they are attained through good vocal habits and various
seating arrangements. As a matter of fact, achieving optimum blend and balance of parts includes a great many factors beyond good vocal production.

> Blend refers to the uniformity of tone within and
> between voice sections; balance refers to the equal-
> ization of the quantity of tone within the voice sec-
> tions. [9]

Blending of the voices in a choral ensemble is significantly affected by the conductor's physical mannerisms. The
"strong arm" of support mentioned previously in this chapter
is vital to the psychological welfare of the singers. Weak
and flabby arm movements discourage timid singers from
singing confidently, and then the more aggressive or independent

singers must assert themselves to maintain the tonal and expressive qualities needed. This factor alone can destroy blend and balance of the group because the more aggressive singers' voices will protrude. Therefore, the choral director must develop a firm technique which establishes a solid rapport with the ensemble, thereby controlling all of the voices in it.

In seeking to accomplish these objectives, the use of homophonic music is an excellent vehicle. Slowing down or even holding certain notes, while advising the singers to listen carefully as to how their parts relate to other sections, is helpful in attaining blend and balance of the parts. Specific vocalises may be useful, but the real value is found in the music itself. Thus, if there is little or no homophonic music in the current repertoire, the director would do well to include some in the next planning session (even for sight-reading purposes). Otherwise, the director may need to rely upon extraneous vocalises to meet these objectives.

Humming is another means of creating a climate in which the singers listen to their neighbors as well as the other sections. However, the humming must be carefully assessed by the director to be certain that the tone quality is not strained. Singers often attempt to hum too loudly, subconsciously feeling that they need to produce sounds comparable to those experienced in singing vowels.

Another excellent aid in making the choristers aware of blend and balance is the use of the tape recorder. Once the group hears individual voices "sticking out" or one section being too dominant, the director has won a significant battle. It is frequently difficult for singers to hear the entire sound from their individual locations, especially in a large choral group. Thus, the use of a tape recorder is an invaluable rehearsal aid.

Good intonation should not be neglected while seeking satisfactory blend and balance. When a particular section flats or sharps, that voice part will be noticed above the others. The choir should be cautioned to listen carefully to the other sections.

An effective means of achieving good listening habits on the part of the choristers is to have various sections face each other. If there are four rows of singers (and ample space) the first two rows should turn around and face the back two rows; or sopranos face altos and tenors face basses. If the group is not too large, form a circle. These formations increase general communication among the singers as well as being a pleasant relief from their regular seating arrangement.

Varying the volume from soft to loud is another good means of achieving good listening habits--and thus improving blend and balance. It is usually easier to attain these objectives when working in the middle range of the singers' voices. The problem is exacerbated when extremes in volume and range are encountered, so these places in the music need to be improved first through effective application of vocal pedagogy. It is ineffective for the director to complain about poor intonation in the extreme ranges if the singers are incapable of singing properly on those levels. They need vocal instruction. It may require special sessions for a particular section having this kind of trouble, but solving the problem for the singers will pay greater dividends later.

Sopranos frequently have the most difficulty in achieving choral blend and balance. Since the correctly produced soprano voice is really the "flute" of the "vocal orchestra," those voices usually have more outstanding vibrati. Also, in non-select choral ensembles there are usually more sopranos than any other voice part. Therefore, choral directors will likely need to concentrate upon that section first to improve blend and balance and to "tone them down."

Altos can offend the listeners' ears when their tone quality is "dry" and "chesty." That kind of flat tone quality certainly can destroy blend and balance. Careful analysis of choral repertoire will reveal that altos are quite largely confined to an octave range from "a" below middle "c" to "a" above middle "c." Thus, they are infrequently required to sing above their high "a" where their passaggio lies. When notes above this level are in the score, altos are prone to carry a chesty tone up two or three notes where their voices will "break." Then they will either make no more sound, or produce a sort of weak falsetto. Almost every director of an amateur choral group will face this problem and, therefore, must seek to remedy it. (See Chapter 4 for vocal pedagogy.)

Tenors are apt to ruin blend and balance when they must sing across the passaggio of their voices (e^1 to g^1). Many of them have never tried to sing correctly in the upper range of their voices because the vocal timbre on those notes

seems so weak and effeminate to them. It is often difficult
to convince tenors to sing falsetto; thus the use of a tape recorder will demonstrate how much better the blend is when
they use this lighter approximation of the vocal folds in the
upper range. It is important to emphasize to all singers that
their upper range singing is more easily heard than the lower;
that when singing in a high tessitura, they need not push their
voices out of focus to be heard.

A strong bass section is the foundation of a choir. In
diatonic music the basses sing the tonic (fundamental) of the
chord more often than any other section. Therefore, strong
blending bass voices can compensate for weaknesses in other
sections, in that the notes in the other voices frequently are
overtones of the basses' fundamental. Basses who sing aggressively often push their voices beyond good tonal focus.
Of course, if the section is very weak as a whole, efficient
remedial section rehearsals may be required in the form of
class voice lessons, using the current repertoire for pedagogical purposes. Like tenors, basses are prone to sing in
their chest voices above their passaggio (c^1 to e^1 flat), especially in loud singing. Here again, as in all cases dealing
with this problem, the tape recorder can be an extremely effective means of making the singers aware of their poor vocal production.

Up to this point the discussion has centered around
internal means of seeking good blend and balance. Another
approach to the problem is external--that of the shifting of
personnel to numerically balance weaker sections. This action should be taken with great caution lest singers be placed
in sections not suitable to their vocal ranges.

Sopranos who are good readers are often asked to sing
alto if the latter section needs reinforcement; similarly, altos
are frequently requested to help reinforce the tenor section.
Unhappily, many alto voices have been ruined singing tenor,
forcing the lower chest tones over a long period of time.
Basses are usually in reasonably good supply, although some
tenors have been known to switch over into the bass section.
The conductor should stress to these persons not to force
their voices singing in another range; when the particular
tessitura goes above or below a comfortable level, they should
return to their own part.

Although this shifting of voices may resolve the blend-
balance dilemma immediately to some degree, the problem

itself remains unsolved. With improved vocal production through vowel purity among the choristers, the alert director may well discover that some voices will emerge as belonging in another section. For instance, many so-called baritones are really "tenors without a top." When these lyric basses learn to sing across the passaggio and utilize their head voices, they are comfortable singing tenor.

Reassigning singers to other sections underscores the need for choral directors to audition all of their singers whenever possible, so as to determine their ranges and vocal timbre. Decisions to change personnel from one section to another should be carefully made, with instruction to those persons not to push their voices beyond a comfortable volume and texture: sopranos should not try to emulate deep altos; altos should not attempt to sound like "chesty" tenors, and tenors should not imitate bravura basses. Harm can be done to the vocal mechanisms by causing the vocal folds to approximate in a position which is too thick for their particular vocal musculature. When singers are required to sing in their lower range, they should be cautioned not to allow too much breath to pass through the vocal folds, even though they may wish to produce more volume. This excessive pressure against the vocal folds only creates a breathy tone. Rather, they should seek more resonance, keeping the larynx low, by the slight yawn, so that the longer loose vocal bands will phonate efficiently in the low range. Resonant sounds produce more volume than do breathy tones. Also, clear, "clean" vowel production will produce better low tones.

There are a few instances in which singers from one section (some or all) can reinforce another section's part. Ideally, this should be done only when the tessitura extends beyond the normal range of the singers for whom the part has been written. However, these choristers should be advised to sing with their native tone quality, not that of the other voice part. In a sense they are adding another dimension to the sections needing reinforcement, i. e., altos singing tenor parts, etc.

A classic example of the use of utilizing one section to aid another is found in Brahms' "How Lovely Is Thy Dwelling Place" (see Figure 39). The second altos can be used to reinforce the tenors throughout the entire ending phrase of the composition. Some, or all second sopranos can be used to aid the altos, who may have difficulty in singing the higher notes of that part; second tenors may aid the basses.

"How Lovely Is Thy Dwelling Place"   Johannes Brahms
(German Requiem)

Fig. 39: Reinforcing Vocal Sections

(However, this action does not preclude the need for pedagogical efforts to help the altos develop their head tones.)

Another example of the use of utilizing one section to
aid another is found in the "pyramiding" of voices in contrapuntal writing. Regardless of the degree of vocal maturity
among the voices, this method works very well to keep the
thematic material outstanding. It avoids a great amount of
verbal effort by the conductor to balance the voices. The
principle is to double the voice parts of each entering section by adding the vocal part above (or below): the tenors
join the basses for their entrance, then "jump up" to their
part with the altos joining them; then the sopranos join the
altos for their entrance until their own part enters. By the
time the soprano section is due to enter, the tessitura is
high enough that the sopranos (though being alone on their
part) carry the thematic material above the others. As each
section "abdicates" the optional part to sing its regular entrance, the subordinate part is then lessened in volume en-
abling the next voice part to more clearly state the thematic
material.

This system of balancing the parts permits strong reinforcement of the thematic material without forcing the voices.
Moreover, it enhances the choristers' cognizance of the musical
sequence of important thematic material wherever it occurs.

RUSHING AND DRAGGING OF TEMPI

"What do I do when the choir rushes or goes too slowly?"
is the question often asked by the tyro conductor. The answer: the director must assert authority. During early periods of rehearsal, some conductors gain attention by stamp-
ing their feet on the podium to establish the correct tempo
(but that is hard on the arches!). Others clap their hands
or strike the music stand with the baton. Still others shout
verbally to speed up or slow down in addition to some of the
above instructions.

In later stages, when the music is more familiar,
conductors should call for the attention of their singers to
look over the tops of their scores to see the beat. This
assumes that the singers have good posture (standing or sitting) and that they are holding their scores in a position
whereby they can easily see the conductors' motions. As
mentioned earlier, previous training during warm-up periods
(Chapter 7) will aid in making the choristers aware of following

MASS IN B-MINOR   J. S. Bach

Fig. 40:   Reinforcing Vocal Sections

MASS IN B-MINOR   J. S. Bach

Fig. 41:   Reinforcing Vocal Sections

the conductor's beat.   It is important to establish early on
that the director is completely in control of the situation.

THE HEMIOLA

One of the most overlooked aspects of interpretation is the
hemiola.   It occurs most often in 3/8 time, usually just before a cadence.   It combines two measures into one, giving
the impression of a 3/4 bar.   Of course, then, the pulse
becomes "one and two and three and," instead of the fast
"1 - 2 - 3," or if the beat is one to a bar, the "and" pulse
is omitted.   Its purpose is to broaden an otherwise fast
tempo, thereby giving special emphasis to the flow of the
music.   In studying their scores, conductors should look for
these opportunities to vary the pulse of the music without interfering with the actual tempo.

        The excerpts from Handel's Messiah and J. S. Bach's
Mass in B-minor in Figures 42 and 43 illustrate how this
broadening effect is applied to enhance the horizontal movement of the musical line.

        In the example of the "Gloria in excelsis" from Bach's
B-Minor Mass, the hemiola serves to establish the quarter
note beat for the change into 4/4 time, thereby allowing for
a very smooth transition to an otherwise awkward change of
tempo.   It also eliminates the "need" for an unnecessary
pause to establish the new quarter note beat.   In effect, the
eighth note value of the 3/8 section remains the same.   That
is, there are eight eighth notes in the bar now instead of only
three.   The major difference is that the emphasis is now on
the quarter note instead of the eighth note.   The hemiola is
a very effective element in interpretation and should be utilized wherever possible in any musical idiom--choral, orchestral or keyboard.

LONG NOTES: THEIR EXPRESSIVE POTENTIAL

Another neglected area of interpretation is that of long (held)
notes.   The tendency is to allow the long note to become
static.   When a section arrives at a place in contrapuntal
music where there is a note held for a whole bar or more,
the choristers may allow it to "die," or at least taper off
into an unsupported tone, while the rest of the voices move
on with faster notes.   Certainly, the long note should not

And the Glory of the Lord (Messiah)   G. F. Handel

Fig. 42: The Hemiola

Gloria in excelsis Deo (<u>Mass in B-Minor</u>)   J. S. Bach

Fig. 43: The Hemiola

override the other moving parts in volume; rather, its purpose is to act as a pivotal point around which the rest of the harmonies move.   Even though the note may decrescendo, it must continue to support the sense of movement--not lose intensity.

Even more noticeable is a long note which occurs in several or all voices simultaneously.   In this more obvious instance, the long note must either expand in volume or diminish.   In any event, it must never become a "dead fish" (static) tone, because intonation will likely suffer from the loss of vitality.   Practicing gradual crescendos and diminuendos, as discussed earlier in this chapter will aid the singers in developing an awareness of anticipating long notes.   These dynamic changes require good tonal support, especially when the volume diminishes.   The main thought to keep in mind is that every long note must "go somewhere."

MELISMAS: MAINTAINING TONAL CONSISTENCY

In Chapter 4 we discussed the problem of losing the vowel sound during the singing of more than one note or a long melisma on one vowel sound.   It seems important to stress again the negative effect that vowel disintegration has upon the interpretation of music.

One of the frustrations of any singer--especially the chorister--is the loss of vocal control (tone) during long musical "runs."   They may begin to sing a few notes strongly, but soon they lose breath control and the fast tones disintegrate into poor vocal production, or the singers drop out. This dilemma is primarily the result of the disintegration of the vowel.

The problem is caused by the choristers' preoccupation with singing all those fast notes for such an extended period of time.   Consequently, the core of the vowel sound is lost. A vowel sound, such as the AH found in "father," will invariably disintegrate into a diffused "uh" sound since all vowels tend to lose their initial identity, and thus tonal focus, during long melismas (see page 93).   In view of this, the singers should write the vowel in each succeeding measure to constantly remind themselves of the proper vowel sound that is to be maintained throughout the length of the melisma. Thereby, the choral balance of voices is more likely to be stable during such fast passages.

SUMMARY

This chapter has stressed important factors that allow musical performance to become something more than the perfunc-
tory, that is, to achieve artistic singing.   The accomplishment of moving beyond the techniques required to merely
"put everything together" should be the objective of every
conductor and choral group.   This objective demands a sincere concern on the part of the conductor to study the score
so thoroughly that the intrinsic values of the music are revealed after technical mastery is realized.   Many of these
subtleties will be revealed while the "mechanics" of the music are being mastered (see Chapter 2).

Finally, historical, theoretical and emotional factors
must be brought together into the context of the whole composition, so that the potential message of the music can be
fulfilled.

NOTES

1.   Eric Blom, ed. , Grove's Dictionary of Music and Mu-
        sicians, 5th edition (New York: St. Martin's Press,
        1955, Vol I), p. 446.
2.   Ibid. , p. 446.
3.   Ibid. , p. 447.
4.   Donald Jay Grout, A History of Western Music, 3rd edi-
        tion (New York: W. W. Norton, 1980), pp. 448-449.
5.   Ibid. , p. 539.
6.   Ray Robinson and Allen Winold, The Choral Experience
        (New York: Harper's College Press, 1976), p. 443.
7.   Louis C. Elson, Elson's Music Dictionary (Philadelphia:
        Oliver Ditson, 1933), p. 108.   (Hardcover edition.)
8.   Ibid. , p. 108.
9.   Harry R. Wilson, Artistic Choral Singing (New York:
        G. Schirmer, 1959), p. 223.

REVIEW QUESTIONS FOR CHAPTER 8

(1)   Why is it so very important to develop a conducting
        style which goes beyond the mere technical demands
        of the music?

(2)   What are some of the important considerations relating
        to interpreting the following periods of music?

   a) Renaissance
   b) Baroque
   c) Classical
   d) Romantic
   e) Contemporary

(3) Discuss the concept of "horizontal movement" of the musical line to achieve a true legato feeling.

(4) What are the major concerns of staccato singing?

(5) Describe marcato singing and its relationship to staccato and legato singing.

(6) Discuss problems of achieving crescendos and diminuendos.

(7) What are the problems encountered in phrasing of strophic songs?

(8) What problems are encountered in phrasing of contrapuntal music?

(9) Discuss the element of rubato in phrasing.

(10) Discuss the two kinds of tenuto found in our musical scores. How does it relate to the fermata?

(11) Discuss the two kinds of fermatas.

(12) Relate the concept of "horizontal movement" of the musical line to all musical phrasing: legato, staccato, and marcato.

(13) What are some means of improving blend and balance in the choral situation?

(14) Discuss problems and solutions to the rushing or dragging of tempi.

(15) Discuss the recognition of and the employment of the hemiola.

(16) What are some interpretative problems relating to long notes and their expressive potential?

(17) What problems are encountered in maintaining tonal consistency on melismas?

● Chapter 9:
   REHEARSAL ROOM CONSIDERATIONS

The condition of the rehearsal room has a significant influence upon the attitude of singers. If rehearsals must be held
in boiler rooms, gymnasiums or other unattractive places,
the director may find low morale among the chcristers. Yet,
difficult situations can be overcome. This writer has known
of some excellent ensemble groups--both instrumental and
vocal--who have been forced by circumstances beyond their
control to rehearse in less than ideal conditions. If the rehearsals are rewarding enough, the ensemble's morale can
overcome many of the disadvantages placed upon it. However, let us consider some rehearsal situations which can
contribute favorably to the morale of an ensemble.

DECOR

Ideally, the rehearsal room should be clean and attractive.
Extraneous materials should be placed out of sight. Chalk
boards should be accessible and clean for each rehearsal.
The piano should be devoid of papers, books, and unnecessary items, and preferably not be a "beaten up" instrument.
The chairs should be of the same style, preferably the kind
that prevents the singers from slumping or "listing" back-
wards. The total setting should "welcome" the entering choristers and present an air of previous planning for the rehearsal. This will subconsciously undergird the feelings of security for the ensemble members by way of good physical organization.

VENTILATION AND TEMPERATURE

The room in which any group assembles should have more
than adequate ventilation. Singers and wind players absorb
a great amount of oxygen. Therefore, exchange of air (sans
drafts) should be a major concern of the director. If the
room becomes more and more "stuffy," the singers will

likely become more and more lethargic. Often, a director
is perplexed by the diminishing returns of the rehearsal, not
realizing that the atmospheric conditions have deteriorated.
When most of the room air is carbon dioxide, the singers'
blood will be starved for oxygen. It is best to take a break
and refresh everyone with time to change the air in the room
when a director realizes that the rehearsal room has reached
this stage.

Another factor to keep in mind is that when many persons are gathered in a room, the temperature will rise noticeably during a one- or two-hour rehearsal. Therefore,
even a slightly subnormal temperature at the beginning of the
rehearsal may avoid discomfort later.

ROOM SET-UP

Not only does the room need to be attractive physically, the
arrangement of chairs, piano, chalk board and recording devices should be in good order. Seating assignments should
be made according to a definite plan, although flexibility in
placement of singers should be open to adjustments as needed.

In assigning seats for the rehearsal, this can be handled
easily by writing the choristers' names on small slips of paper and placing them on the appropriate chairs. This saves
time and any discussion as to "who sits where."

Ideally, the chairs (formation of the group) should be
in a semicircle so that there is adequate audiovisual communication among the singers--especially for those on the ends
of the rows who have more difficulty in hearing the total
sound of the group than do those near the center. In view
of this condition, it is good "therapy" for all singers to reverse rows or change seating periodically.

ROOM ACOUSTICS

One of the most easily overlooked frustrations for the conductor is that of the acoustics of the room in which the rehearsal takes place. Often it is too "dry" or too uncontrollably reverberant (see pages 203-04). Tempi and vocal texture are important considerations in adjusting to room acoustics.

When the ensemble moves to the concert hall or sanctuary, the acoustical changes may radically alter the sound
and the "feel" from that to which the group is accustomed.
Therefore, the conductor must be ever aware of this possibility and advise the group accordingly.

The Excessively Resonant Hall

In this instance, the tempi may need to be slowed
down to accommodate the reverberations of the resonant room.
Care must be taken to articulate the sounds (especially melismas) more cleanly than ever before. The use of "d," "l"
or "t" consonants before each note of a fast passage may be
necessary, although this should be employed with great care
and only under the most extreme conditions of uncontrolled
resonance: dah, dee, day, doh; la, lee, lay, loh; or tah,
tee, tay, toh. Caution: the use of these consonants tends
to make the notes too short and thus produce choppy singing.
The singers must be advised to keep the purity of the vowel
in mind.

The Excessively "Dry" Hall

When this acoustical condition is encountered, the
singers feel they have lost all of their tonal power and thus,
begin to force their voices in the attempt to compensate for
this loss of resonance. In this case the director must caution the singers to be especially concerned with producing vibrant tones via clean, clear vowel production. The purity of
the deeply-set vowel will produce the best results, regardless
of their initial perceptions. Also, tempi in "dry" rooms can
be increased slightly to the advantage of both choristers and
listeners.

Acoustical shells help to concentrate choral sound in
unresonant concert halls.

THE USE OF RECORDING EQUIPMENT

Audio Equipment

The employment of recording equipment to monitor
every rehearsal is so important to the improvement of both
the ensemble and the conductor that it needs a special emphasis

in this book. Many directors opine that they cannot be bothered with extraneous mechanical equipment because valuable
time and effort will be taken from the rehearsal. Yet, with
experience and proper organizational procedures, these mechanical devices will save a significant amount of time in preparing the music. As with any skill, it requires patience
and perseverance to develop the use of audiovisual equipment
effectively.

Ideally, the director should have someone to tape record every rehearsal, so as not to be personally concerned
with the manipulation of the instrument. However, when this
is not possible, the director should try to obtain an uncomplicated machine to fulfill this need. Relatively simple port-
able recording mechanisms of reasonable quality are available
for prices within almost any modest capital institutional budget. Permanent installments would be preferable, but even
a small cassette recorder can reveal a great deal of information for the conductor or choral group.

It is imperative that directors become familiar with
the mechanical operation of recording equipment, so as to
utilize them for study purposes. Modern machines can run
for at least forty-five minutes per side of a cassette or reel
to reel tape. Therefore, the director can pre-set the proper
dynamic level and be relatively free of concern over the recording. The review of this tape after a rehearsal can be a
most rewarding experience for the director. It permits assessment of the efficiency and progress of each rehearsal.
Furthermore, it can reveal the conductor's own strengths
and weaknesses. A tape recording of a rehearsal can dis-
close many things about the conductor's efficacy, such as
inadvertently talking too much, or not giving directions clearly
and concisely, or pausing too long before analyzing problems
occurring during the rehearsal.

For many years, this writer has benefited from recording almost every rehearsal (including the dress rehearsal)
to review what may have transpired unnoticed by him. Suggestions are then notated for section leaders and for himself
in order to prepare for the next rehearsal or the concert.
It is often surprising to note the errors which went undetected
during the rehearsal.

Playing back selected passages of the rehearsal tape
to the ensemble will inform the singers of their shortcomings
more effectively than any verbal descriptions of the errors.

Moreover, the ensemble can then initiate its own response to the error at the time of the replay. This reinforces learning and provides a more positive input on the part of the choristers for correcting their mistakes.

Audiovisual Equipment

Any director will find audiovisual recordings of a rehearsal an invaluable aid in self-evaluation. The visual aspect of watching one's conducting gestures as well as the verbal comments will bring about some startling revelations. Whenever possible, all conductors should take advantage of the availability of a videotape machine to record actions and gestures made in front of an ensemble. One's ingrained habits may have become very comfortable, even when they are ineffective or incorrect.

A television camera and playback mechanism purchase is a very valuable teaching tool for any school or college. It can be used by theater, speech, and many other departments, so as to share the overall cost of the equipment. Many colleges and universities have rather elaborate facilities for audiovisual instructional services. The use of such equipment by conductors (students or teachers) is of enormous pedagogical value.

REVIEW QUESTIONS FOR CHAPTER 9

(1) How do the following physical conditions of the rehearsal room affect the morale and motivation of the singers?
a) decor
b) ventilation and temperature
c) room arrangement
d) acoustics

(2) What values are gleaned from the use of recording equipment used in a rehearsal?

(3) What values accrue from the use of audiovisual equipment to aid and analyze rehearsal efforts?

PART IV:

CONSIDERATIONS RELATING TO CHURCH CHOIRS

● Chapter 10:
CHURCH CHOIR ORIENTATION

There is a great need for part-time as well as full-time
church musicians to understand the nature of worship and the
role that music plays in our efforts to worship God. Lack
of understanding of these two factors, as well as how they
may relate to the individual parish situation, creates many
of the problems found in church music efforts. The following discussion concerns some of the basic elements which
involve worship and music.

WORSHIP AND MUSIC

Of the two general categories of worship, private and corporate, this study concerns itself with the latter aspect of
worship--that which is performed in a social setting.

The first consideration in the discussion of worship is
recognition of the wide variety of modes of corporate worship
and the role that music should ideally play in the particular
liturgy of the church in which it functions. As we well know,
there are significant differences in practice among Protestant
churches in the amount and style of formal liturgy used.
There are contrasts between the ritualistic practices of the
"free" Protestant churches and those of the liturgically oriented churches. Moreover, there are significant liturgical
differences among Lutheran congregations. The orthodox and
conservative Hebrew, Greek Orthodox, Roman Catholic, and
Anglican Church liturgies are so highly structured as to be
foreign to the "free" church practices, which might be labeled
as informal liturgy.

HISTORICAL PERSPECTIVE

To understand more fully the relationship of music to corporate worship, some historical perspective seems to be in
order. If we trace this history from the Liturgical Movement

of the early twentieth century back to the origins of religious rites, we can easily determine that this great span of time produced many variations of communal worship experiences found in the Judeo-Christian religious practices.

Music of the Hebrews

As was noted in Chapter 1, the Jews of the Old Testament utilized a significant amount of liturgy, using instruments as well as voices. "The music of the Temple at Jerusalem was probably very elaborate, being performed by a large choir of Levites and an orchestra composed of varied instruments."[1] No authentic records exist as to the exact nature of the music since the tradition of temple worship ended abruptly with the fall of Jerusalem in A.D. 70.[2] We do know, however, that a scale similar to the present pentatonic scale was used,[3] and from this primitive scale stems much of our Western musical heritage. (If we add the missing fourth and seventh notes to the pentatonic scale, we have, of course, our common diatonic scale.)

Music of the Greeks

The culture of the Greeks and Jews was obviously diverse. As the Jewish nation disintegrated, the Greek nation was on the upgrade and theirs was considered to be an advanced form of civilization. Greek music did not exist as an independent art. It was monodic and incidental to drama and dance, supporting of those art forms. The sequence of sounds was intuitive, rather than logical, again reproducing the pentatonic scale. Eventually, Terpander (in 670 B.C.) and later Pythagoras (582-507 B.C.) opened the doors to a more scientific base upon which to explore musical expression[4] (see Chapter 1).

Early Christian Liturgy

During the latter part of the first century, the apostle Paul and his fellow Christians made their first missionary journeys to Greece, which had been subject to Rome for nearly two centuries. However, even though the Greeks were ruled by Rome, their culture flourished. In fact, the Romans relied upon the Greeks for most of their cultural inspiration and expression. While music was not a dominant factor in

religious expression at that time, eventually people's need to
enlarge their mode of religious feelings and demonstration led
to the forms of chanting cited in Chapter 1. Thus, liturgy
developed through vocalizing these feelings.

It is especially significant to note at this juncture that
the early Christian missionaries faced a problem. If the
liturgy was to be sung in Greek, the music had to accomo-
date that language. Therefore, the early Christian music in
the larger world of Greece, and eventually all of Rome, had
to be based upon the Greek language.

> ... [I]t was the policy of the Jewish missionaries
> to pour the new wine of Christianity into the new
> bottle of Greek civilization, to refrain from forcing
> converts to accept Jewish rites and customs and
> language that might prove stumbling blocks in the
> work of evangelization. In keeping with this policy,
> it was only natural that the Greeks be permitted
> and encouraged to use their own music. [5]

Thus, it was the common people who formed the liturgical responses. There were no Hebrew Levites to act as
cantors, or to train special choirs. Eventually, most leaders of the services were Greeks. If the Jews had used only
their own monody, very likely music would not have entered
the scene of Christian worship. For instance, the phrase
"Kyrie eleison" (Lord, have mercy), one of the basic pillars
of Christian expression, is Greek, not Latin. Thus, we
must not ignore the role of Grecian influence upon our liturgical heritage. Philo, the Jewish philosopher of Alexandria
(30 B.C.-A.D. 45), described the singing of the new Christian
congregations as similar to the chanting of Hebrew sects. It
is probable the choral music of the early Christian church
included the singing of antiphonal and responsorial psalm texts
on a style similar to that practiced in the temple. [6]

That the early Christian Church encountered violent
persecution from the Romans is common knowledge. Nevertheless, musical expression continued until the latter part of
the fourth century. By that time the Christian Church was
emerging predominantly in Western civilization, but still re-
taining strong Roman influence. Although the Romans had
little culture of their own (in the sense of the Greeks), they
attempted to adopt many Greek manifestations of that culture.

But the adoption was far from being an assimilation.

> Whereas the Greeks were inherently aesthetic, the
> Romans acquired culture from without, donning it
> like an ill-fitting garment that had been designed
> for others.   They failed to appreciate the subtleties,
> the shades, the overtones that were so obvious to
> the Greeks. 7

Music in the Early Christian Church

The fact that chanting and singing was popular in the
early Roman Catholic Church is found in the writings of the
church leaders of that time.   Pope Leo I, who lived during
the fifth century, related that the "Psalms of David are pi-
ously sung everywhere in the Church. "8

As songs and chants were adopted by the early Christian service, the liturgical demands were adapted to the local
melodic customs.

> Those who preached Christianity brought with them
> their songs, but new communities of Christians
> praised the Lord in their own fashion.   Thus arose
> the different chants and liturgies of the various
> churches, Syrian, Greek-Alexandrian, Byzantine,
> East and West Syrian, Coptic, Abyssinian, Armen-
> ian and Roman. 9

As a result, we have the great variety of liturgies,
all reflecting the adaptation of Christian expression of thought
to the local language and customs.

The Pagan Influence

As Christianity asserted its "world" dominance in the
fourth century, it was being subjected to the test of pagan
influence, and musical expression was at the forefront of this
challenge.   Even though Christian cult-music had remained
aloof from other ancient musical influences, an eventual compromise was inevitable.   Accordingly, Christians began to
adopt pagan customs and expressions.   Many of our established Western Christmas customs reflect the adaptation of
these pagan ideas: the English holly and the ivy; the laurel
and dove, emblems of peace and the joy of Roman victories;
the mistletoe from Scandinavian lore to ward off evil spirits
(later adapted to refer to the power of Christ); the Druids'

custom of lighting fires during the Yule season to burn out the sins and evils of the past year; the candles adapted to the Christian belief of the Light of the World.

As the early Christian Church spread throughout Asia Minor, Europe, and even into Africa, it naturally adopted the musical and other cultural elements of these areas. Psalms and hymns found their way via Syria to Byzantium and thence to Milan and northward throughout what is now Europe.*

> The canticles of the Byzantine Church, with one exception still remain today in the liturgy of the Roman Catholic Church.[10]

It was Bishop Ambrose of Milan (A.D. 374-397) who first introduced antiphonal psalmody to the West, later to be known as the Ambrosian Chant. Yet it was the role of Pope Gregory to reform the entire liturgy in a codified manner at the end of the sixth century; a somewhat different version of chanting. While the Ambrosian Chant was highly ornamented, the Gregorian Chant tended toward more simplicity.[11]

Emergence of the Gregorian Chant

The fourth and fifth centuries A.D. were confronted with the problem of the precise relationship between liturgy and music in worship. As new forms of verbal expression were being introduced as a result of the expansion of Christianity, new chants and songs emerged. The Oriental (Eastern Orthodox) concept of religion was one of contemplation. In contrast, the new Christian view expressed an exuberant outlook. The conflict had to be resolved. It was Pope Gregory the Great (590-604) who established a rigid liturgical set of modes, which became the backbone of the medieval Christian Church. Improvisation no longer was tolerated. This was a true victory for the Western arm of the Christian Church over the Eastern body of Constantinople (now Istanbul). This treasure of Western civilization is one of the "noblest artistic works ever created in pure melody."[12]

---

*For a comprehensive view of early Christian church music, Donald Grout's monumental A History of Western Music is important reading (see Bibliography).

Schola Cantorum

What was needed now was a reliable system of notation to be certain that all liturgy was perpetuated accurately
for future generations.   The system of indicating intervals
was finally brought to final fruition in about the eighth century with the permanent establishment of the Schola Cantorum
(school of singing).   These singers (boys and men) and teachers were employed by the Church.   It was first envisioned
by Pope Sylvester (A. D. 341-335) and reorganized as a prac-
ticum by St. Gregory I at the end of the sixth century.   Central to the Schola was a leader who acted as cantor (chief solo
singer), a practice inherited from the Hebrew liturgy.

However, total acceptance of the Gregorian Chant was
not easily accomplished.   Travel and communication being
very slow during the early Middle Ages (usually known as
the "Dark Ages") retarded total acceptance of the Chant.   A
notable example of this was evidenced by the fact that Charlemagne (Charles the Great, A. D. 742-814) was forced to give
up his plan for complete unity of church chant.   Finally, the
Frankish kingdom accepted and coordinated it around the ninth
century among the many Germanic kingdoms.   Thus, there
was established a more or less "universal" unity of liturgy.

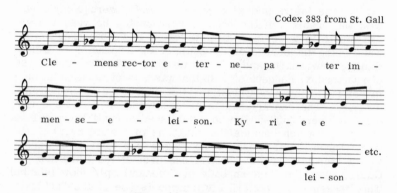

Fig. 44:   The Trope

Considering this multiplicity of versions of the liturgical chant, the creation in this vicinity [Italian,
Gallic and Spanish] of a vital center for the Roman
tradition was of capital importance in the endeavor
to achieve unity.[13]

New Forms of Liturgical Music

The Gregorian Chant seemed doomed to fight for its existence as to domination of the worship scene. In the ninth century inroads were made into the realm of the Chant through the introduction of the Trope. It was a new, expressive form of church music and literary form which aimed at revitalizing the rigidity of the established Chant, both in shape and in conception. [14] The Tropes ranged from a few amplifying words interpolated between the Kyrie eleison to lengthy explanatory sentences. Entire poems were placed between two words of an authentic text. [15]

Following the same form as the Tropes, the sequence (prose) was introduced to reshape the melismatic sections of the Chant as they were attached to the Alleluia jubilus with their own tunes. They reflected the provincial tastes of the clergy and were well-established by the twelfth and thirteenth centuries. They further reflected the personal piety of the church leaders and eventually were used outside the divine service.

Out of this effort a new form of personal expression of religious thought emerged, called the "Cantio." These melodic cantiones (spiritual songs) were born of popular musical experiences. They were termed "Pilgrim Songs" of the eleventh and twelfth centuries.

An off-shoot of the Cantio gradually emerged in the form of rhymed liturgy--still in Latin, however. It was referred to as the "Rhymed Office." It is interesting to note that the Franciscan and Dominican Breviaries (ecclesiastical book of hymns, offices and prayers for the canonical hours) still retain this form. [16]

The logical progression of the development (or transition) cited above of the Chant emerged in the form of native hymns. The emergence of a desire and need to interpret the Latin texts in the vernacular, particularly among the independent-minded Germanic peoples, produced popular hymns as early as the ninth century. This form of ecclesiastical folk custom greatly aided the pastoral work of the clergy. Herein lie the roots of the German hymnody expression which led to strophes (verses) and eventually the hymn-style of the Reformation. They became the popular musical language of the thirteenth and fourteenth centuries.

An overlapping development during this time was the introduction of religious drama by way of the division of the trope into dialogue. Thus, the special celebrations of the Church (Christmas, Easter) as well as other significant biblical accounts, were dramatized in the vernacular. Of course, the natural outcome of this drama was to introduce musical themes to intensify or modify the dramatic material--the development of a musico-literary form.[17]

The Middle Ages Potpourri

As one can quite readily observe, the maintenance of unity of musical and theological expression during the Middle Ages was exceedingly difficult for the Roman Catholic hierarchy. The power and influence of the Church was growing faster than could be easily controlled. The independent progress of the Celts (in what is now the British Isles) during the early Middle Ages brought additional problems to Rome. The Northerners, under missionary Patrick, had been permitted to adapt their own customs and language to the Christian liturgy, thereby creating a great difference in liturgical practice and tradition from those in Rome.

After their invasion of Britain, the Normans attempted to force the Celts to adapt their customs, including the French manner of singing the liturgy.

> The Anglo-Saxon Chronicle tells us that, in 1083, the Abbot of Glastonbury posted archers in the clerestory with orders to shoot down the stubborn monks who persisted in singing the office in the English manner which they considered to be proper.[18]

Furthermore, secular music was making inroads on church music as the age of poet-musicians, minstrels in England, troubadours (trouveres) in France, and Minnesingers in Germany became popular entities. The movement began with the nobility and later migrated to the cultured middle-class citizens. Along with that activity, monophonic religious songs appeared. They were not used in religious services, but were used as vernacular hymns, sometimes combining plainchant and popular folk song material.

Meanwhile, another development within the Gregorian Chant had taken place--the development of organum. The single note melodies had given way to octaves, which the

trained singers of the Schola Cantorum could easily handle.
However, the movement toward harmony was hastened by the
fact that the lower clergy in the monasteries found these
plainsong melodies out of their vocal ranges--too high and
too low at the extremes.   Thus, this failure to be able to
match pitches led to the organum at the fourth and fifth (four
and five notes below melody line), and eventually there developed a kind of polyphony resulting from two independent
lines.   This surely broke the bond of control which the
Church had strived to maintain over the sacredness of the
Gregorian melodies.

Sit glo - ri - a Do-mi-ni in se-cu-la

(v.p. = vox principalis;
v.o. = vox organalis)

Rex   coe - li Do-mi-ne mar-is un-di-so - ni

Fig. 45:   Organum at the Fourth and Fifth

The Beginnings of Polyphony

Inevitably, improvisation of music had to give way to
composition.   By the eleventh century (the time of the Norman conquest of Britain), composing a melody for posterity,
instead of simply varying it at each rendition, became an attractive activity.   Once people learned this new "language"
of notation, the music could be perpetuated more readily in
its original form.   Modes and rhythms began to be codified
and then rules of consonance in harmony were set up.   However, definitive personalities who led this new movement
were not recorded.   It seemed to be a rather general striving
caused by the natural evolution of music and history itself.
Thus, polyphony began to emerge without any sudden discon-
tinuance from the monadic plain song form.   As a matter of
fact, early polyphony borrowed heavily from plainchant.   Grout
believes that polyphony existed in Europe long before it was
identified as such.

It was probably used in nonliturgical sacred music;
it may have been employed also in folk music, and
probably consisted of melodic doubling at the third,
fourth, or fifth, along with a more or less syste-
matic practice of heterophony--that is, by performing the same melody simultaneously in ornamented
or unornamented form.[19]

As organum became more and more complex both in
harmonic and melodic parameters, the Church was confronted
with added problems of control over the simple Gregorian
chants.   In 1324 Pope John XXII issued an encyclical emphasizing the central position of the liturgical melodies.   Fellerer
concludes,

But the new art [of polyphony] had stifled the Gregorian cantus firmus and thus estranged itself even
from the liturgical link that helped to make polyphony ecclesiastical music.[20]

At this juncture it was the hope of the Church leadership that polyphony would serve only to embellish the recognized musical liturgy, rather than become an entity unto itself.   However, this was not realized because the Church was
no longer the controlling force in musical matters.

Therefore, in the course of history, ecclesiastical
polyphony has stiffened into a mere backward-looking
formalism only during those periods when religious
attitude lost its power to create its own means of
composition and give material at hand ecclesiastical
significance.[21]

Thus, the Church lost its absolute control over the
musical portions of the Mass and gradually polyphony became
the new model for liturgical purposes.   That is not to say,
however, that the chants were banished.   Rather, the melodic
shape of the Gregorian liturgy was considerably changed, such
as shifting the melodic center of the chant, changing tempi
and shortening melismas.

The musical evolution eventually separated the polyphonic movement from Gregorian Chant so that the shift was
away from the cantus firmus to that of contrapuntal composition.   This development greatly accelerated the art of composing because the complexity of this new musical form demanded that there be a means of controlling the voices.

Another significant development came in the form of free organum, that is, the adaptation of florid lines to the basic
tunes.   Naturally, this opened the way toward more and more
independence from the confines of Gregorian Chant.

By the thirteenth century polyphony had developed a
chordal manner of writing called "conductus."   Even though
the voices (usually three) moved independently, there was un-
mistakable harmony which resulted from the juxtaposition of
the voices.

Gloria from the Mass of Tournay

Do - mi - ne__ De - us__ A - gnus De - i

Fig. 46: Conductus

This example illustrates the employment of Gregorian
melody in an elaborated form.   Even in the fourteenth century the link with the Gregorian Chant was no longer considered essential, thus opening the way toward greater freedom
in sacred compositions and the development of polyphony.

The Motet

Probably the most distinctive feature to emerge from
this transition from plainsong to harmony was the development of the motet.   The term derives its source from the
French word "mot," meaning "word."   It became the most
important form of early polyphonic music and dominated the
ecclesiastical musical scene from about 1250 to 1750.   It
was usually sung unaccompanied based on a Latin sacred text,
mostly of biblical origin.   (Later developments, however,
brought other religious vernacular texts into the form.)   English motets eventually were called anthems, and in later years
of development used instrumental accompaniment as well as
a cappella singing.

Actually, there were three distinct periods or forms of the motet: the medieval (c. 1225-1450), or ars antiqua (old art); the Flemish ars nova (1450-1600) (new art); and the Baroque (1600-1750). It is not within the realm of this treatise to go into detail describing and illustrating this vast collection of liturgical and sacred music. Suffice it to say that the motet serves as the basis of most choral music of the Protestant and Roman Catholic churches of the twentieth century, even though some "high churches" of the Roman tradition still chant portions of the liturgy.

New Developments in Choral Style

The fourteenth century produced a great schism in the Roman Catholic Church. The supremacy of the pope was widely questioned throughout much of Christendom. There were rival claimants to the Papacy as well as corruption within the higher clergy. This led eventually to the Protestant Reformation and the eventual separation of Church and State in later centuries. As independent powers became established, the various rulers vied for prestige by becoming patrons of the arts, further diffusing the power of the Church. The separate kingdoms, "dukedoms" and the like, encouraged the development of the secular form of the arts, and also supported the clergy as long as the latter did not interfere with political affairs. In this sense the Church became subject to the secular.

Everywhere music flourished from the fourteenth century onward. Composers of our major sources of choral music began to emerge, such as these:

> Guillame de Marchant, c. 1300-1377
> John Dunstable, c. 1370-1453
> Gilles Binchois, c. 1400-1460
> Guillame Dufay, c. 1400-1474
> Jean Ockeghm, c. 1430-1495
> Josquin des Pres, c. 1450-1521
> Adrian Willaert, c. 1480-1562
> Christopher Tye, c. 1497-1572
> Andraes Gabrieli, 1520-1586
> Thomas Tallis, 1505-1585
> Giovanni Pierluige da Palestrina 1525-1594
> Orlando de Lassus, c. 1532-1594
> William Byrd, 1543-1623
> Guilio Caccini, c. 1546-1618

Giovanni Gabrieli, c. 1557-1612
Thomas Morley, 1557-1602

These names are but a few of the early composers of
polyphony whose music is accessible to us in modern times,
but they serve as a background of information for any choral
conductor to explore. The age of discovery--of experimentation and initiative--was born and matured during these centuries.

Before the invention of printing presses in early fifteenth century Netherlands, the laborious method of hand
printing a composer's manuscript retarded the wide dissemi-
nation of musical works. Only the Church could afford the
manpower, time and skill to make copies which were thought
to be worthy of preservation. Even then, few copies were
reliable. However, there came the German, Johann Gutenberg in the middle of the fifteenth century, who is usually
credited with perfecting a practical method of reproduction
of words and eventually of music. This, in turn, provided
the impetus for standardizing notation.

The German Reformation

No other movement in history had greater effect upon
church music than did Martin Luther's break with the Vatican.
Among Luther's many objectives for reform was the active
participation of the laity in public worship. He drew freely
from familiar secular songs, but he also composed hymns,
the most familiar of which is "Ein' Feste Burg ist unser Gott."
He also translated some Latin hymns into German, "adapting
plain-song melodies to accommodate the translation where necessary, and adding harmonies."22 In addition to being a
cleric, he was a sound musician. Eventually, he compiled
several hymn books, which were to act as a catalyst for future German composers, such as Hans Hassler (1564-1612)
and Johann Crüger (1598-1662)

Yet, Luther's music was not accepted outside of Germany because the greater part of Europe remained Roman
Catholic. In addition, the Calvinists frowned on church music and made a complete break away from the Church. They
wanted only the simplest forms of music in public worship.
For them traditional forms of worship had lost their original
purposes and meanings.

> Where Luther sought to restore to music its proper
> function as an aid to worship, the Calvinists threw
> it out almost completely. 23

There is evidence that there were few musicians in
the early refugee Calvinistic movement located in Geneva.
So, without competent musicians to provide direction, organized music was discontinued from their worship practices.
Instead, metrical Psalms were paraphrased for worship from
the Vulgate Bible.   The tunes were borrowed from Dutch folk
songs, one example being the Souter Liedekens (1540) first
published in Antwerp.

Erik Routly, in his concise treatise on the church and
music, cites three precepts which Calvin stated as the doctrine for church music:

> 1.   Music is for the people, so it must be simple;
> 2.   Music is for God, so it must be modest;
> 3.   These objects are best attained by the music
>   of the unaccompanied voice. 24

The English Reformation

King Henry VIII brought about his separation from
Rome in 1534, but the actual reformation action was delayed
until after his death in 1547.   Henry had been appointed "De-
fender of the Faith" by Pope Leo X and he remained a devout
Catholic despite his split with the Papacy.   Archbishop of
Canterbury, Thomas Cranmer, was the prime mover to bring
about reform in the guise of a compromise between Romanism
and Calvinism.   The repeal of the Roman dogma (Statute of
the Six Articles) opened the way for the eventual Thirty-nine
Articles of Religion, which established the Church of England.
Music was given a high priority in the new church giving
John Merbecke the opportunity to adapt the old Latin liturgy
to the English language.   His Book of Common Prayer became the backbone of Anglican Church liturgy.   He disliked
contrapuntal motets because they obscured the words.   Therefore, he urged composers to write simply--one note to each
syllable.   This led directly to the chordal style of writing
exploited so adroitly by Thomas Tallis and Christopher Tye.
However, anthems and motets were performed mostly in the
cathedrals and large city churches with their trained choirs
--a carry-over from Roman Catholic times.

But all was not smooth for the English Reformation. When devout Catholic Queen Mary I succeeded to the throne upon the death of young King Edward VI in 1553, it was her aim to kill the Protestant movement. During the persecution that followed, the church musicians retreated to save their lives, and as a result, very little church music was composed. In 1558 Queen Elizabeth I ascended the throne and the country returned to Protestantism with all of the former Anglican church rites restored. Yet, it took several years to regain the musical momentum enjoyed before Queen Mary's reign, although liturgical service books soon began to appear. When it seemed evident that Protestantism was reinstated permanently, Tye and Tallis began again to write for the Anglican Church. Young William Byrd, an avowed Roman Catholic, was appointed organist at Lincoln Cathedral (Anglican) during this period. He contributed significantly to English church music while still composing Latin masses and motets. During the Elizabethan Age, England prospered greatly. Literature, art, and music developed to tremendous heights producing Shakespeare and his contemporaries; in music, men like Tye, Tallis, Orlando Gibbons, Thomas Weelkes and Thomas Tomkins composed freely.

Again, the English Reformation faced violent change. During the reigns of James I and Charles I (Stuarts) the Calvinists dominated the religiopolitical scene, with that era seeing the establishment of Puritanism. The result of this trauma (civil war) was the establishment of the Commonwealth in 1649. Under Protector Oliver Cromwell, the liturgy, prayerbook, choirs, and organs were abolished from worship. Only the simplest metrical psalms were permitted.[25] The repertoire of the Tudor regime was lost for many years. The music of the church after the Restoration (1660) became the product of a new age. From this new era the English Anthem came into being.

The Baroque Era (1600-1750)

By the year 1600 the musical world was searching for new means of expression. According to the Harvard Dictionary of Music, the term "baroque" probably originated from the Portuguese word barrocco, a pearl of irregular form. Applied to music, it defines a style which was described over the years of its predominance in artistic life as being overly ornate. In art and architecture it was considered to be "overladen with scroll-work." But generally speaking, the Baroque period represents "an era of ecstasy and exuberance."26

Most persons who have studied music seriously have been exposed to the music of such Baroque masters as Palestrina, the Gabrielis, Monteverdi, Gibbons (early period), Schütz, Lully, Corelli, Purcell (middle period), J. S. Bach, Handel and Telemann (late period). Their works (as well as those of others too numerous to list here) remain as monuments to an era in which all musical development (secular as well as sacred music) made magnanimous strides. This period gave great impetus to the rise of opera, oratorio and cantata forms. By 1750, the Baroque musical form was apparently considered to have exhausted all that it was capable of saying and was punctuated by the deaths of Bach in 1750 and Handel in 1759. Although a number of good composers continued to write in this idiom after 1750, the period, for all practical purposes of historical "calendarization," was over. It is difficult to draw arbitrary lines of periods because the influences of each "period" carried over into others. For instance, Early Baroque composition reflects strong influences of late Renaissance style music; early Classical (Rococo) period had great amounts of ornamentation. The Romantic period certainly relied upon the elements of the Classical period, and so on. However, for purposes of this study it seems important to examine some of the influences in brief specificity.

Baroque Stylistic Practices

Every choral conductor should become thoroughly acquainted with the stylistic practices of this period--all periods, for that matter. During the Baroque era, great strides in instrumental development took place. Organs, string and wind instruments were significantly perfected, and subsequently used widely in churches. This development gave rise to new musical forms, such as passions and dramatic masses with orchestral accompaniment. The eagerness for a new style of musical expression opened new avenues of polyphonic experimentation. Overlapping Renaissance and early Baroque periods, Orlando di Lasso (c. 1532-1594) began fuller use of chromatics, although most of his works reflect the unaccompanied Renaissance. Giovanni Gabrieli (1557-1612) introduced the concept of multiple choirs placed around the sanctuary with instruments doubling the parts, greatly expanding the scope of church music.

The emergence of the thorough-bass, or <u>basso con-</u>
<u>tinuo</u>, to undergird the vocal forces became one of the major
identifying elements of middle and late eras of Baroque music.   The figures for harmonization of melodies were written
below the lowest line of the staves.   Added to this technical
development was the emergence of a more emotional quality
of musical expression.   Some musicologists believe that all
Baroque music should be metrical (objective) and devoid of
emotion; that dynamic markings included only piano and forte;
that crescendos were forbidden.   These notions are likely
derived from the fact that the organs of that period contained
no expression (crescendo) pedal.   All dynamics were made
by the use of stops on the organ console.   In those days an
organist had to have an assistant standing by to change stops
quickly while he presided at the keyboard.   Those organs also
required a person to manually pump the bellows for air in
the wind chest.   It seems logical, then, that any hard and
fast rules of this kind as to dynamics may fall short of total
historical accuracy.   For instance, the voice and other wind
instruments have the capability of singing through a wide
range of gradual dynamics.   It is impossible to believe that
medium loud or medium soft dynamics were not used--inad-
vertently at least--by singers and wind players.   Even the
harmonies, as they develop in Baroque music, tend to build
dynamics and create crescendo effects.

Probably the most outstanding example of a composer
who maintained the ties with earlier ecclesiastical music
along with the innovations of the new era was Claudio Monteverdi (1567-1643).   His compositions frequently incorporated
the chant as <u>cantus firmus</u> along with the new style to become
known as concertante (church and secular) music.   In the
secular world of music, Monteverdi's contribution to the
emergence of opera is most significant.   Although Jacapo
Peri (1561-1633) and Guilio Caccini (1546-1618) are considered to be the "fathers" of opera, it was Monteverdi who
brought the early form into prominence.   Monteverdi's contribution to church music was equally significant.   His (along
with Giovanni Gabrieli's) many Psalms combined the style of
concertante (which reached its apex in eighteenth-century developments), which led to the solo <u>parlando</u> expression.   This,
in turn, led to the recitative of the middle and late Baroque
eras.   The term "concertante" may be described as a composition for orchestra in which there were parts for solo instruments, and also sometimes pieces written for several
solo instruments without orchestra.   Soli singers were also
employed in this concertante fashion.

In Germany the concertante style was outstandingly
applied to vocal forces by Franz Heinrich Biber (1644-1704)
in a contrapuntal use of voices, with the instruments becoming an extension of the vocal parts harmonically and rhythmically.   In other words, the entire forces combined to make a
total orchestral-choral effect of equal importance.   Heinrich
Schütz's compositions developed the recitative along with
choral-instrumental forces that so ably laid the foundation
for the late (high) Baroque concertato compositions as observed in the compositions by J. S. Bach and the Bach family of musicians.   "Concertato" connotes "sounding together,"
but also to contend or dispute.

> The stile concertato--in the form of solos, duets,
> dialogues, trios, choruses and diverse small or
> large combinations of voices and instruments--was
> applied to both motets and masses.[27]

This new stile moderno in vocal church music was
often combined with stile antico--the use of ancient chants.
However, these melodies were often altered almost beyond
recognition.[28]   Another composer who effectively utilized
this combined form of writing was Michael Praetorious in
the seventeenth century.

> Canon and cantus firmus gave this form of compo-
> sition archaic interest and at times, too, the im-
> pression of scholarliness.[29]

The Roman Catholic mass has two forms--the Ordinary
(regular, consisting of Kyrie Eleison, Gloria, Credo, Sanctus,
Osanna, Benedictus, Agnus Dei, and Dona Nobis Pacem), and
the Proper, or Service for Special Occasions.   Among the
special masses is the Requiem Mass celebrated for the dead
to be sung on the day of burial and anniversaries of that date
or celebrated on the third, seventh or thirteenth day after
death.   It is interesting to note that most composers wrote
only one Requiem, perhaps their own in mind.

The first extant polyphonic Requiem is believed to
have been written by Johannes Ockeghem, a Netherlander
(c. 1420-1495).   It is a combination of monophony and polyphony.[30]   "His achievements in the art of imitative counterpoint unquestionably make his music a milestone on the way
to the a cappella style of coming generations."[31]   The polyphonic style of writing eventually became established as an
integral part of the Roman Catholic mass and remains so today despite occasional efforts by the hierarchy to ban it.

The Passions and Magnificats

Polyphonic settings of the Passions date back to about the middle of the fifteenth century in England, particularly the accounts of St. Matthew and St. Luke. However, these works contained plainsong movements as well. In the latter part of the sixteenth century, Spanish composers such as Francisco Guerro (1528-1599) and Tomas Luis de Victoria (1549-1611), further developed the use of polyphony, but still on a very modest scale. The same practice was applied to compositions based on the Magnificat. Eventually, the polyphonic practice "invaded" Germany where the Lutherans adopted it, despite their aversion to worship of the Virgin Mary. In England it was adopted as a part of evening worship. Thus, the mingling of each country's vernacular liturgy continued to keep its ties with the Roman Catholic Church.

It was during the years of the High Baroque (about 1675 to 1750) that polyphony reached its highest state of development--epitomized by Johann Sebastian Bach. Ironically, Bach confessed at one point during his mature years that the study of counterpoint was exceedingly difficult for him to master; this from the man who is universally regarded as the greatest composer of polyphonic music in all of musical history. It is hard to accept the fact that during his lifetime, J. S. Bach was known widely throughout Europe as a brilliant organist, but not as a composer. Could it have been because his music was so complex (particularly his choral polyphony) that his inadequate vocal forces could not do justice to it? It was one hundred years after the completion of Bach's Passion According to St. Matthew that Felix Mendelssohn revived it in 1829, although in a greatly romanticized version. In this passion, Bach's writing reaches the most exalted ideal of Lutheran Church music:

> [I]n it the chorale, the concertato style, the recitative, the arioso and the da capo aria are united under the ruling majesty of the central religious theme. [32]

The Cantata and Oratorio

With the development of opera, the latter part of the seventeenth century witnessed the emergence of the cantata. In a sense, the cantata represented a conservative version or off-shoot of the operatic form. In the early versions of the

cantata, during the first half of the seventeenth century, the
cantata was monadic and strophic with many short, contrasting sections. It first appeared in Italy and then spread quickly
to other parts of Europe because of its expressive-dramatic
qualities. "[I]t differed from opera chiefly in that both poetry
and music were on a more intimate scale."33

Of course, not being staged, the cantata differed considerably in the visual message that could be conveyed by the
performers. The cantata form first featured the solo soprano
voice with continuo support and later involved duets. It eventually included choral forces. At the height of the Baroque
period, J. S. Bach composed more than three hundred cantatas (mostly sacred) of which over two hundred are extant.
His cantatas exemplify the highest development of this choral
cantata form. "Bach had no real model for the chorale cantata; he evolved it himself with the aid of the Leipsig poet,
Picander...."34

Bach's cantatas are composed of fundamental groupings. Each grouping is a "mini-orchestra" in effect: the
strings (being separated by cello-bass continuo), the wood-
winds and the brass-percussion group. Scores should be
studied carefully in regard to the relationship which each
"orchestra" has to the other parts in the concertato form
of composition. Often there will be four or more concerti
groups interacting with the choral forces. In some cases
a single section or wind instrument (oboe or flute, for instance) will be acting in the concertato role. Examples of
this feature are abundant in Bach's Mass in B-Minor (composed in separate parts over a period of many years, the
sections of which are titled: [1] Missa, [2] Symbolum Nicenum,
[3] Sanctus, [4] Osanna, Benedictus, Agnus Dei, and [5] et
Dona nobis pacem). One illustration is found in the "Credo"
in which the plainchant melody of the four choral voices are
supported by the basso-continuo line (with keyboard continuo).
The contrapuntal writing has each voice entering followed by
violin I entrance and then violin II, making a six-voiced canon
--another example of the genius of Johann Sebastian Bach!
Truly, it can be said that Johann Sebastian Bach was the capstone of all the musical development which preceded him and
the cornerstone of the music which has followed his work.

Early Baroque music may be characterized as an "accumulation of fundamental ... and ornamental instruments."35
Middle Baroque orchestration witnessed the advent of continuo
emphasis. Late (high) Baroque music embraced the concept

of equality of all voices, totally integrated as interacting entities.

George Frideric Handel needs little or no introduction as the other giant of the late Baroque period. Unlike the mystic Bach, who died in obscurity, Handel was a composer of international stature. He was much more conscious of the larger world and his secular as well as church orientation to it. He created his music for large audience appeal-- commercial, if you will. He was a monetary speculator who died a wealthy man. Bach remained an orthodox Lutheran all through his life while "Handel did not deny religion; rather, like a good Englishman, he settled with it."[36] He truly affirmed the joys of this life--to be creative in living for one's given purposes in a visible world, rather than a world to come.

> He is pagan and yet Christian, sensuous and yet
> spiritual, his men, though mythical heroes, are
> entirely human, and his women are both his lovers
> and his sisters.[37]

We can never really compare Bach and Handel. They are two different composers who used similar vehicles of expression, but emerged with completely different results.

Protestant Substitutes for the Mass
(17th and 18th Centuries)

In post-Reformation England, the mass was replaced by the Anglican Service as the dominant form of worship. Although the basic format of the Roman liturgy was followed, certain substitutions were made. The Te Deum replaced Matins; the Benedictus Dominus replaced Lauds; the Kyrie and Nicene Creed (Credo) from the ordinary of the mass were used with the exception of the Gloria (not regularly included) --all done in English rather than Latin. Composers following the lead of Byrd and Morley were John Blow (1649-1708), Henry Purcell (c. 1659-1695) and William Croft (1678-1727), who contributed significantly to the Anglican Service.

In sixteenth-century Germany, the mass was occasionally sung in Latin, but chorales with other responses in the German language were also included. There were Latin plainsong pieces, Introits and Alleluias, as well as songs in both Latin and German.[38] In other words, Latin and German continued side by side in Germany.

> Had Luther's German Mass [Deutsche Messe] been
> adopted as a basic pattern, it would have had as
> great an effect upon Lutheran liturgical practice as
> the formulation of a standard pattern in English had
> upon the Anglican Service. [39]

J. S. Bach wrote four Missae Brevis (brief masses)
as one example of the Latin-German bed-fellow arrangement
in the regular worship of the German Baroque church service;
the choral music being in Latin, but the hymns and preaching being in German.   Also, his great B-Minor Mass stemmed
from the concept of the brief mass.   However, it certainly
became much more than a Missa Brevis when finally assembled.   That is why even today there is controversy over the
knowledge as to whether or not Bach himself conceived of
the separate sections as a unified whole.   The only resolu-
tion comes from the decision that the entire work, as it remains, is a universal mass--devoid of any denominational or
sectarian claims.   "The MASS in B-Minor is as ecumenical
a gesture as the World Council of Churches."[40]

The Eighteenth-Century Classical Period (1750-1850)

The advent of new modes of thinking during the years
following the end of the Baroque period was led by Carl Philipp Emanuel Bach (commonly known as C. P. E.) and Franz
Joseph Haydn.   By 1750 the development of music was noticeably divorced from the church.   During the preceding
two hundred years composers even related their secular music to church modes, disguising secular songs in the polyphonic motet genre. [41]   By the middle and late eighteenth century the emphasis was on secular music.   Concert halls were
built to accommodate large crowds of music lovers, and from
that time on composers relied less and less upon the Protestant and Roman Catholic arms of the Christian church for
monetary support.

Along with this development came the change of emphasis from polyphony to a homophonic style "featuring a
melodic line with accompaniment built on basic chords...."[42]
One need only compare the style of Haydn, Mozart, Beethoven, and Schubert to note the comparative lack of complexity
as compared to J. S. Bach's music.

In England, church music deteriorated because of many
factors, the chief one of which was that the choice of music

was made by the clergy rather than the organist.   Even
though the great composers wrote oratorios, masses, motets
and songs based upon "religious" texts, their music was rejected by the Church hierarchy as "being too worldly and lacking in seriousness."[43] Conditions became so bad in England
that some cathedrals had no choirs at all, while in smaller
churches the choral offerings were very poor.   Many organs
had been destroyed during England's Commonwealth Period.
Only the wealthier congregations replaced them in later years.
In some cases amateur church orchestras were organized,
but the attitudes and quality of performance left much to be
desired.   Thus, the cleft between clergy and church music
was exacerbated.   The situation deteriorated so badly that,
in the 1770's, the "barrel organ" made its entry into the
English church.   It is believed that the first "barrel organ,"
an automatic instrument, was invented in the early eighteenth
century and was slowly perfected over the span of about one
hundred years.   Its use was mostly confined to England and
the Continent, especially Germany.   The instrument consisted
of a series of metal pins arranged on revolving drums which
then opened pre-set pipes on each barrel.   These "organs"
could play up to ten hymns per barrel (see Grove's Dictionary of Music and Musicians, 5th ed. Vol. I, p. 456 for a
detailed description).   It was a self-contained unit, probably
the predecessor of the large music boxes of the nineteenth
century which made pitches (sound) by tiny metal pins.   At
least there was more accuracy in the hymn-playing, but the
condition of music in the church remained pitiful with little
or no monetary support from church leaders.[44]

Eventually (1729), John and Charles Wesley began a
movement called Methodism, which began to change the texture of English musical life.   Though the Wesleys brought
about theological change, they still adhered to the basic ten-
ets of the Anglican Church.

> [Charles] Wesley's own views on music were those
> of the theologian who knows the principles without
> having specialized knowledge. He knew what sort
> of music was fit to use, even if he committed him-
> self to no dogmatism on the matter.[45]

We can look to his great emphasis upon hymnody, however,
as being the basic musical influence within his doctrinal concepts.   He wrote more than seven thousand hymns which were
set to many new tunes.

The Methodists were greatly in need of new tunes, not because they rejected the old, but because their hymns [texts] were written in a wide variety of meters for which no tunes were available. Their leaders were too sound musicians to permit the distortion of traditional psalm tunes to fit new hymns. 46

The Congregationalists, still freer in their view of Anglican Church practices organized singing classes, and eventually they embraced instrumental as well as vocal music in their church worship.

The Baptists, as can be expected, evidenced a great variety of musical practices. Having no titular church hierarchy above them to dictate behavior, some Baptists "not only performed music incidental to public worship, but sang Handel's oratorios. "47

The Presbyterians of Scotland are not to be ignored in this overview of music trends of the eighteenth century. An English soldier stationed in Aberdeen was even relieved of his military duties to teach Scottish congregations to sing. 48

The most important element in this entire discussion of post Baroque church music in England is that the emphasis of music development was placed on the hymn and the improvement in its execution and theological enlightenment.

The American Scene (1730-1850)

Boston, New York, and Philadelphia abounded in good musical fare, as did even Charlestown, South Carolina. The singing of psalms and hymns was evident throughout the various denominations. In addition, choral societies were founded. Singing schools became well-established, although there was an abundance of self-styled instructors who tended to lower standards.

The Moravian (Czech) immigrants contributed greatly to the musical life of young America. Of course, they brought with them their great tradition of music and then continued to develop it in this country both vocally and instrumentally. John Antes was one of the great figures of the Moravians. He was born near Bethlehem, Pennsylvania in 1740. Antes was the son of the founder of the Moravian congregation in

Pennsylvania.   Eventually, he became leader of the United
Brethren in Northwestern Pennsylvania.   He composed very
little music, but was a great force in spreading the "gospel"
of better music among American pioneers.

William Billings (1746-1800), the tanner-amateur musician, is well-known among choral directors of the twentieth century.   He published six music books, specializing
in what came to be known as "fuguing tunes."   His style was
widely imitated and his songs were very popular among the
non-musically educated populace.

Eventually, the Eastern populace was weaned away
from the Billings influence and in the early nineteenth century more dignified hymns and psalm tunes were given preference.   Interestingly, this movement toward better hymns
was led by the clergy. [49]

However, in the American West, where there was
great isolation in the nineteenth century, the situation naturally was fertile ground for the kind of "soul music" so
characteristic of the revival trend.   The highly emotional
qualities of the texts and music brought by the itinerant
preacher and his colleague, the singer-song leader, offered
the settlers an opportunity to vent their emotions to the point
of frenzy.   The "saw-dust trail" became the familiar path
down which many persons walked or crawled in order to be
"saved."   Basically, this is not too different from the responses of the early Christians, who intoned their "amens"
and "hallelujahs."   Some published collections of hymns represented in these camp meetings were Davisson's "Kentucky
Harmony" (1820), Walker's "Southern Harmony" and the famous "The Sacred Harp" by White and King.   Many of these
hymns are still in use today, particularly in the Southeast.

The Negro spiritual's development and assimilation
into American musical culture is of great importance.   The
chief characteristics of the Afro-American's basically vocal
music was a strong sense of rhythm, the frequent use of the
pentatonic scale (African heritage), and a text that promised
emancipation from the burdens of this world.   Since little or
none of this music was notated, the music was greatly improvised and ornamented as per individual feelings.   It has
come through the years by way of rote and should not be confused with the white man's versions of the Spiritual, which
are frequently unauthentic.

The Oratorio-Passion Development of the
18th and 19th Centuries

Before we leave discussion of the music during the Classical and Romantic periods, we should mention some facts which have stabilized our heritage of these significant eras of musical development.

As has been noted previously, the oratorio style has its seeds dating back to the liturgical dramas of the Middle Ages. Seventeenth-century opera laid the real foundation for the mature oratorio and passion style. Instrumental development provided the impetus for the "invasion" of these forces into church music, even though the clergy rebuffed this music initially as being pagan and unfit for public worship. The contribution of Heinrich Schütz to the Baroque era cannot be ignored as a transitional force to further development of the style. He combined the German practices with the Venetian by utilizing plain chants in a highly structured manner and also using musical symbolism to enhance the dramatic features of the text and music.

We have also discussed the impact of J. S. Bach's style upon the oratorio-passion-cantata forms. Yet, "[e]ven though the Bach passions stand out above similar works of the period, there is no line of succession in their style."[50]

Gradually, the oratorio style was secularized and this opened the door to the development of the musical idiom by men like Haydn. Meanwhile, in England, there were imitative attempts by "lesser" composers to create works in this idiom, but, alas, by the last quarter of the eighteenth century, the form had disintegrated into a pitiful condition.

It was left to Haydn, Mozart, and Beethoven to develop further the large-scale choral composition. In contrast, English church music began to utilize the anthem form as part of the liturgy, however pitiful that was in terms of performance. Generally, choral music was no longer considered to be solely in the realm of the church. As an example, Haydn's The Creation and The Seasons, though biblically oriented, developed the form as a new, dramatic style. Following this, Beethoven's Christ on the Mount of Olives (Op. 85) was another large step in the oratorio field. The musical treatment produced an intensive dramatic and operatic effect for the entire work. Mendelssohn's revival of Bach's Passion According to St. Matthew (though highly romanticized and altered) tended to further heighten interest in the concertized oratorio. The German Requiem of Johannes Brahms (1833-1897) finally made its way back into the church when it was performed in the Bremen Cathedral on Good Friday of 1868.[51] This work, like Bach's B-Minor Mass, has almost universal appeal, crossing sectarian religious lines. The contribution of the Romantic era composers was to bequeath to us a musical vocabulary capable of freely expressing human emotion. This is not to imply that the music of preceding centuries lacked emotion, but rather, the new mode of musical expression more freely utilized emotional concepts (9th, 11th and 13th chords and melodic lines which elicit emotion) that had not been used before this time. Now the emphasis seemed to be "playing to an audience," rather than playing or singing for each other or for the church service. Performing forces were becoming larger and the concept of music as entertainment (whether sacred or secular in nature) became an openly admitted fact. The conductor became the focal point of the performance both for the performers and the listeners.

Erik Routley summarizes this vital change in musical "thought-form." First, the use of counterpoint was thrust into the background of composition, whereas counterpoint occupied the foreground of sixteenth-century music.[52] It was now relegated to a less important role or technique. J. S. Bach was the eighteenth-century musical giant whose polyphony became the standard for his successors to follow. In contrast, Brahms employed contrapuntal techniques, but in a very subtle manner, though he understood polyphony exceptionally well. His motet "A Crown of Grace for Man Is Wrought" is a classic example of Brahms' ability to write in the style of eighteenth-century counterpoint following the precepts established by Bach. Secondly, Romanticists' musical statements (thematic materials) became greatly extended in terms of time and space, rather than the terse statements which characterized earlier music. That is to say, melodic phrases tended to become longer and intervals farther apart. (However, some of Bach's fugues are also very long and complicated in thematic development, such as that found in the double fugue first movement of his motet No. 1, "Singet dem Herrn.") Thirdly, ecclesiastical modes disappeared and were replaced by classical scales and key-relationships.

> This was to polarize music on an outer axis of "major and minor" modes and an inner axis of "tonic and dominant."[53]

Routley extends his discussion, stating that the new emotionalism of nineteenth-century music and other artistic forms elicit non-musical ideas and responses from performers and listeners, becoming a "tool" rather than an entity unto itself. He implies that imitators of Brahms, Liszt, Wagner and other great composers of the Romantic era were incapable of composing music with integrity.

> The vice of Victorian music is often said to be "sentimentality," and if sentimentality is emotional content backed by no solid truth, a show of feeling with no intention of consequent honesty, the description is an accurate one. 54

We can observe the progression of church music (both Catholic and Protestant) through the nineteenth century, as follows.

Dwight L. Moody and musician Ira D. Sankey in the United States brought their religious revival efforts from America to England, further "corrupting the standards" of church music. Such hymns as "There Were Ninety and Nine" aptly illustrate the musical and textual "quality" of the hymns introduced into the Protestant service. 55

The "decline" in the "quality" of music in the Lutheran and Roman Catholic churches on the Continent in the nineteenth century also became evident. These churches had an enormous treasury of music dating from antiquity. Yet, European composers, during the Classical and Romantic era, became preoccupied with music which the Church rejected as being unsuitable for worship. Also, during the heyday of grand opera, Giuseppe Verdi (1813-1901) and Pietro Mascagni (1863-1945) in Italy, Georges Bizet (1838-1875) and Camille Saint-Saëns (1835-1921) in France, as well as Joseph Rheinberger (1839-1901), Franz Liszt (1811-1866), and Anton Bruckner (1824-1896) of Germany, to name but a few, composed sacred music in that operatic style. This was highly offensive to the Vatican, and consequently the controversy developed which is still in effect in the late twentieth century. True, there were efforts early in the nineteenth century to revive the Gregorian Chant in Germany, France, and Italy, but they received little more than passing recognition. By the middle of that century, the movement became paralyzed by the dominance of religiously oriented concert music of requiems and masses.

The Liturgical Movement

In 1886 Pope Leo XIII issued a decree restricting the use of the organ in church music. The Benedictines of Solesmes began the publication of their Paleographia Musicale in 1889, which set the standards for all modern editions of the Gregorian plainchant. 56

The emergence of the Caecilian Society in 1868, begun by Franz Xaver Witt (1834-1888), brought church-music reform to the Germanic speaking countries. The Caecilian groups spread prolifically to France, Belgium and even to the United States. The movement in the United States was largely the result of efforts made by John B. Singenberger (1848-1924), although a Society was actually begun in Cincinnati in 1838. 57 As a result, the Chant and vernacular hymns were given a new lease on life in America.

By the end of the nineteenth century the influence of the Caecilian Movement began to wane and it became an organization in place of a movement. 58 The effect of the demise of this Movement was to create great concern on the part of the Vatican. Early in the twentieth century a new edict was made.

The Motu Proprio of 1903

On November 22, 1903, Pope Pius X issued a basic document of church-music legislation evaluating the issues and antithesis of the nineteenth century. This edict stated that the traditional Gregorian Chant "occupies the first place in church music."59 Following this in order of importance was to be the ancient classical polyphony of the Roman school of Palestrina. Last in order of importance was modern music with its many stylistic forms, insofar as they were appropriate to the liturgical texts, and insofar as they avoided all that is theatrical and unseemly. Instrumental accompaniment other than the organ was forbidden. In effect, all music which glorified the performer(s) was regarded as completely unacceptable.

Other papal pronouncements followed:

> 1912: the Regolamento for church music in Rome brought clarifications and supplementary regulations.

1917: the Codex juris canonici stated more general
requirements

1928: the Divini cultus sanctitatem of Pius XI,
wherein certain particulars were stated concerning the training of clergy, liturgical (boys')
choirs, congregational chant and organ playing. [60]

Thus, in the early twentieth century the Liturgical
Movement gained new impetus throughout Europe and America. In the United States the Movement was fostered by Dom
Virgil Michel of St. John's Abbey in Collegeville, Minnesota.
A new music publisher emerged in 1906, McLaughlin & Reilly
in Boston specializing in approved music for the Roman Catholic service. (At this writing the firm is no longer in business.) In 1913 the Society of St. Gregory of America was
formed. It had the same general aims as the Caecilian Society, but was unrelated. The St. Gregory Society published
a "White List" which had a decided impact upon Catholic
church music practices, although it primarily informed church
musicians what they were forbidden to use. The St. Gregory
Hymnal, first published in 1921 and revised in 1940, was the
most widely used hymnal in the United States and English-
speaking Canada[61] until McLaughlin & Reilly published The
Pius X Hymnal on May 1, 1953 (the Golden Jubilee of the
Motu Proprio). It was compiled, arranged, and edited by
the faculty of Pius Tenth School of Liturgical Music, Manhat-
tanville College of the Sacred Heart in Purchase, New York.
The hymnal includes examples of the plainchant Tones and
Modes (eight) for the celebrations of the Church as well as
vernacular hymns. It also includes a short mass by Henri
Potiron (1882- ?), entitled "Missa de Sancto Joanne." The
names of many familiar composers are included among the
hymns and responses: Palestrina, Lotti, Viadana, Victoria,
and even Flor Peters of contemporary times. Also included
are Psalm tones stated first in Latin, then in English. This
is an outstanding and valuable publication.

THE TWENTIETH CENTURY

The "symphonic mass" (employing large orchestral and choral
forces) which was developed to such a great extent by Beethoven, Brahms, Bruckner, Berlioz, and other nineteenth-century
composers, set examples for twentieth-century writers, such
as Ralph Vaughan Williams (1872-1958) of England, Igor Stravinski (1882-1971) of Russia, Francis Poulenc (1899-1963) of

France, Arnold Schönberg (1874-1951) of Germany, Leonard
Bernstein (1918-) of the United States, and Krzysztof Penderecki (1933-) of Poland. Heinz Werner Zimmerman,
contemporary German composer, should be singled out for
his ability to combine a contemporary jazz type of writing
with the established principles of bygone eras. His "Psalm-
konzert" proves that jazz need not be out of character with
religious expression. [62] His music serves to bridge a gap
between the usually conservative attitude in churches with
the avant-garde jazz movement in church music. These contemporary composers have left us a heritage of great religious concert music. Yet, this music is rarely suited for
church use as a whole works, being that it is generally too
long and complicated. However, excerpts of movements from
some of these works are used as anthems in a few churches
having advanced music programs.

What has happened to church music during the period
between 1930 and 1980 in Europe and the United States? Research indicates that this period of church music history is,
at best, spotty in terms of definite musical trends. The
Lutheran Church in Germany still encourages concerted mus-
sic in special programs and church celebrations. In the average German church, musical life is quite sterile. The
larger churches have their festivities, but the local church
choirs are sometimes rather poor. In England, among the
various "free" denominations, there are a few good choirs,
while the large Anglican Cathedrals still have their boy choirs
and choir schools to nurture them. In Italy (and to some extent all European Roman Catholicism) the compromise of
Pope Paul VI in 1963 authorized celebrating certain parts of
the Mass in the vernacular in order to infuse new life into
the ailing music of the Roman Church.

In the United States and Canada, the musical tapestry
is freely painted with the gamut of colors and shapes. In
the large, wealthy Protestant churches, choral music is frequently outstanding. As has been historically the case, many
of the small Protestant churches continue to struggle with
undistinguished music for the most part. The vital fundamen-
talistic churches, on the other hand, have great numbers of
people participating in worship services. Many of them have
fine, well-balanced choirs, which perform Romantic style
music, even though much of it has been composed by contemporary writers.

A relatively small Protestant denomination is the

Christian Reformed Church. Though not large in numbers,
their musical efforts usually produce better than average results. Their excellent private schools have strong music
programs, thus providing an excellent base, which continues
to enhance appreciation and performance of music within the
Church. This is not to say, however, that some of their
congregations and choirs avoid nineteenth-century gospel music.

Since the end of World War II the Southern Baptist
denomination has built tremendous musical programs based
upon the Graded Choir System--a choir for each grade of
the Sunday School. This program, along with well-organized
summer conferences in music for all age groups, has significantly improved the status of music in this denomination.
They have bonafide Ministers of Music possessing bachelor's,
master's and doctoral degrees in church music from their
seminaries. Much of their music tends to be gospel-oriented,
but many of the larger (and some smaller) churches are embracing music of a substantial nature.

Currently, in Roman Catholic churches, the spectrum
of musical life is similar to that of mainline Protestant
churches. In large Catholic cathedrals and churches the music is frequently good or better than average with professional
or semi-professional leadership, adhering to the Motu Proprio of Pius X, the apostolic constitution Pius XI (1928), or
the encyclical Mediator Dei of Pius XII (1947). These edicts
emphasized the significance of church music and pointed to
its place in the liturgy. The Christmas season of 1955 witnessed another encyclical to preserve Gregorian Chant, also
by Pius XII, entitled Musicae Sacrae Disciplina. An encyclical entitled Musicam Sacram of 1967 was the result of the
Second Vatican Ecumenical Council. It sought liturgical re-
newal and more formality in worship in the Universal Church.

In the United States many Catholic bishops have attempted through recent years to "upgrade" liturgy and music
in this church body. New orders of the mass have been pro-
claimed, such as "The General Instruction and The New Order of Mass" by the International Committee on English in
the Liturgy (1969). This directive was approved by Pope
Paul VI, and it reflects the latest encyclical concerning liturgical and musical deliberations of the Second Vatican Council. These documents were published in 1975. This huge
study included the role of music in the Roman Catholic Church
with recognition of its value in worship and its influence upon
the quality of experience ideally sought for worshipers. [63]

In many Catholic and Protestant churches the "guitar syndrome," began in the 1960's, forced local parishes to accept vernacular music which sprang from the folk-rock influence of young people. This style of music is, unfortunately, still the practice among many Roman Catholic Churches. The distinction between low and high mass also has been largely eliminated in most churches of this faith. Thus, some congregations may have two to six persons leading them (frequently with guitars) in the musical portions of the liturgy. To better understand the dilemma of the contemporary Roman Catholic Church, a review of that body's association with Gregorian Chant is necessary.

The Gregorian Chant Today

The contemporary Roman Catholic Church is involved in a dilemma. It is obliged by history and custom to revere Gregorian Chant, but it is also faced with the fact that the chant does not appear to serve the emotional worship needs of the laity of the twentieth century. This gradual evolution had its genesis in the nineteenth century through the influence of the Romantic style of music of that era. The Papacy declared that the churches were using music which was histrionic and "profane"; that it glorified the performing forces rather than God. That led to the Motu Proprio of Pope Pius X in 1903. Thus, an entire set of liturgical standards was outlined for the Universal Roman Catholic Church in an effort to revitalize its music. From that time until the present there has been a concerted effort by the Vatican to maintain the custom established by the early Church fathers. However, the worldwide decline of the Latin language has caused the Vatican to recognize that the influence of the Church is being eroded by vernacular and secular influences. Therefore, some of the strict demands of the Motu Proprio have been modified to include the notion that a new view of Roman Catholic liturgy is necessary in order to serve the needs of the twentieth-century Catholic.

So, while the contemporary Roman Catholic Church respects the Gregorian Chant in name, it is attempting to modernize its liturgy to meet the demands of the laity. Therefore, the central musical standard--the Gregorian Chant --has come into question as being unsuitable for modern needs. "It is no longer sufficient to have the keys of the past to open the doors of the future."[64]

It is recognized, then, that music as a unifying element

for the congregation is needed, and that there must be an
adaptation of the Church's liturgy to present day demands.
Therefore, intonations in the vernacular (in the United States
in English) are being sought by courageous clerical leaders
determined to revitalize liturgical and musical practices for
the Roman Church. It may be some years hence before this
dilemma--the anathema to the Gregorian liturgy--is resolved.

In the Episcopal Church in America some of the larger
congregations have maintained the tradition of male choirs
(boys and men) for use in their major services, although many
churches with strong music programs have embraced the high-
church liturgy by employing mixed-voice choirs in formal
services. Latin anthems are used freely, although the rest
of the Episcopal mass is said in English. The lesser services usually have simpler liturgy involving the congregation
in all responses (similar to Roman Catholic custom) led by
the organist and clergy, sans choir. Some small Episcopal
churches have choirs which sing the chants and responses
mostly in unison from the Book of Common Prayer, newly
revised and published in 1977. At this writing, work is being done to supersede the 1940 Episcopal hymnal, with projected publication in the late 1980's.

SUMMARY

Since the objective of this book is to contribute to the improvement of choral procedures in the many phases of the field,
the singing in corporate religious activity demands a significant amount of attention. As the historical overview above
has attempted to delineate, it is religiously inspired music
that has been the catalyst for most of the choral music progress through the ages. Therefore, persons involved in church
music (including all of the clergy) should be vitally concerned
with achieving a level of performance and repertoire which
significantly enhances the act of corporate worship. We have
observed that there has been a demise in the influence of
church music over the centuries. As a whole, church music
leadership has relinquished its effectiveness, and this state
of affairs is to be deplored. In the interest of up-grading
the quality of all church music, it is this writer's hope that
strong, imaginative leadership among all persons now involved
in the field (as well as coming generations) will aggressively
pursue a renaissance in the quality of its musical offerings.
This charge strongly implies the recognition that religious
orders must undergird such a movement with funds adequate

to meet these needs--limited as they may be in the difficult
economic climate in which we find ourselves.

NOTES

1. Charles L. Etherington, Protestant Worship Music, Its
   History and Practice (New York: Holt, Rinehart and
   Winston, 1962), p. 15.
2. Ibid., p. 15.
3. Ibid., p. 16.
4. Ibid., p. 20.
5. Ibid., p. 23.
6. Ray Robinson and Allen Winold, The Choral Experience
   (New York: Harper's College Press, Harper & Row,
   1976), p. 10.
7. Etherington, op. cit., p. 26.
8. Robinson & Winold, op. cit., p. 10.
9. Karl Gustav Fellerer, The History of Catholic Church
   Music (Baltimore: Helicon Press, 1961), p. 9.
10. Donald Jay Grout, A History of Western Music, rev.
    ed. (New York: W.W. Norton, 1973), p. 14.
11. Willi Apel, Harvard Dictionary of Music (Cambridge:
    Harvard University Press, 1964), p. 24.
12. Grout, op. cit., p. 22.
13. Fellerer, op. cit., p. 34.
14. Ibid., p. 37.
15. Apel, op. cit., p. 768.
16. Fellerer, op. cit., p. 41.
17. Ibid., p. 44.
18. Etherington, op. cit., p. 47.
19. Grout, op. cit., p. 70.
20. Fellerer, op. cit., p. 55.
21. Ibid., p. 56.
22. Etherington, op. cit., p. 93.
23. Ibid., p. 98.
24. Erik Routley, The Church and Music (London: Gerald
    Duckworth, 1950), p. 125.
25. Etherington, op. cit., p. 110.
26. Apel, op. cit., p. 76.
27. Grout, op. cit., p. 322.
28. Fellerer, op. cit., p. 127.
29. Ibid., p. 128.
30. Elwyn A. Wienandt, Choral Music of the Church (New
    York: The Free Press, 1965), p. 105.
31. Baker's Biographical Dictionary of Musicians, 4th rev.
    ed. (New York: G. Schirmer, 1940), p. 801.

32. Grout, op. cit., p. 434.
33. Ibid., p. 355.
34. Manfred F. Bukofzer, Music in the Baroque Era (New York: W.W. Norton, 1947), p. 293.
35. Ibid., p. 381.
36. Paul Henry Lang, Handel (New York: W.W. Norton, 1966), p. 692.
37. Ibid., p. 696.
38. Wienandt, op. cit., p. 186.
39. Ibid., p. 186.
40. Routley, op. cit., p. 157.
41. Etherington, op. cit., p. 152.
42. Ibid., p. 153.
43. Ibid., p. 154.
44. Ibid., p. 155-156.
45. Routley, op. cit., p. 159.
46. Etherington, op. cit., p. 161.
47. Ibid., p. 463.
48. Ibid., p. 163.
49. Ibid., p. 167.
50. Wienandt, op. cit., p. 309.
51. Ibid., p. 369.
52. Routley, op. cit., p. 175.
53. Ibid., pp. 174-176.
54. Ibid., pp. 177-180.
55. Ibid., pp. 186-191.
56. Ibid., pp. 194-195.
57. Fellerer, op. cit., pp. 168-191.
58. Ibid., p. 193.
59. Ibid., p. 195.
60. Ibid., p. 195-196.
61. Ibid., p. 197.
62. Wienandt, op. cit., p. 437.
63. Austin Flannery, O. P., General Editor, Vatican Council II (Collegeville, Minn.: The Liturgical Press, 1975), pp. 80-97.
64. Lucien Deiss, C. S. Sp., Spirit and Song of the New Liturgy (Cincinnati: World Library Publications, 1970), p. 18.

REVIEW QUESTIONS FOR CHAPTER 10

(1) What are the two factors which are especially pertinent for the church choir director to consider in dealing with his/her ensembles?

(2) What role does liturgy play in the church choir situation?

(3) Cite the influence of Greek culture (especially music) in the development of our musical heritage.

(4) What role did music play in early Christian liturgy?

(5) How did pagan practices affect our early Christian church music?

(6) What effect did Gregorian chant have upon early church music?

(7) Cite the influence of the Trope upon early church music.

(8) Discuss the conditions in Europe during the Middle Ages which affected (and conditioned) music in the church.

(9) What was (is) organum, and how did it influence the development of church music composition?

(10) What effect did the emergence of polyphony have upon the Gregorian chant?

(11) What was (is) "conductus"?

(12) Describe the evolution of the motet and its characteristics.

(13) What effect did the German Reformation have upon church music?

(14) Discuss the effect which the English Reformation had upon church music in England.

(15) Why was the Baroque Period of music history so influential in developing church music of that period?

(16) Discuss the character of the Passions and Magnificats in sixteenth- to eighteenth-century Europe and England and the influence polyphony had upon musical development of those centuries.

(17) With the emergence of the cantata and oratorio, what changes occurred in musical composition?

(18)   What were the Protestant substitutions for the Mass, and how did this effort influence church music?

(19)   What effect did Methodism and the Wesleys have upon English church music?

(20)   Describe the American scene of choral music from circa 1730 to 1850.

(21)   Trace the status of the Liturgical Movement of the Roman Catholic Church and its influence (or lack of it) upon musical practices of that church.

(22)   What role does the "symphonic mass" play in contemporary church and/or concerted music in Europe and the United States and Canada?

(23)   What efforts have been made by Roman Catholic bishops to "upgrade" liturgical music?

(24)   What is the role of the Gregorian chant in today's Roman Catholic and liturgical Protestant churches?

● Chapter 11:
CONTEMPORARY CHURCH MUSIC CONCEPTS

The rapidly changing world of the last two decades of the twentieth century may defy any generalization about what church music will be like at the dawn of the twenty-first century. The worship of deities from the beginning of time has never really changed due to humanity's need for and desire to express recognition of a superior, mysterious force. No matter how religiously sophisticated the human being becomes, there is still that basic component of striving for contact with an existing force beyond.

DEFINING WORSHIP

The following definitions are presented in an effort to arrive at a basic understanding concerning the nature of worship and, consequently, the role that music plays in the act of corporate worship.

> The term "worship" is used to denote a wide range of activities, from inner states of mind to overt acts, simple or complex. [1]

According to Dr. John Spencer, Professor of Religion at Kalamazoo College, the word "worship" has a variety of connotations, some of which may be described as follows:

> It is a relationship, rather than a psychological quality, which really cannot be defined.

> It is acknowledgment and celebration of worth.

> It is a sense of awe which renders us completely helpless to predict or control our relationship with God--the ultimate reality of life.

> In worship we celebrate a God which is utterly beyond human manipulation.

The great nineteenth-century philosopher Martin Buber
has stated that worship is the response to that which is
"wholly other." It is a person's sense of dependence and
also recognition of that dependency.

The Interpreter's Dictionary of the Bible, Volume IV,
states that the word "worship" derives from the Saxon "worth-
ship," and means literally the "attitude and activity designed
to recognize and describe worth."

According to the Reverend Dr. Byron Bangert, "[w]or-
ship always has a ritual.... Our various rituals constitute
the form or pattern, in terms of which the drama of the worship service unfolds. To worship is to participate in a
drama, the story of who we are, and who God is, and what
that means. Above all, this drama is the story of our life
together with God."

MUSIC AND WORSHIP

Lovelace and Rice cite "four main characteristics of music
which give it an organic relation to worship":

1. The element of mystery which surrounds both
    [music and worship].

2. Music and worship are interwoven with the
    emotions; ... "both are capable of expression
    that is personal and universal."

3. The third point of contact between worship and
    music lies in their creativity. Worship is
    man's creative encounter with God.... Music
    is closely related to this point of creativity,
    for the source of all great church music is the
    elusive moment of inspiration which is a glimpse
    of God revealed to the composer....

4. Music has an affinity to language, for both are
    forms of communication evolving from the im-
    pulse to give voice to the feelings and express
    thoughts. [2]

The expression of worship in the company of others
"stands out for the total orientation of life towards God; expressed both through stylized liturgical action, and spontaneous
common praise." [3]

Worship as an Art

Some persons may be reluctant to consider worship
as an art, or the arts in worship, for fear that such an interpretation will detract from their worship experience.   However, Wolfe, Dickinson, and Dickinson have stated the issue
concisely:

> Worship is an art in that, like other arts, it has
> something to say about the spiritual life of man and,
> like them, it utilizes materials and instruments to
> say it.... Increase of awareness, greater depths
> of feeling, greater riches of meaning--these are the
> contributions of the arts to worship.   They enable
> the church to appeal to the whole being of man,
> heart, mind, soul and strength. [4]

Since the fine arts include music, architecture, poetry, and drama, which are predominant in a corporate worship service, one may conclude that to conduct public worship
properly and to better serve the worshiper, an understanding
of these subjects is essential.   The appeal of these arts is

> ... largely to the imagination.   It should be clear,
> therefore, that public worship is closer to the fine
> arts than to the practical.   At least among Chris-
> tians, public worship seems to be best of all the
> fine arts. [5]

> Man turns to music and other arts to enrich his
> life, and to express his deepest needs and emotions.
> In the church, music is an applied art--it is Art
> with a purpose--not just art for art's sake. [6]

Church music makes an important contribution to the elements
of worship chiefly through its emotional appeal.   In vocal music, however, there is also the added element of instruction
through the text.

> Church music should be to illuminate, to enrich,
> and to aid in the mystical process of communicating
> --man to man, man to God, and even more impor-
> tantly, God to man....   An anthem can teach,
> preach, comment, enrich and support the message
> the minister wishes to convey. [7]

Moreover, by serving the elements of worship, church music

has the potential of improving the quality of the worship experience for the congregation as well as for the choir.

Music in Worship

Church music is a form of worship; it does not just
set the stage for worship. Its performance or reception is
an integral part of the act of worship. The choir rehearsal
also may be considered an act of worship in that it is dedicated to serving loftier purposes than personal desires.
Careful preparation of significant music for the church service can provide a kind of religious experience for choristers.
The final objective of the program should be to achieve a high
level of worship experience for both performers and congregation.

The Status of Music in Worship

A controversial question in the field of church music
is the status of music in the worship service. Ministers and
church musicians have often been at odds concerning the role
which music plays in worship. One of the problems involves
order--that is, at what intervals in the service should the
music be introduced. When church music is considered to
be an integral part of worship, rather than an embellishment
of worship, it is better able to function in its intended capacity. Church music should not play a merely "decorative"
role; rather it should become that integral part of worship
which will allow it to function advantageously and effectively
in the worship service.

Edith Lovell Thomas describes the role of music in
worship as

> ... first, the preparation and presentation in the
> worship services of such religious music as is
> worthy of being offered up to the Almighty God
> and of being shared with those who make up the
> fellowship of the church. We believe that music
> should be performed not as an end in itself, but
> always within the objective of more meaningful
> worship for all who attend. The second purpose
> ... is ... to provide many opportunities for indi-
> vidual growth and expression. 8

Mursell states,

> Music, in fact, does convey, not the intellectual,
> but the emotional meanings of human life and ex-
> perience. [9]

The statements above imply that one's life can be
more meaningful through church musical experiences.   When
the church choir experience is significant, it eases the difficult task of choir recruitment.   It minimizes the elements of
duty or service and stresses satisfaction through participation.
Choir members have a right to expect this church activity to
be musically and spiritually rewarding to them.   The preparation of the music as well as its performance can enhance
the worship experience for the choir members.

> Since music is the expression of feeling, and one's
> feelings are of the spirit, it is one of the unique
> characteristics of music that it can satisfy the na-
> tural urge to find contact with the spiritual forces
> beyond one's self and to become identified with
> them. [10]

Hartshorn's statement brings into sharp focus the fact
that through music, especially church music, one can satisfy
a desire to make contact with the spiritual forces that are
"beyond one's self."   These are expressed as follows with
musical expression woven into the fabric of the corporate
worship framework:

1.   Litany--acts of prayer and praise, with a fixed
     response on the part of the choir and the congre-
     gation.

2.   Psalms--adoration and dependence, chanted in
     some liturgies.

3.   Collects--communal prayers (usually not musical).

4.   Sacred chants, hymns and anthems.

Music, then, should be regarded as a form of worship
rather than an adjunct to the worship service.   It is from
this vantage that the philosophy of church music should be
formulated.   Proceeding from this orientation to other considerations, church music can be most meaningful for both
congregation and choir.   Dr. Bangert further states, "[I]t

helps me to think of the anthem or other music as an expression of faith, or beauty, or love, that is offered by some member or members to the rest of us as a gift ... and it is offered for the refreshment of our souls. "

Lovelace and Rice cite four chief characteristics of music which give it an organic relationship to worship:

1. "The first similarity between music and worship lies in the element of mystery which surrounds both. Beauty cannot be easily explained and defined.... Why does a particular chord in one composition add mystery and excitement while in another it is tame and even tasteless? No one can say. "[11]

2. Music and worship are both inextricably intertwined with emotions.

    Music is a language in its own right, and, as an art, a means of communication. [12]

3. A third point of contact between worship and music lies in their interacting creativity.

    Worship is a creative encounter of man with God.... Each moment of worship is a new, fresh, creative, and spiritual quest. [13]

4. Music has an affinity to language; it can be the means of expression of thoughts, especially when wedded to a text.   Language and music are

    ... forms of communication evolving from the impulse to give voice to the feelings and to express thoughts. Plainsong and the chant are merely heightened speech, making use of the rising and falling inflections of the words themselves to provide the melodic line. The use of high and low pitches heightens the emotional impact of words, and the timbre or quality of the voice in speech ... is merely sustained or dramatized in song. [14]

MUSICAL PERFORMANCE AND WORSHIP

The Roman Catholic Papacy has discouraged the use of any music which attracts attention to the individual rather than

to the act of worship.   This introduces the concept that both
the character of the music and the attitude of the performer(s)
must be subservient to the worship goals of the church service.   The objective of the church music program should be
to provide leadership in the act of worship; it should never
be presented for the sake of performance alone.   However,
the very location of some choir lofts puts the choir at a disadvantage in its leadership of worship.   Palmer states,

> The worst thing about our church music is not apt
> to be the quality but the location of the singers and
> the concert psychology which results therefrom. [15]

The Choir Loft and Worship

In churches which have a split chancel, obvious movements and mechanical details involved in the presentation of
music in the service are kept to a minimum.   Obviously,
then, the more a choir is exposed, the more distracting are
the physical movements that occur in performance.   Palmer
presents a caricature of a typical choir situation:

> Perch a lot of people up in serried rows behind
> the minister and under the constant gaze of the con-
> gregation, and then have a director stand up on a
> stool beside the pulpit with his back to the congre-
> gation, coat-tails flying, and wave a baton with all
> the fervent gyrations of an orchestra director, and
> you may have a concert but hardly a service of
> worship. [16]

The director and certainly the choir members must always
remember that in most choir lofts every movement is under
surveillance.   Restlessness, whispering and inattention are
distracting to the congregation as well as to the other choir
members.   Often the "offender" does not realize how conspicuous such actions are to others.   The good example set
by the choir director should be the basis for establishing
choir loft deportment.   Usually, for adult choirs, a simple
statement to remind the members that they are being observed
at all times is sufficient.   Social pressure of the group can
also solve the problem.   Often, the choir president will be
the most appropriate person to speak to an "offender."

The placement of choir lofts in newly built or remod-
eled Protestant churches has experienced a radical change in

recent years.   Choir lofts and organs are now installed in
the rear of many sanctuaries, thus reflecting the more formal
atmosphere and influence of the Roman Catholic and Lutheran
liturgical practices.   This ancient tradition obviously documents the belief that church music should be devoid of glo-
rifying the individual rather than God; that seeing the performing forces tends to detract the congregation from the act of
worshiping God.

Worship Attitude

        It is important for all people involved in church music,
including the pastor, to be aware of the tendency of the non-
liturgical church service toward the "concert psychology" referred to in Palmer's quote above.   Music in these more informal worship services often tends to divide the elements of
the worship ritual into fragments.   This, in turn, breaks the
continuity of the worship service sequence.   Church musicians
and clergymen should analyze the elements of worship for continuity and effectiveness and then attempt to minimize any apparent irregularities or inordinately abrupt changes.

        Hartshorn, in discussing the effect of music upon the
emotions of people, makes a statement which is valuable in
gaining a clearer perspective on the matter of worship attitude in relation to music:

            Music ... is expressive of and appeals to the same
            qualities of mind and spirit which have led men to
            great religion, great art and idealistic forms of
            government.   By its very nature, music intensifies
            and emotionalizes the ideas with which it is asso-
            ciated.   [Classic examples of this are musical set-
            tings of the Twenty-third Psalm, the Lord's Prayer
            and the Beatitudes.]
            ... In fact, music is such a potent means of ex-
            pression that it is impossible to exercise care and
            discrimination in selecting the concepts with which
            it is to be associated in order that the emotions
            will be related to the areas of experience that con-
            tribute to the betterment of human life.[17]

        The statement quoted above is brought into sharper
focus regarding worship through music in a statement by Davies and Grace:

> ... the hearers are not an audience, but a gather-
> ing of fellow-worshippers whose primary interest
> in the proceedings is not [necessarily] musical. 18

To some people, music can conceivably be a foreign
or disturbing element in their worship experiece. The service of the Society of Friends (Quakers), for instance, is aus-
tere, devoid of liturgy, preaching, or music. (Some of their
congregations in the Midwest, however, have preachers and
choirs.) Most corporate worship experiences do require
some degree of verbal expression. In this way, the congregation is mentally prepared to respond to individual and/or
group leadership in worship. There are times, nevertheless,
when church music seems to be a distraction to the worship
experience of the congregation. This condition is probably
the result of one or more of four factors:

1. The poor quality of the musical performance;

2. The unconscious attitude on the part of the choir
    and congregation that church music is entertain-
    ment;

3. The sequence of the music in relation to the rest
    of the service;

4. The attitude of some clergymen and music direc-
    tors that the place and function of music in wor-
    ship need not be directly related to the theme and
    mood of the service.

Quality of Performance

Poor quality of a musical performance usually is the
result of insufficient rehearsal and/or inadequate technique
by the choir. There surely can be no argument against the
ideal of continually raising the performance standards of
church choirs. This study is devoted to the techniques and
procedures which should aid choir directors in improving the
quality of performance of their choirs.

The Attitude of the Director and Singers

A "prima donna" attitude on the part of some directors and singers (whether solo or ensemble) may create a

climate alien to the worship needs of the congregation.   A
sincere, personal dedication to the worship objectives of a
particular church service is a prerequisite to any musical
offering for that purpose.   There is evidence that people oc-
cupying the pews are quick to sense a detached or apathetic
attitude on the part of a person or persons involved in the
presentation of church music.

    An official statement, which defines the standards for
church music and musicians in the Roman Catholic Church,
cites the following ideals:

> ... Church music cannot in any sense be "enter-
> tainment" music, however inspirational or lofty.
>
> ... There must be exclusion of any church music
> which evinces a spirit of egoism on the part of the
> composer, or music which would appear simply as
> a challenge to musical skill.
>
> ... There must be the indispensable quality of
> reverence, the music must be recognizably "holy."
>
> ... Church music must exclude whatever is bom-
> bastic, contrived, merely dramatic, ingenuous,
> sensuous, borrowed from worldly associations, friv-
> olous, trite or too esoteric or "arty."
>
> ... Church music is used with liturgy for the edi-
> fication of the faithful.   It is necessary, therefore,
> that the music for divine worship be apprehended
> as a means of promoting in the faithful a sense of
> God's presence and of the serious need to pray.... [19]

    Perhaps these Roman Catholic conventions are too in-
hibiting for some Protestant congregations.   Some persons
respond very "favorably" to dramatic music which acts as an
exclamation mark when set to a biblical text.   Free church
Protestants have purposely avoided Roman Catholic liturgy
because they felt it was stereotyped, ornate, or uninspiring.
Thus, the quotes above should be applied to individual congregations as they suit the situation.

    However, another significant comment which Dr. Ban-
gart makes is that lectionaries for strict liturgical services
often do not relate to the minister's thoughts regarding contemporary concerns of the congregation, or of society as a

whole.   Therefore, in the "free church" tradition the liturgical dictates for a given Sunday worship service do not necessarily speak to the immediate concerns of a pastor or congregation.   Consequently, many clergymen follow their inclinations to deviate from prescribed liturgical patterns, and
thus, there needs to be great flexibility in the vocal music
of such churches.

The Sequence of Music in Worship

Church music is often ineffective, regardless of how
well it is presented, when it is either isolated or placed in
an incongruous sequence relating to the continuity of the
church service.   The musical offerings should be incorporated
in such a manner that there is logical thematic progression
of ideas.   The musical contribution should never be inserted
into the liturgical pattern of the worship service without a
specific purpose in mind.

The status given to music in worship has been cited
above as extremely important to the effectiveness of its contribution to the worship service.   If one consults the bulle-
tins of many churches, it will be observed that the greater
the departure from liturgy, the more the elements of the
worship service tend to lose their continuity.   For instance,
the anthem and offertory selections should never assume the
aspect of "special music."   Announcements of musical offerings by the minister tend to relegate the musical efforts to
a special place outside the context of the worship sequence.
These "credits" may be given in a sincere attempt to emphasize the importance of the music or the individual(s) performing it; however, comments about the "special music" are
usually out of place in any normal service sequence.

"We shall now be favored by a vocal selection by
Miss Mary Jones."   Each time such an announcement is made, something happens to the spirit of
the service akin to what happens to an electric current every time the line is grounded. [20]

If a worship service is systematically planned and the
bulletin carefully printed, there should be little or no need
for verbal announcement regarding selection and sequence.
It seems quite obvious, then, that when the musical portion
of the service is a "special" by the choir or soloist, it is
most difficult for those performing as well as listening to

overcome the feeling that the selection is really not a part
of the service. When this occurs, church music tends to
assume the role of a concert performance rather than an act
of worship. It is, therefore, imperative that church musicians and ministers realistically and carefully examine this
problem as it relates to their individual situations.

On the other hand, in formal liturgical services, where
the order of worship is memorized, there is danger that the
sequence may become a sterile, meaningless ritual through
which the worshiper passes as a matter of habit.   In contrast, the freer, less formal order of worship often provides
a fresh, spontaneous experience for the worshipers.   It is
the responsibility of leaders of worship in either category of
service, therefore, to anticipate pitfalls such as those cited
above, and then seek to avoid those elements.

The Attitude of the Clergy

The attitude of the clergy can either ensure or under-
mine the status of music as an integral part of worship.
Abrupt breaks of any sort, such as announcements or unrelated comments at the close of musical selections, can mar
an important moment of worship for musicians and congregation.   However, this is not to say that a period of announcements is necessarily out of place in a worship sequence.   It
may begin with words of greeting and welcome to members
and visitors, informing them that this particular congregation
is open in its fellowship and worship to all who come and
want to share mutual concerns which identify those present
as a community.   Such communication can provide substance
to the worship of God, and the witness to the one body which
is comprised of the individual members.   This portion can be
considered as a part of the liturgical progression of the service if it is conducted with care and dignity.

Ministers who consider church music as merely background while seating people, opening windows, "stirring up
people," and creating a "breather" for them in the worship
routine prostitute the role of music in worship.   This predi-
lection tends to cause a similar attitude on the part of the
congregation.   Therefore, it is the minister who must set
an example of respect toward the music which should be consonant with the worship atmosphere.

THE MINISTRY OF MUSIC

Definition

The ministry of music, like any other ministry, represents more than a program of activities. The title itself implies the serving of people in one of the most important facets
of church life, namely, the musical entity.

The ministry of music is a distinct ministry in itself.
It ministers through music, just as religious education serves
through the church school program. It should be wide in
scope; it should not be just a performance by one or more
choirs.

> ... the music ministry in a church is an agency
> existing on an organized basis for the purpose of
> developing a comprehensive music education pro-
> gram that will minister to all areas of church
> life. [21]

The Need That It Serves

The primary service that the ministry of music ren-
ders occurs during the corporate worship periods of the congregation and church school programs. The secondary service that it performs is to provide religious and music education through preparation of programs for these corporate worship experiences.

Obviously, these two categories cannot be distinctly
separated from each other. Corporate worship is also a
form of religious education. Furthermore, religious education and music education are inseparable in church musical
activities.

> The ministry of music is designed for all the
> [church] members. It exists for the masses as
> well as for the talented. It finds expression in
> every area of worship, education and evangelism....
> It is a church program for all the church. [22]

Church Music a Means to an End

The church music program is not an end in itself,

but a means of achieving a more meaningful religious experience.   It is a vehicle through which men "practice the presence of God. "   If one accepts this premise, then church music must be presented as an act of worship rather than as
a musical performance primarily for exploitation, entertainment, or personal gratification.

Central Objective

No organizational structure can become a substitute
for an inspiring experience for the singers or the congregation.   Thus, the chief objective of the ministry of music
must be to prepare the music of the worship service in the
best manner possible within the limitations of the group or
individuals participating.   All other factors entering the picture are secondary.

AREAS AND SCOPE OF FUNCTION

It has been stated that the ministry of music should provide
varied experiences for all church members, listeners as
well as participants.   Ideally, in addition to adult choir activities and congregational singing, there should be an extensive program of choral work for younger age groups.

> No church choral program, and no school music
> program will ever be successful unless there is
> a broadened program of singing activities. 23

Multiple-choir Programs

There seems to be little disagreement in the field of
church music as to the desirability of a multiple-choir program serving the needs of a total church program.   Some
churches have double morning worship services; others also
have evening services in addition to the morning worship.
Thus, the services of at least two choirs are needed.   Rarely
is any one choir requested to perform for more than one
service per week.   There are still a few choirs which sing
at two identical morning worship services, but the trend seems
to be to utilize youth or children's choirs to sing regularly at
one of these two identical services.   A multiple-choir program can effectively serve the church program in religious
education if it is well-coordinated with church school and

youth activities.   Evening youth programs afford ideal time
slots for youth choir rehearsals as a regular part of the
schedule.   Younger age choirs may also profit by rehearsals
conducted during "junior church" sessions (when children leave
the adult church service to have their own activities).

Obviously, most churches cannot accommodate multiple
choirs regularly in their formal church worship services.
Therefore, some provision should be made for these younger
choirs to serve in the church school worship.   Unless a choir
has definite responsibilities and motivations for its existence
--beyond the mere learning of music--it will have difficulty
in maintaining interest and high standards.   There must exist
an experience-centered goal of sharing the values in the music and the text.   Music and religious education evolve as a
natural concomitant to a significant experience for those persons involved.   Getting together to sing and to learn music
and scripture is valuable in itself, but, in order for a group
to attain its maximum potentialities, the preparation efforts
must culminate in the presentation and sharing the results of
its work with others.   In other words, the desire to perform
must be directed into more significant channels than a mere
display of talent or proficiency in musical endeavor.   Ideally,
it might be characterized by the following saying: "I have
tasted something good; now I want to share it with you," or,
"I have learned something valuable and I want to tell you
about it."   The performance in this instance is not the ex-
hibition of talent and accomplishment, but the offering of these
gifts is a capacity of leadership in worship.

Choirs and the Church School

Fortunate are the congregations whose church school
personnel is aware of the contribution which an organized
music effort can make to its program.   Unfortunately, however, since short periods of time are allocated to church
school activity, most of these people conclude that there is
insufficient time to include organized musical activity is as
part of their program.   They may think that music is not
actually a form of religious education, whereas, "[m]usic
is many times a means of spiritual interpretation that succeeds where nothing else can."[24]

Religious Education Through Church Music

Interviews with individuals who have had significant

long-term choir experiences have indicated that, for the most part, they have learned more scriptural passages and have arrived at a deeper meaning of the scriptures through singing sacred music than through their religious education activities. In spite of the mechanical problems involved in finding time and place for music in the church school curriculum, there should be no fundamental reason why some degree of music education cannot become an integral part of that program. This could logically be a choir (large or small) in each church school grade or department, depending upon enrollment. In smaller churches there can be a "cherub" choir for very young children, a primary age choir, junior age choir, and a junior-senior high school age choir. Furthermore, where can church leadership training be utilized to better advantage than in the church educational program? What better place can exist, then, besides regular school musical experiences, for the adult choir singer of the future to begin training and to acquire experience in church music leadership? A reappraisal of the place of music in religious education by both church school and church music personnel seems necessary so that each can be informed how to best serve the other.

> Close correlation of the music taught in the choir with the curriculum the choristers are studying in their church school is an imperative commonly disregarded. Sometimes the two programs are rivals or even opposed to each other. How the singers function as live worshipers in both church and school is a responsibility that rests squarely on the shoulders of music leaders and teachers. Rewarding results come only from careful, cooperative planning. Without this, boys and girls receive fragmentary impressions due to disparate efforts and uncoordinated fare.[25]

If church musicians and church school leaders can be made aware of the possibilities of religious education through music, they will probably make more serious attempts to include music in the total church curriculum. Realistically, it behooves them to become familiar with each other's resources in order to correlate material or to suggest new material. The challenge presented here demands that religious educators and church musicians spend more time and effort exploring the possibilities of this ideal.

The Role of Adult Choir Leadership

Even though multiple choirs serve specific needs of a church music program, in reality the leadership and inspiration starts at the "top" and "works down." The adult choir, then, should assume the responsibility for stimulating interest and setting an example for emulation throughout the church choir program. The members of all the other choirs should aspire to eventual membership in this adult group, which should represent the highest achievement and best possible opportunity for service through music in that church. If the over-all choral program is to grow and improve, continual development of the adult choir is imperative.

One of the church music programs that was reviewed for this study revealed that at one time the high school choir was a stronger and better singing organization than the adult choir. The director, who was unable to work well with the adult group at the time this situation existed, was loved by the young people. The result was that morale was so poor among the adults, they felt unneeded, and the adult choir disintegrated. The youth had little or no respect for the adult choir, nor did they have the desire to become members of the senior group when they became eligible. The attitude of the high school group was entirely changed when the adult choir, under a new director, increased its membership and demonstrated unusually high standards of performance. Consequently, the young people now had an excellent example to emulate.

The role of music in the church is more than an effective organization--a busy program. Rather, it must be concerned with the church as a living organism, which acts as a magnet to draw the whole person into a meaningful relationship with God in whatever manner each individual deems to define it.

Vocal and personal development will follow logically if the techniques that are used are based upon sound principles of both music and religious education.

THE ROLE OF THE MINISTER OF MUSIC

Definition and Function

Traditionally, the person responsible for the choral

efforts in a church is called the choir director, choirmaster
(common in Europe), or the organist-director. With the
emergence of larger-scale church choral activities requiring
a full-time staff member, the term "minister of music" has
come into wider use. The name itself implies that church
music, being a spiritual influence, is comparable to that of
the other ministries of the church. In some instances,
churches combine the positions of the minister of religious
education and minister of music.

Presbyterians and Southern Baptists have pioneered the
bestowal of ministerial status upon the church musician. The
Westminster Presbyterian Choir School is the oldest one of
its kind in the country. The Southern Baptists have incorporated separate schools of church music in some of their
seminaries and Lutheran Seminaries also give music a great
deal of emphasis.

Most churches are forced by size and financial condition to seek part-time music personnel. All too often, these
persons are attracted to the church music position, not through
a sense of "calling," but as a means of earning extra income.
This attitude of materialism may limit the effectiveness of a
church music program. However, it is not to be assumed
that a person on a part-time basis cannot have a sense of
being called to the work.

> And this ... leader in the church must understand
> that he is not merely a musician. His work in-
> volves all that the secular profession of music does
> and much more. In the church, he is a leader of
> worship and a religious educator. He falls short
> of a true conception of his responsibility and priv-
> ilege, unless he comes to his work with a definite
> and conscious purpose to enrich the lives of people
> and to lead them into ways of spiritual impression,
> expression and experience. [26]

Regardless of the place of music in a given church,
it is the degree of self-consecration on the part of the music director which should be the guiding factor in determining his status in the church. The term "minister of music"
will be used frequently to refer to any person responsible
for the functioning of one or more choirs in the church. The
terms "director of music," "choir director," and "choirmaster" will also be used where applicable.

Relationship with the Pastor

The minister of music should recognize the pastor as the leader of all church life, a factor which ambitious choir directors sometimes overlook. Music has great latitude within the scope of church life, but the extent of its incorporation with the spiritual experiences of the congregation is dependent upon the attitude of the pastor. If the music program is unrelated to the needs of the congregation in the worship experience, it is possibly the result of the pastor's attitude or the inability of pastor and music director to work together effectively. Therefore, it is the obligation of the clergy to make a conscious effort to improve their knowledge of the place and function of music in the worship service with a sensitivity to the potential of music as a handmaiden of religious education.

It is important to underscore the fact that the minister of music and the pastor should have personal respect, trust, and vocational admiration for each other. Unconscious petty jealousies can develop on the part of both minister of music and pastor. Usually, friction arises through misunderstanding of purpose or lack of communication. Pastors often expect choir directors to "sense" what they need and want, without benefit of direct communication. An alert church musician can often compensate for this lack of consideration. However, the most satisfactory program is one that is planned in a staff meeting or individual conference. The basis for successful teamwork between pastor and minister of music should be mutual respect and confidence. Upon this foundation a policy can be developed to successfully serve the church under the leadership of the pastor. However, the final success of this music program depends a great deal upon the leadership qualities of the minister of music.

Relationships with the Music Committee or Council

The music committee of many Protestant churches consists of one or more members of the board of trustees and/or representatives from the board of deacons. This committee can cause problems for a music program, depending upon how musically oriented these persons are. Since only a few people are involved in this administrational structure, however, there is likely to be less friction with which to cope than would be experienced with an entire church board.

This arrangement ideally suits the church leadership whose
policy generally is "hands off the music as long as there
are no major problems."

There is an organizational tool which can be helpful
in the coordination of a total church music program: that
of a music council,

> ... upon whom rests the responsibility for the de-
> velopment of the graded music education program
> of the church. This includes the pastor (ex-officio),
> minister of music or director, the congregational
> song leader if other than the director, the church
> organist and/or church pianist, director of each
> choir, director of instrumental groups, an active
> deacon, president of the church choir, general
> chairman of choir sponsors, the associate super-
> intendent of training of the Sunday School, the song
> leader of the Training Union and other church lead-
> ers as needed. Additional personnel may be en-
> listed at the discretion of the minister of music
> and the pastor. If the church has a music com-
> mittee other than the music council, the chairman
> of this committee should also be a member. [27]

Dr. Sims indicates in the statement above that the
music council should meet at least monthly "for planning the
many phases of music activity." The duties of such a council are circumscribed by their need to develop a church-wide
music program. Some of the specific responsibilities of the
council are these

> 1. Develop promotional materials and projects
> 2. Plan yearly calendar of musical events
> 3. Plan music budget
> 4. Keep the objective of service through music
>   before music groups
> 5. Study objectives and plan and execute means of
>   meeting them. [28]

Relationships with the Congregation

Rapport between the choir and congregation (those oc-
cupying the pews) is one of the important, though unrecog-
nized, concerns of church life. The physical or "geograph-
ical" barrier--the location of the choir loft--which separates

the choir from any personal contact with the congregation, makes it difficult for the congregation to respond intimately to the efforts of the choir.

The full-time music staff member has a distinct advantage over the part-time music director. The former is more likely to meet the congregation in many surroundings other than just the formal worship services and, thus, may be able to assess the personal desires and attitudes of the congregation-at-large. In addition to contacts which the minister of music has with the music committee, he/she should also establish good rapport with the congregation as a whole.

The second major barrier to choir-congregation affinity is psychological. If a choir does not sing very well, the congregation is likely to develop an attitude of forebearance and/ or indifference. It is difficult under such circumstances to recruit new members because there is little incentive for people to join the group. On the other hand, when a choir is very proficient prospective choristers in the congregation may be discouraged from joining the group because they may feel incapable of attaining the high standards of the choir. Therefore, the choir director must try to convince the church-at-large that potentially the best sounding choirs are made up of "grass roots" singers. With encouragement and proper training these persons can eventually make a valuable contribution to the efforts of the choir. They must be assured that even if they do not have solo voices, they can be of significant value to the group, providing that the director is capable and patient leader. Later in this chapter there will be specific suggestions in regard to the problems of choir member recruitment from the ranks of the congregation.

THE CHURCH CHOIR

Many persons consider the adult church choir to be a chorus of voices singing only for the church services. A church choir, however, should be more than a group of singers. Therefore, it is important to discuss some definitions and functions of the church choir.

Definition and Function of the Choir

It might be said of the church choir that the members are "corporate preachers." According to Davies and Grace,

> The church choir is a section of church workers
> drawn from the congregation.... A church choir
> is therefore not an independent organization, but a
> small section of the congregation--we might call it
> an executive committee in the most literal sense,
> with the choirmaster as chairman--charged with the
> musical interests of the congregation. [29]

Wilson and Lyall emphasize the service element by saying,
"Singing in the church choir is an adventure in human service."[30]   Representing the Lutheran Church, Halter writes,
"The choir is part of the congregation and exists by its will
and permission."[31]   A point of view held by Methodist leadership states that a choir is a "dedicated group of people who
have joyfully accepted the opportunities provided by the choir
for advancing the Kingdom of God."[32]

        Probably the most comprehensive, and yet concise,
definition of the church choir is one made over a half century ago by Waldo W. Pratt, Professor in the Hartford Theological Seminary, and Lecturer in the Institute of Musical
Art:

> The choir is a properly specialized branch of the
> ministry and exists for the same purpose.   Like
> the ministry, it is to serve the congregation not
> only as leader in whatever it can do itself, and
> not only as substitute and representative in what-
> ever it cannot do itself directly, but also as teacher
> and inspirer of the congregation. [33]

Later in his book, Pratt concludes that the choir is "necessary to the fulfillment of music's mission as a handmaid of
religion."[34]

        From the quotes above three generalizations emerge:

1.   The choir is a leader in worship.
2.   The choir is a leader in religious education and
      music education.
3.   The choir personnel is drawn from the ranks of
      the congregation.

Some other factors to consider are the function of the choir
in relation to the general aims of the church, and the responsibilities of the choir as an organized unit of the church program, the congregation at large, and the individual choir member.

THE CHOIR MEMBER

Many churches invite non-members to sing in their choirs.
In these situations directors extend an eager welcome to anyone who can satisfy the musical demands of the ensemble.
Some ideas pertaining to church choir membership are cited
below.   They are not necessarily in agreement with each
other and are presented here to point to a diversity of opinion among the various church denominations.

Election by the Congregation

Some church policies embrace the philosophy of consonant moral and spiritual views on the part of choir members so as to be able to "minister through music."   The
member is "elected" during an official service of the congregation, or during a choir dedication service.   The newly-
elected member must be a bonafide member of the church
before being accepted as a member of the choir.   Choir
members are considered to be servants of the church in the
same manner as the church school teachers.   Unquestionably,
this concept of church choir membership places its personnel
in an ideal position.   Few persons involved in church music
would contend that this is not a visionary concept of the choir
situation in regard to personal qualifications of the members.

> Choir members must be selected with care.   To
> invite any and all people to sing in the choir is a
> serious mistake and frequently results in unpleasant
> episodes.   The choir proclaims the gospel through
> song just as the minister proclaims it through ser-
> mon.   Should not the choir member be as conse-
> crated and devoted to his task as the minister?
> Some standards should be set up and met.   When
> this is done, choir membership will be a greater
> spiritual force within the church. [35]

This Southern Baptist viewpoint above is to require
the choir member to be a consecrated Christian and member
of the church. [36]   Other church bodies which do not officially
set any specific requirements for choir membership feel that
too much rigidity will discourage growth of the choir.   Halter states a less rigid, yet specific attitude concerning church
choir membership:

> The ideal singer is first of all a Christian in more

than name.   Christianity is for him not an institu-
tion, but a way of life and a cause to be served....
He has spiritual understanding and balance. 37

The choir director, then, must by example, attempt
to bring all choir members closer to this ideal concept of
"choir member spirituality." However, most church governing bodies do not have official standards for church choir
membership.   Some Protestant church groups regard the
choir as an evangelistic arm of the church.   This "evangelistic arm" can hold two very important views.

1.   A fine choir may serve as a recruiting device to
     attract new members into the church through the
     choir.

2.   The other view is that a choir of professing Chris-
     tians can, through their personal actions and sing-
     ing ministry, influence "non-believers," thereby
     leading them into church membership.

In regard to the earlier viewpoint, it should be recognized that there are people for whom the preaching ministry
--and even the church itself--has lost some appeal, whose
enthusiasm might be rekindled through a significant church
music experience.   These persons are not necessarily insen-
sitive, selfish individuals with low moral standards.   On the
contrary, they may be sensitive people with attitudes reflecting the highest ideals of the church with possibilities of developing into devoted and dedicated church leaders.   The degree of spiritual leadership and musicianship of the choirmaster will certainly determine the effect of the music and
educative materials upon such an individual as described
above.

Those who criticize this mode of thinking cited here
concerning church choir membership requisites usually do so
on the basis of extreme examples, stating that they do not
want any persons ministering to them "who are not Christians" or whose morality does not suit their particular concepts.   It is not the purpose of this project to support or
refute the value of either notion regarding church choir membership.   It is rather to show that there is distinct value in
each conviction and that the individual's make-up and philosophy must govern the decision as to eligibility for choir membership.   In any church choir situation, it is the quality of
spiritual and musical leadership which significantly influences
the total development of its membership.

The Choir Member Cannot Be Stereotyped

An accurate or even adequate description of the typical church choir member is obviously impossible, if one takes into consideration individual differences among people. Conceivably, the choir member will be a person possessing some skill or potential in vocal production and musicianship. The range of ability of the participant can embrace novices as well as highly-trained musicians if the leader has the personal and professional capacity to bring together what each has to contribute to the whole. When people with great diversity can submerge their individual identities in the process of achieving the objectives of the choir, a powerful force can be unleashed in choral singing. One person's most significant contribution to the choir may be a sense of humor-- a leavening force in a rehearsal. Others may possess superior sight-reading skills and/or an excellent voice. These are all important factors in the maintenance of strong group morale. One may consider, therefore, that understanding and sincerity are the most important qualities for members of a volunteer church choir.

> All human beings possess the same sort of capacities; however, they may vary in the degree to which we possess them. [38]

It seems logical to conclude, on the basis of the quoted statement above, that the aim in choral singing should be to bring to as many people as possible a greater realization of their potential capacity to contribute to the group. It is ordinarily more difficult to work with a larger, less proficient choir than with a highly selective group. However, the church choir director should seek to widen the scope of participation, so that more people might benefit from stimulating musical experiences. A small, select group of highly trained people can be used when special occasions require performers with greater skill and technical perfection.

Potential Choir Members

The next step in this concept of the nature of the church choir member is to regard practically everyone in the congregation as a potential choir member. This idea is prevalent in the concept of membership for children's choirs, why not for adult choirs? Is this due to lack of means for motivating and educating potential adult choir singers? According to Leeder and Haynie,

> About 95 percent of our total population is estimated
> to be capable of musical response. We must recog-
> nize our responsibility to cultivate that need. 39

Obviously, it can be neither expected nor desired that
everyone sing in a church choir. There must be some "con-
sumers. " Yet, the quotation above implies that, in most
churches, more persons should be encouraged to participate
in the singing program. Among church musicians, it is generally agreed that at least 10 percent of the congregation
should be represented in the music program.

Therefore, instead of a select choir satisfying only
the requirements of the worship service and the director,
the objective also should be that of serving the needs of the
individual members for self-expression through music. In
accordance with this concept, it should be the aim of the director to see that all choir members find a meaningful experience through the preparation and the presentation of the
music of the church. Is there a better vehicle in the field
of general adult music education than the volunteer church
choir when the objectives include this concept of growth? If
this concept is to be honored, the demand for creative leadership by the director of music cannot be ignored. This realistic objective has support from Broudy, who states,

> As used in art, realism refers to both a kind of
> subject matter and a way of presenting it. Realis-
> tic art utilizes for its subject matter the objects
> and actions of ordinary people in ordinary life as
> opposed to highly idealized or romanticized scenes,
> characters and actions. 40

This, however, does not discharge the obligation of
the choir director to seek new materials and higher levels
of experience for his/her group. The objectives of most
people can be raised to new levels of aspiration as a result
of the vision and inspiration of the choir director's leadership. The educational aim of the minister of music, or
choir director, then, must be to bring as many people as
possible to a greater realization of their capacities--in this
case to make music which is dedicated to God in the worship
experience.

The desire to perform some act for the approval of
others is an established psychological concept. Therefore,
it is probable that a significant number of persons sitting in

the congregation would really like to be in the choir sharing
that experience of leadership and approval.   These laypeople
most likely have no illusions about their ability to perform
as soloists, but they probably harbor a desire to experience
something in the arts beyond their capabilities as individual
performers ("grass roots" concept).   The church choir can
be the means through which many more persons can find opportunity for self-expression.   The program of recruitment
must be organized so as to seek out and personally encourage
the individual to join the group.   Choir members' inducement
of these prospective members to join can greatly aid the director's recruitment efforts.

FACTORS NECESSARY FOR SERVING
CHOIR MEMBERS' NEEDS

Facilitating Learning

The specific and immediate needs of church choir
members, their role as choir singers, and the nature of
these needs, are not easily identified.   There are nine factors in learning, outlined in Symonds' articles published in
a series in the Teachers College Record (1955-1959), entitled,
"What Education Has to Learn from Psychology."   The articles were reprinted in booklet form in 1958 under the same
title.   (Chapter 3 should also be consulted for further information.)   The nine elements are considered by Symonds as
major factors governing learning.   They are listed under
these headings:

      1.   Motivation
      2.   Reward
      3.   Punishment
      4.   Learning is reacting
      5.   Whole versus part learning
      6.   Emotion and learning
      7.   Transfer and formal discipline
      8.   Individual differences
      9.   Origins of personality[41]

These factors of learning help to reveal some of the
needs of church choir members as they function in the capacity
of learners.   Each of the above, with possibly the exception
of "Punishment" and "Origins of personality," has a specific
relationship to the church choir situation:

Motivation (also see Chapter 3)

        The choir member should be strongly motivated to ful-
fill the role of choir singer. Symonds reminds us that interest is a strong motivating force; that the theory of "drive" is
"the basic motivating principle underlying human behavior."[42]
Symonds identifies these drives as "goals of human striving."[43]
Furthermore,

            Psychology would teach us that the motives for
            most human striving reside in the interpersonal re-
            lationship, for it is acceptance and approval that
            human beings most crave.[44]

        This is a point which the choir director often ignores
when failing to provide acceptance and approval for every
member, regardless of musical ability. "... [B]ehind mastery is the need for proving oneself and winning the approval
of others in almost every normal case."[45]

        Understanding the need for proving oneself and winning
the approval of others is reinforced by the seven "goals of
human striving" cited by Symonds.

            1.   The satisfaction of physiological needs
            2.   Safety
            3.   Acceptance
            4.   Approval, prestige, status
            5.   Self-esteem
            6.   Mastery, success, achievement
            7.   Independence[46]

        Of these seven categories of human striving, there are
four areas described which refer specifically to the needs of
the person filling the role of choir singer:

            1.   Acceptance
            2.   Approval, prestige, status
            3.   Self-esteem, self-respect, self-satisfaction
            4.   Mastery, success, achievement[47]

All four of these categories revolve around the individual's
need for some kind of reward for effort expended, and they
strongly influence continued interest in the choir in addition
to the "call of duty."

Reward

The element of reward serves to sustain interest and thus continues motivation toward seeking more and better experiences. Conversely, lack of success in any of the four areas listed above is likely to diminish the choir member's interest in the group and its activities. These four "goals of human striving," which find their orientation in the church choir situation, can be described as follows.

1. Acceptance--the feeling of being necessary to the welfare and goals of the organization, regardless of technical proficiency. A telephone call to the most humble choir member, indicating that he or she was missed at a rehearsal or a worship service, will quite likely renew that singer's interest in the organization--the feeling of being wanted. This underscores the need for "belonging."

2. Desire for approval and status by the choir member is sometimes overlooked by the choir director in the zeal to prepare the choir for its performances. The director must remember that a general compliment to the choir for any accomplishment, no matter how small, can be interpreted personally by each member, since each person is a part of that achievement. Even though accepted by their peers, the choir members' ultimate approval is dependent upon the "authority-figure" (the director). "[A]cceptance by peers is in part a function of and dependent upon acceptance by authority figures."[48]

3. Self-esteem or self-respect (or to a degree, self-satisfaction) is closely linked to the feeling of approval by the director. Symonds tells us,

> If our parents find pleasures in us, we find pleasure in ourselves; if they tend to admire us, we tend to admire ourselves; if they approve of us, we begin to approve of ourselves.[49]

In this context, when the choir director expresses congeniality toward and approval of the choir members (a parental relationship), they will usually develop a sense of self-esteem.

4. The element of mastery might be categorized better under the heading of "learning" for the purposes of our consideration. In order to progress, learners must have confidence in and respect for their leader. The director's attitude

and techniques must provide a solid psychological and technical basis upon which the singer can build.   An awareness
of having learned something is a form of reward for the individual.   The element of mastery and the achievement of
success play a great role in motivating choir members toward seeking more of the same kinds of experiences.   One
of the rewards for their efforts is the realization that they
are having experiences which will help them develop their
potentialities as singers.   The cliché "Nothing succeeds like
success" takes on real meaning for the church choir director.
As cited previously, one of the most significant comments
which directors can receive is to be told by choir members
that they dislike being absent from rehearsal for fear they
will miss some vitally interesting information about singing
or music literature.   A stimulating and/or elucidating musical experience creates a feeling of pride among the members
of the group which, in turn, maintains a high degree of motivation.

Professional musicians, such as choral directors,
must keep in mind at all times that the volunteer singers
with whom they are dealing are frequently professionals in
their own fields of endeavor.   They may have enough musical
background to be interested in and/or qualify for the church
choir, but, after all, they are not usually professional musicians; otherwise, they would, themselves, be directing or
singing in a professional group elsewhere.   Frequently, musicians are scornful of persons who are not knowledgeable or
proficient in music and they sometimes ridicule their choir
members or else "talk down" to them.   The rewards for the
director who is patient, yet firm and consistently positive,
are far greater than for one who is negative and sarcastic.

Learning Is Reacting

When the choir director has complete control of the
rehearsal (or performance) the above phrase "learning is reacting" has special meaning.   That is to say, the choir members react positively to effective leadership, and as a result,
learning takes place.   The learning may be in the form of
theoretical or vocal concepts in the rehearsal, or it may be
experienced as an inspirational episode through interpretation
of the music.   The central objective for the director, then,
is to attempt to make each encounter--rehearsal or perform-
ance--a vital developmental experience for the choir members.

Whole Versus Part Learning

Throughout this text there have been references to the Gestalt concept of learning as it applies to the choral environment. Chapters 2, 3, and 6 emphasize the developmental concept of learning. Suffice it to say that the most rewarding learning experiences are those in which the whole is never lost while dealing with the parts.

Emotion and Learning

Chapter 3 deals with the important role which positive emotions play in learning the tasks at hand. In the church choir situation, mere duty is rarely sufficient to maintain strong morale among the members. Rewards for time expended in the effort are necessary for individual and group development. One learns best in a positive environment. A person must desire to learn whatever is needed for achieving specific goals.

Transfer of Learning and Formal Discipline

Even in the choral rehearsal, a significant degree of formal discipline must be employed. The well-structured rehearsal, having been thoroughly planned in advance by the director, provides security for the singers. The disciplined rehearsal will provide the means by which the choristers will learn what is necessary so as to realize the intrinsic values to be found in the music. However, the whole (anthem or movement of a large work) must be kept in mind during the learning process. That is why synthesis is so important to "tie together" the analysis efforts as the group works to solve problems and perfect the whole. (See the discussion on S-A-S in Chapter 3.)

Individual Differences

It is imperative for the choral director to be aware that the choristers are individuals, and as such, they are likely to possess a variety of tastes, attitudes, and "talent." Likely, there are quick learners, slow learners, and many in between. The choir director must channel all of these people into a unified group without threatening the ego of any member. Most certainly, there will be conflicts or tensions

which will arise occasionally, but these episodes should not
be a serious threat if the director demonstrates respect for
each individual.   Finally, solid musical technique and an attractive personality are traits which will aid in establishing
a successful, satisfying experience for all concerned.

Blame or Disapproval

So much of the choir rehearsal time is spent pointing
out incorrectly sung notes and unacceptable tone quality that
it is quite easy for directors to become critically negative.
They must avoid censure, ridicule, and sarcasm and be quick
to indicate in an affirmative and kindly manner what is desired in place of the unacceptable performance.   In all cases,
the choir members' feelings of failure must be avoided, since
"this failure-induced behavior alienates the environment."[50]
In summation, then, "[l]earning takes place best in an atmosphere of incentive, and opportunity, not in an atmosphere of
punishment."[51]

Learning Is Reacting

Symonds states, "It seems to be generally agreed
among psychologists today that one learns what, and only what,
one does."[52]   The application of this principle to the church
choir environment is through understanding the learning situation at the proficiency level of the choir members.   If the
music is too difficult for most of the choristers, they will
likely become frustrated and negative in their attitude.   Therefore, the choice of music for any given ensemble must be
within some realistic grasp of the group.   Also, when the
atmosphere is congenial, the learners will desire to continue
this experience.

> ... Personality and behavior have been learned
> through the selection of responses that are reward-
> ing and bring success to the individual.[53]

Again the factor of reward through successful achievement and
acceptance is seen as extremely important to the learning
process in the church choir.   For more detail concerning
music education, including synthesis-analysis-synthesis, through
the choral experience, consult Chapter 2.

THE ADMINISTRATION OF CHURCH CHOIRS

The Place of Administration in the Choir Program

Common reference to the choir as the "war department" places church music in an unfavorable position; this is an appellation which is sometimes justly earned by church choirs, and one which is hard to overcome. Typically, jealousies occur over who sings solos or who seems to have special privileges, or who sits in the most prominent place in a section. Therefore, the administration of church choirs must be the framework through which human problems, as well as musical and mechanical problems, can be understood. A manual containing pertinent information may be helpful in orienting choir members to choir responsibilities, especially new members. Another means of communication on specific issues or problems is through letters to the choir by the director or choir president.

Organizational Structure of the Choir

It is possible to over-organize the choir program. Organization for its own sake, or because it has proved effective in another situation, is insufficient justification for the use of a particular structure. Detailed systems consisting of data cards on file for both personnel and music are no substitute for a sincere administrative concern to serve the needs of the choir personnel. An excessive number of officers and rules might succeed only in separating the choir members from the director. Thus, there must be an organizational structure which cares for those needs without becoming a formidable object itself. Its purpose basically is to achieve the final goal of the choir--that of performing effectively to enhance the total worship experience.

A Choir Constitution

Some choirs operate satisfactorily without a constitution. However, it can be an effective instrument for administration of a church choir when it meets the practical (defined) needs of the choral organization. It should be a frame of reference defining the duties of the choir officers and the function of the choir. The primary consideration is that there must be a definite need for the application of every item in

the constitution.   It is also logical to expect that a large organization would need more people in leadership capacities
to serve its needs than a smaller, more intimate one.

Choir Attendance

The best way to encourage steady choir attendance is
to ensure that the choir members have interesting and stimulating experiences resulting from the investment of their time
and energies and that they feel important to the welfare of
the group.   Moreover, there are important follow-up procedures which will assist the director in maintaining good attendance at rehearsals and performances of the choir.

The Need for Attendance Records

In discussing the necessity for keeping a record of
choir attendance, Sunderman states,

> Individual importance in an ensemble is greatly em-
> phasized if he knows that there is insistence upon
> his presence at each rehearsal.   Whenever a choir
> meets or performs, there must be insistence upon
> attendance.   There is no such thing as a balanced
> organization without it.   Rehearsal effectiveness is
> lost without it.   Without it the morale of the organ-
> ization suffers. [54]

There are several effective means of keeping attendance
records.

The Roll Book

An official choir list of personnel is, of course, a
necessity; every director should have a complete list of names,
addresses, and telephone numbers of the group.   Data beyond
this are effective to the degree to which they are used.   Further information, such as background, ability, and other details, should be kept by the director in a confidential card
file for reference.

Traditionally, the choir recording secretary marks the
roll book or chart, or it can be checked off by the members
individually each time the choir assembles, provided the chart

is kept in a conspicuous place; or a paper can be passed
around for the choir members to sign, which can be re-
entered later in the roll book.   The most important factor
to consider in keeping attendance is that it be done in a
manner that avoids "school room psychology," especially
among adults.

As has been said, one of the most important responsibilities of the director is to inspire confidence among the
choir members, not only musically, but also personally.   In
working with adults, it should be kept uppermost in mind that
an adult choir is composed of mature, conscientious people
who are there voluntarily.   These individuals should be kept
interested and active through utilizing to the best advantage
various abilities of volunteers.   If these principles are put
into practice, there will be little need to check on absentees.
It is important, however, that when people are absent from
the choir, they give a reason for their absence.   Consequently,
the roll book or chart becomes necessary in its traditional
sense, but plays a very important part in indicating the dates
when individuals must be absent.   Except for illness, most
people know in advance when they must be away from rehearsals or performances of the choir.   The calendar chart of
the choir membership, posted on the bulletin board in the
rehearsal room, permits the members to check in advance
when they expect to be absent from rehearsals and church
services.   Therefore, the indication of expected absences
on an open record has a twofold advantage for the director.

First, it tends to reinforce in the minds of choir
members that they have good reason to be away when they
must be (rather than are) absent--AWON (absent without notice); that they are all expected to be present, except in cases
of emergency, unless they have marked an "A" (absent) on
the posted chart.   This is an effective method for stressing
individual responsibility for the welfare of the choir.

Second, this method of marking the chart in advance
gives the director some indication of how many members will
be present, especially when there are additional choir members who must be absent for business or personal reasons.
For example, if the director has planned a seven- or eight-
part a cappella anthem for a service, poor balance of parts
will obviously result in an inferior performance.   It is con-
ceivable that almost an entire section could be absent for good
reasons, which may happen in volunteer choir situations.
Therefore, the director can avoid scheduling an ambitious

anthem requiring the maximum number of parts, provided the members have kept the attendance book or chart up to date. With this system of record keeping the choir director is able to choose music that will suit the balance of a limited number of singers. This alternative is better than an ambitious anthem poorly sung. Such a plan tends to ensure a consistently satisfactory level of performance by the choir.

Some Means of Improving Choir Attendance and Punctuality

Occasionally, a choir director may experience attendance or other problems, despite sincere efforts to avoid these circumstances. Below are some suggestions for dealing with these concerns.

1. Post cards. A hand-written note by the director or choir officer is an effective means of telling an absentee that he or she was missed and is necessary for the welfare of the organization.

2. General letters to the choir by the director expressing concern about attendance and/or any other problems which have arisen are sometimes necessary and quite effective if written in a forthright, positive manner. However, chronic attendance problems probably indicate that the director should carefully assess his or her leadership, which may be the cause of poor attendance.

3. A candid talk with habitual absentees can result in a better understanding of the problem by the absentee member and director or choir president.

4. Telephone calls are often effective in contacting the individual when it is impossible to make a personal visit.

Graphs

Charts and graphs indicating attendance at rehearsals, services, and special occasions can provide both the director and choir members with an accurate analysis of attendance throughout the year. They can be posted on a bulletin board in a conspicuous place, so that the entire choir membership can observe the attendance profile of the choir. This chart can reinforce the need for regular attendance, in some instances, better than any other type of communication.

Tardiness

The first step in preventing tardiness is to start the rehearsals on time. One might ask, "How can I start without a reasonably balanced choir?"

First of all, by beginning the rehearsal promptly, even with only one or two members present, the director establishes the fact that all rehearsals will begin punctually. As mentioned previously, when it is time to begin the rehearsal and only a few persons are present, the director can start with voice lessons. Such lessons will not only be helpful to those receiving them but can have a startling psychological effect upon the tardy members who might be more inclined to take advantage of this opportunity for vocal training.

In all efforts to deal with tardiness, the director must firmly insist that the choir members arrive promptly at the specified times. If certain persons persist in arriving late to choir functions, a private talk with them individually is far more effective than a "lecture" to the entire choir about "the evils of tardiness." It is also possible that a latecomer has had certain mechanical difficulties or personal problems which resulted in tardiness. The private interview also affords the opportunity of establishing better understanding between the individual and the choirmaster. The informal conference should lead to a solution of the problem. Finally, the choir director must admit to an awareness of individual problems and be sympathetic toward them; yet, establish the fact that it is of utmost importance to all concerned that rehearsals begin promptly.

RECRUITMENT

The truism "nothing succeeds like success" can be applied to choir member recruitment. A well-balanced, successful choir has little trouble maintaining its membership. But how does one solve the problem of building a choir that has known little success? It is desirable that the director

be able to attract people through his or her own personality as well as through musical sensitivity;

be musically outstanding so as to command the respect and admiration of choir members;

use varied techniques of recruitment to attract members from the congregation, such as these;

1. Utilizing choir members as emissaries. Their
    enthusiasm can be a vital force in recruiting new
    personnel.

2. Enlisting the help of selected people in the congre-
    gation to introduce prospective choir members to
    the director when they hear persons around them
    during the church service who sing well.

3. Seeking cooperation from the minister for secur-
    ing information about the musical background of
    new or prospective church members.

4. Promoting membership campaigns.

5. Asking the minister to make special announcements
    from the pulpit and in news letters. (This is
    probably the least effective means of recruitment,
    except in original organization attempts--starting
    from "scratch.")

The Choir Members as Emissaries

If the choir members themselves are enthusiastic about
the choir activity, then they, in turn, will tend to invite others
to join the choir. The members should be reminded often to
increase their efforts to find singers among their friends,
acquaintances, and the congregation at large who might be
potential choir members. A choir party, dance, banquet,
outing or even a musicale by choir soloists for the entire
congregation might be a successful means of acquainting potential singers with the choir personnel.

The Congregation Can Be Recruiters

Members of the Boards of Trustees, Deacons and Dea-
conesses are potential representatives of the choir. When
visiting new church members, invitations to join the choir
should be extended to those who indicate musical interest.
This is specifically part of the function of the official boards
in many churches. Also, other persons interested in the welfare of the choir, including relatives of choir members not

in the choir, might be requested to recruit possible choir members in the congregation.

Personal Calls by Ministerial Staff

When ministers call upon a new family in the church, or a prospective one, they should always inquire as to the musical interests of that household. The names of such persons can be referred to the choir director for follow-up letters or for calls by the choir membership chairman, any member of his committee, and/or the director. This method of recruitment is one of the best means of finding new choir members. All-church survey cards, indicating various categories of church interest, are also useful in discovering prospects for the choir.

Membership Campaigns

This method, while effective in some churches, tends to imply that the choir is not functioning well, and needs to be strengthened. Few people can be induced to join a group which they regard as weak. If choir membership campaigns are used, however, definite periods of the year should be selected for such efforts, since they require a great deal of organization to be successful. Wilson and Lyall suggest that January, May, and September are the best months for such campaigns:

> January--because of the psychological impact of the New Year, and the stimulation of musical interest by Christmas music and the attraction of approaching Easter music. May--because of the interest stimulated from the Easter music, return of college students and the possibility of a summer music concert. September--because of the beginning of the new season of activities and cooler weather and the incentive of the approaching Thanksgiving and Christmas music. [55]

Pulpit Emphasis

Encouragement by the pastor can sometimes induce individuals to join the choir. However, the manner in which the pastor states this plea can often be discouraging as well

as encouraging to prospective choir members. The pastor
must not suggest in any way that the choir is so weak that
they are begging for help. Therefore, such announcements,
as well as printed statements in the weekly bulletin or newsletter, should be worded in a positive fashion. It is important psychologically to indicate that the choir is doing well,
but that new qualified members are welcome.

In the final analysis recruitment depends upon the following:

1. Personal contacts by the choir personnel.

2. The ability of the existing choir to interest pro-
    spective members through inspiring musical per-
    formances. Music performed well with good tone
    quality will tend to attract qualified personnel.

3. Individual contacts with these prospects can do
    much to encourage people to join the choir. If
    the choir members are cordial to new and pro-
    spective members, recruitment efforts will be
    effective.

4. A challenging program, good repertoire, combined
    with effective conducting techniques and attractive
    personal qualities on the part of the director, will
    provide strong incentive for new members to join
    the group.

AUDITIONS

Most churches are not in a position to hold auditions for new
choir members, since formal auditions tend to discourage
many prospective choir members. Usually, persons need
encouragement to join rather than have obstacles to overcome.
Wilson and Lyall describe three approaches used in testing
the voices of the choir. A summary and interpolation of these
three methods follows.

1. No vocal try-outs. Under this system people are
    assigned a seat in the section in which they choose
    to sing. An experienced director can determine
    how the person is functioning, providing the sec-
    tion is not very large. This plan works best in
    choirs with fewer than twenty-five voices. In large

choirs the director may need to consult the members on each side of the new singer for information regarding the new-comer.

2.   The "vocal conference" is a compromise to the audition plan.   It should avoid implications of being an audition, per se, since a "vocal try-out" tends to create a feeling of insecurity and nervousness among many prospective members.   The "vocal conference" can be successful on either an individual or group basis, depending upon the preference of the director.   If conducted by the group process, it may be helpful to have a quartet of experienced members present to reinforce each voice part, thus avoiding any potential embarrassment for one of the new persons involved in the conference.   Hymns and simple anthems are valuable material to be used in such a situation. The director may request the individual to sing a stanza of a hymn as a solo with the group humming for reinforcement.   This approach affords the director a good opportunity to assess the qualities of the new members vocally and personally without undue embarrassment.

3.   The individual audition is successful under certain conditions: a) a completely full quota of singers which necessitates a waiting list, and b) a tradition of auditioning.   The audition tends to be more successful when conducted in the form of a personal interview rather than a vocal try-out.   The audition should be routine enough to be standardized, so that all applicants have similar tests to follow.   A sample test might be this:

Singing the melody of a familiar hymn chosen by the applicant.   Then moving to more complex material, such as counterpoint, or independent vocal lines.   The accompanist can fill in the other voice lines if desired.

Repeating tonal patterns of various notes on a selected vowel played on the piano or sung by the director and various intervalic skips, both chromatic and diatonic.

The use of arpeggios (or a preferred vocalise) to discover the range of the voice. 56

If the audition standards are too rigid, many potential
choir singers will eliminate themselves out of fear.   Auditions
should be used by the director to determine the ability of each
applicant to sing and to read music.   This affords the director the opportunity to become personally acquainted with each
new singer.   The audition may add some prestige to the choir
activity inasmuch as it implies that there are certain standards
necessary for membership.

RAPPORT WITH THE CONGREGATION

This study has previously discussed the need for a harmon-
ious and pleasant relationship between choir and congregation.
There are definite means through which the choir and congregation can become more closely associated in function and in
understanding.

So as to gain the respect and admiration of the congregation, the choir must first of all produce a good sound which
is inspiring and stimulating.   If a positive reaction toward the
choir is present, it can result in additional good relationships.

Christmas Carol services in which the congregation
participates and caroling for shut-ins are activities that can
bring choir and members of the congregation together in a
common effort.   It is probable that, through these activities,
many people who are not in the church choir will realize that
they too can find satisfaction in singing, and thus may join
the group.

The congregation-wide hymn service is also a means
through which the choir and congregation can share in the
music for all people in the church.   Brief accounts of the
history of the hymns can be interesting and helpful addition
to the activity.   A congregational hymn-rehearsal is another
means of cooperative activity by a parish.   For variety on
such occasions the choir might preview some anthems so that
the congregation may better understand them when the music
is presented in the formal worship service.

A pictorial brochure, which lists all church organizations, will inform the congregation of the role which music
plays in the life of the church.   In one parish a photographer,
as his contribution to his church, produced a montage of outstanding musical services performed in the church.   This was
included in the annual report of the church and was distributed

to every home on the church membership roll as a way of
pointing out the areas in which music is an important entity
in the life of the church.

PLANNING THE MUSICAL PROGRAM

The Yearly Calendar

A general calendar of activities ideally should be
planned together by the entire church staff. This helps to
coordinate church school, music, and general church activities. If the minister, and/or church school, has a series
of special themes, the music program can help to emphasize
and implement them. The text of an oratorio or cantata may
reinforce thematic material for the church school program or
sermons. When the various church staff members meet together and plan the church calendar for the year, this in itself has merit because it combines the efforts of all groups
in the church. In one instance, a minister of music, inter-
viewed for this book, indicated that he intended to present
Mendelssohn's Elijah oratorio in an evening concert the first
Sunday in June of that church year. The minister promptly
planned a series of sermons during the month of May on the
life and accomplishments of Elijah. The director, in turn,
chose to have the choir present several of the oratorio choruses as anthems each Sunday during the month of May. The
twofold advantage of this plan for the choir was first, it acquainted the congregation with the music and thematic material
of Elijah; second, it permitted the choir to prepare the difficult, but rewarding, choruses of this long work more gradually as well as having the joy of performing them more than
only one time.

Ideally, the meeting for preparing the yearly calendar
should be held during the summer. Specific planning sessions
should then be held at least once a month during the church
year to discuss and alter plans as required. Some churches
find that weekly staff meetings coordinating the total church
program are most helpful. In these weekly meetings, the
immediate program plans can be coordinated; the sermon
topics and appropriate music can be discussed or assigned.
These regular staff meetings can help the pastors realize
that volunteer choirs require at least four to six weeks advance notice in order to prepare their music properly. Therefore, if the music is to be consonant with the worship themes,
the minister must plan his sermon themes at least four to six
weeks in advance.

Some examples of advance planning are done by several larger churches known to this writer. Each summer the staffs, including the minister of music, plan the entire year's church program around major themes and festivals of the church year. This enables the director to publish a calendar of events which is distributed among choir members. Even though adjustments may have to be made from time to time, the choir personnel has a definite idea of what is expected of them. It can be expected that choir members will tend to feel more confident and enthusiastic when they know that the singing activity is well planned and has a definite, important place in the life of the church.

A calendar need not be confined to ecclesiastical apportionment of the Christian church year, but may be based upon biblical highlights, such as these suggested by Richmond Bryan Brown:

> Emphasis on patriarchs, Moses, David, prophets, creation, Providence, Covenant, et cetera.
> Season of Preparation for the Advent of Christ--December
> Emphasis on Old Testament prophecies, John the Baptist "fullness of time."
> Season of the Life and Teaching of Christ--January, February
> Emphasis on great events: Sermon on the Mount, parables, miracles, healings, et cetera.
> Season of Preparation for Easter--March
> Emphasis on self-examination, repentance, prayer, reconciliation, renewal, cross.
> Season of Easter--April, May
> The risen Christ, the cosmic Christ in Acts and the Epistles.
> Season of Pentecost--June
> Seven weeks after Easter; emphasis on Holy Spirit, inner life translated to outer witness.
> Season of the Life of Deeds of the Church--June, July, August
> Doctrine of the church: fellowship, ordinances, beliefs, practical application of faith to the problems of everyday life. [57]

A calendar of themes for the entire church permits coordination of topics for the church school and the minister. Thus, the congregation is made aware of the fact that church life is important in all areas.

Fifty-two Weeks a Year

Many directors assume that their choir as a group needs a vacation during the summer months. If the ideal choir experience is attained, members might well prefer to continue to sing during the summer except when they are away on vacation. The idea of choir summer hiatus conveys to the choir members that they are not always needed for every church service. As previously explained in this project, whenever choir members feel their services are dispensable, a strong motivating force to sing is lost.

The "Summer Choir"

A change of pace may be necessary during the summer months, but that does not mean that the choir is not needed. Following are some suggestions which have proven effective for this writer over the years of working with a variety of choirs.

The Psychological Preparations. Most importantly, if all through the year choir members feel needed and feel responsible for the welfare of the group, on the whole, they will be responsive to the idea of singing during the summer months also. There is usually a change of pace with a more relaxed atmosphere during the summer. Instead of weekly evening rehearsals, it is often more convenient to have a thirty- to forty-five-minute rehearsal held just before the church service. Most churches having double services from September to June hold only one service during July and August, leaving ample time to rehearse in the cool of the morning.

The summer season, with its less intensive and extensive rehearsals, would likely require more modest S-A-T-B music and selections with impressive organ accompaniment and hymn arrangements. Repeating favorite anthems of the previous season, since this music is still quite familiar to the singers, also supplies a fine incentive to keep up attendance. "On the spot" arrangements of hymns are often effective. Some verses--or parts of them--can be sung in unison, or as solos to vary the harmonic emphasis. An effective practice is to have the altos and men sing unison on the last stanza while the sopranos (those capable of singing a high tessitura) sing the alto line an octave higher as a descant. With good keyboard support playing the harmony, the effect can be very impressive. Special quartets, trios, duets and other ensemble combinations afford great opportunities for adding variety to the summer program of music.

Consolidating the high school and adult choirs will augment the summer choral forces, thus creating a feeling of solidarity both in number and in sound. College students, home on vacation, can add a significant amount of quality and quantity to summer choral efforts.

Physical Arrangements for the Summer Choir. Summer robes of light material might be provided, or the choir could be permitted to dispense with robes entirely if the sanctuary is not air-conditioned. The choir should be asked to dress conservatively in the latter case: white summer blouses for women and white shirts being appropriate in some non-liturgical churches.

Summer attendance. In order to calculate the number of singers likely to be present for a given service, the bulletin board chart described earlier in this chapter is useful. Since most people know a week or more in advance what their summer weekend plans are, they can indicate on the chart when they will be absent from choir. If members recognize that the director and the other choir personnel are expecting them, they are more apt to make a special effort to be present. The chart also enables the director to more intelligently select the music which will be suitable for the size of the group that can be expected for a given service.

An interesting example of a summer choir assignment schedule is that of a very successful forty-five-voice choir in a church of 400 members in New Jersey. In May, choir members are asked to indicate on the master chart when they plan to be away from church during the summer. When the information is complete, the director constructs and posts a "Summer Choir Assignment Schedule." The schedule lists a smaller, but balanced, choir for each Sunday during July and August, relieving certain members from "duty" according to the information on the chart and in view of a vocally balanced group. The singers are then expected to be present at the pre-service rehearsal and worship on the day on which their names appear. If they find that they cannot be present on that day, they must notify the director or choir president and/or find a substitute to take their place. The rotating "reserve force" of singers is comprised of regular singers along with high school and college students who are home for

the summer.   Quite obviously, this kind of program can be
implemented only in instances in which there is a relatively
large, well-balanced pool of singers from which to draw.

A combination of youth and adult choirs in the summer
may provide a choir as large as (or possibly larger than) the
established regular choir.   Furthermore, a successful summer
choir experience will provide continuity to the choral program
with very little effort, while at the same time adding to the
quality of the summer worship services.   The atmosphere of
the summer choir and summer church service can be an informal yet meaningful experience for choir and congregation
alike.

PAID SINGERS

The issue of paying singers for their services is one which
each congregation or music committee must resolve individually.   If a quartet or any paid singer is hired, however,
there is an important factor to consider regarding choir morale.   To assure the volunteer singers that they are equally
important to the choir, and to avoid unfair discrimination,
the director must never give the paid singer(s) preferential
treatment.   Indeed, if there is to be any difference in status,
the paid singer should be considered as a section leader--a
person who works as a colleague of the volunteer.   If the
paid singer is a hard worker and a congenial leader, instead
of a prima donna (or don), the choir members will admire
and respect the "professional" among them.   Some paid singers may "save" their voices for the solo parts.   This quite
naturally can cause the volunteer to resent that person.
Therefore, it behooves the director to encourage teamwork
and camaraderie among all of the choristers, so as to achieve
a unified feeling of working toward the objectives of the group.

Choirs Without Paid Soloists

Churches whose policy or finances prevent them from
hiring paid choir singers often find themselves without able
soloists.   If there are no individuals in the choir capable of
singing solos, it is possible to have entire sections sing the
parts written for the solo voice.   Complete sections of melodic arias from oratorios and cantatas can be sung as one
voice.   For example, a section of sopranos singing the aria
"I Know That My Redeemer Liveth" from Handel's Messiah

can be equally effective as the solo part alone because of the long phrases. A whole soprano section, or small group of them, can sing the melodic lines with great ease and grace by "snatching" breaths, thereby contributing to a smooth musical line and thus to the overall beauty of the aria.

MULTIPLE CHOIRS

Many churches, desirous of developing a graded choir system (a choir for almost every grade or age level in the church), are overwhelmed by the organizational and administrational problems of these younger choirs. Parishes desiring more than one or two choirs might achieve greater success in a program of multiple choirs if they begin with fewer choirs and wider spans of ages. The principle involved here is one of overlapping ages; i. e. some young people singing in two choirs. In one choir they would be leaders because they would be older than most of the group; in the other choir they would be "apprentices" because they would be the younger members of the group. This kind of situation serves the twofold purpose of providing a balance of leadership and apprenticeship during the same period in a young person's life. The success of building these choirs requires that there be an efficient director in charge, and that there will be a reasonably large resource from which to draw. It may be necessary to combine these limited age groups until the choirs become large enough to be effective numerically and vocally in the multiple-choir situation. In some churches, this age span may be the norm for all time, but these choirs could become the staple of the younger church music program.

Young voices particularly need the security of numbers so that their voices are not strained in attempting to achieve the vocal demands of the music. In a reasonably large sanctuary, most children's and youth choirs need at least thirty voices to provide sufficient volume for interesting musical expression in terms of dynamics and tone quality. Some possible structures of younger choirs are as follows:

1. Young people of high school age can sing in the adult choir, where they are "apprentices," if they qualify vocally and musically. It has been the experience of this writer that mature high school age singers can demonstrate vocal, musical, and personal maturity equal to that of adults. It is a mistake to assume that high school age persons are too immature to associate with older people. This may not be true in every locality, but it is a safe generalization to make.

2. Youth of high school and junior high school age may be combined. Again, it is a mistake to assume that the two age groups are not compatible for singing. Of course, if the director assumes that these two age groups are incompatible, they might, quite naturally, live up to that expectation. On the other hand, if the group of high school age is challenged to set an example for behavior and vocal achievement for the junior high group, they will likely try to prove their maturity. Moreover, if the younger members of the group are informed that they must exhibit the same level of maturity expected of the high school group, they will usually respond accordingly. This plan has proven successful in several churches investigated for this study.

3. Another choir may be formed using 4th, 5th, and 6th graders, with the 7th graders included from the Junior-Senior High School Choir as leaders of this "junior age" group.

The arrangement of choirs is illustrated as follows:

Adult and senior high
   Senior high and junior high
      Junior high and junior age (4th, 5th, 6th, and
      7th graders)

Another workable age grouping is this:

Elementary choir	Grades 3-5
Preparatory choir	Grades 5-7
Youth Choir	Grades 7-9
High School Choir	Grades 9-12
Adult Choir	Grade 12

When the choirs develop in proficiency and increase in size so as to be completely self-sufficient, the age limit for membership may be drawn more sharply. This suggested plan does not dispense with the graded choir system. Rather, it permits a church with a smaller membership to have an effective multiple-choir program.

Recruiting and Sustaining the Interest of
Younger Choir Members

The greatest handicap young children have as choir members is a short span of attention. One must use various methods to challenge them:

1.   The music not only must capture their interest from the start, but it must also be at their level of understanding.   A very young group (6- to 8-year-olds) will be satisfied with unison singing; children 9 to 11 generally need something more difficult, such as a descant and/or two-part music to challenge them.   Music that is too simple is as unsatisfactory as that which is too difficult.

2.   The choirs should have a regular place to meet and specified times for rehearsals and performances.   It is also a great incentive to wear a robe and stand before parents and friends as a singing group.   Parents and others in the congregation might well be asked to make robes for the younger choir personnel.

3.   The practice of serving refreshments after rehearsals once a month (or more often) can add much to the camaraderie of young singers.   Before refreshments, a few of the members might perform for their peers in vocal and instrumental solos, reciting and so forth.   This should be done for two reasons: the desire for solo performance is being satisfied for some, and at the same time the varied individual talents of the children are displayed for others to emulate and enjoy.

CARE OF MUSIC

Each choir director hopes that every singer will take good care of the music assigned to the membership.   However, occasionally there are those who tend to be a bit careless about property which is not their own.   Therefore, it is best to have specific rules to remind the choir that each person is responsible for the assigned music.   Complex filing systems are not needed for this purpose.

Assignment of Music

Each member can be given a large envelope with a string to prevent the music from slipping out accidentally. If black folders are preferred for performances, the music can be placed in the folder weekly by each singer from the supply in the large envelope.   Some octavo-sized folders have elastic bands which hold several pieces of music.

Ideally, all music should be numbered and assigned to

the members, being certain there is a sufficient quantity.
Thus, each person can be held responsible for his or her
music. In instances where each person cannot have a copy,
a joint folder assignment could be made.

Filing

        The less complicated a filing system is, the easier
it will be to keep track of the music. It can be readily
identified by alphabetically listing the composers and the
titles of the selections whether placed in manila folders in
a filing cabinet or in special boxes on shelves. If there is
more than one selection by a composer, each anthem should
be listed in alphabetical order under the composer's name.
Seasonal music, such as that used for Advent, Christmas,
Lent and Easter, may be more accessible if filed separately
from the "general" anthems. In addition, a card file is desirable for quick reference for the director. It should contain
composer's name, title, publisher, date of publication and
quantity of octavos. The director will probably wish to keep
one copy of every selection in the library in a separate file
for ready reference.

CONCLUSION

Currently, there is a wide variety of modes of worship among
religious denominations and sects with music playing a significant role in most contemporary churches. Moreover, even
among churches closely related to formal liturgy there is a
diversity of practices and forms which are employed for the
worship needs of the various congregations. Orthodox and
Conservative Jewish congregations have little or no choral
music in their services, the cantors supplying the liturgical
music. The larger Reformed congregations tend to have
choirs, as well as cantors.

        A historical view of liturgical practices reveals human-
kind's desire to explore new modes of worship. For instance,
many Protestant groups have rejected the traditional--the
seemingly impersonal--liturgical observances. Through the
ages, the pendulum has swung back and forth from extreme
rigidity to "free-style" worship modes.

        Church musicians have often found themselves in diffi-
cult positions when attempting to serve the objectives of a

particular convention or style of worship while still holding
firm to their own musical standards in addition to their main
purpose as educators, which is to serve the needs of their
choristers as well as the tastes of the congregation. This
presents the problem of how to best serve the various needs
of all concerned in church life.

Choir directors must first help the volunteer singers
to fit into the scheme of worship, challenging them to develop
their potential as they experience satisfaction in giving their
talents and limited time to this end. Church music leaders,
being educators, should be aware of and practice basic concepts of educational psychology.

Church music programs should be realistic in concept.
They should be designed to serve the needs of the church
through service to the individuals involved in the program(s)
and to the worship demands. Organization for the sake of
organization (an elaborate constitution or endless rules) will
not guarantee a successful church music program. Instead,
the framework of the entire program should be designed and
administered according to a thorough analysis of the needs
that conform to the financial and personnel parameters of the
total church organization.

We have emphasized the fact that the church music
leader must be a well prepared, broadly oriented person in
order to build and maintain a successful program. However,
it is also necessary for the church congregation to respond
with financial and moral support to undergird the efforts of
the dedicated music director.

NOTES

1. R. S. Lee, Psychology and Worship. Burroughs Memor-
    ial Lectures, University of Leeds, S. C. M. Press,
    Ltd. , London, 1955 (London and Southhampton: Came-
    lot Press, 1955), p. 11.
2. Austin C. Lovelace and William C. Rice, Music and
    Worship in the Church (Nashville: Abingdon Press,
    1960), pp. 15-19.
3. Evelyn Underhill, Worship (New York: Harper and Broth-
    ers, 1936), p. 84.
4. Paul A. Wolfe and Helen and Clarence Dickinson, The
    Choir Loft and the Pulpit (New York: H. W. Gray,
    1943), pp. 13, 15.

5. Andrew W. Blackwood, The Fine Art of Public Worship
    (New York: Abingdon Press, 1939), p. 14.
6. Louis Diercks, "Church Music Corner," Resound, Cen-
    tral ACDA Divisional Newsletter, Feb. 1981, Vol. 4,
    No. 2.
7. Ibid.
8. Edith Lovell Thomas, Music in Christian Education
    (Nashville: Abingdon Press, 1953), p. 114.
9. James L. Mursell, Music Education Principles and Pro-
    grams (Morristown, N.J.: Silver Burdett, 1956), p. 66.
10. William C. Hartshorn, Address to the American Asso-
    ciation of School Administrators, Atlantic City, Feb-
    ruary 17, 1959.
11. Lovelace and Rice, op. cit., p. 15.
12. Ibid., pp. 15-16.
13. Ibid., p. 18.
14. Ibid., p. 19.
15. Albert W. Palmer, The Art of Conducting Public Wor-
    ship (New York: Macmillan, 1953), p. 9.
16. Ibid., p. 9.
17. Hartshorn, op. cit.
18. Walford Davies and Harvey Grace, Music and Worship
    (New York: H. W. Gray, 1939), p. 88.
19. Joseph A. Murphy, "Church Music Standards," The
    Catholic Choirmaster, 46:4, Spring 1960.
20. Palmer, op. cit., p. 113.
21. W. Hines Sims, Church Music Manual (Nashville: Con-
    vention Press, 1957), pp. 4-5.
22. Ibid., p. 5.
23. Lloyd F. Sunderman, Organization of the Church Choir
    (Rockville Center, N.Y.: Belwin, 1954), p. 14.
24. Thomas, op. cit., p. 112.
25. Ibid., p. 108.
26. Earl E. Harper, Church Music and Worship (New York:
    Abingdon Press, 1924), p. 64.
27. Sims, op. cit., p. 13.
28. Ibid., p. 14.
29. Davies and Grace, op. cit., pp. 87-88.
30. Harry R. Wilson and J. W. Lyall, Building a Church
    Choir (Minneapolis: Hall and McCreary, 1957), p. 13.
31. Carl Halter, The Christian Choir Member (St. Louis:
    Concordia Publishing House, 1959), p. 23.
32. Lovelace and Rice, op. cit., p. 88.
33. Waldo S. Pratt, Musical Ministries in the Church (New
    York: G. Schirmer, 1901), p. 100.
34. Ibid., p. 105.
35. The Church Choir, Church Music Department, Education

            Division of the Baptist (Southern) Sunday School Board,
            p. 3.
36.   Ibid.
37.   Halter, op. cit. , p. 19.
38.   Harry S. Broudy, "A Realistic Philosophy of Music Ed-
            ucation," Basic Concepts in Music Education, National
            Society for the Study of Education, 57th Yearbook, p.
            76.
39.   Joseph Leeder and William Haynie, Music Education in
            the High School (Englewood Cliffs, N. J.:   Prentice-
            Hall, 1958), p. 21.
40.   Broudy, op. cit. , p. 63.
41.   Percival M. Symonds, What Education Has to Learn from
            Psychology (New York: Bureau of Publications, Teach-
            ers College, Columbia University, 1958), passim.
42.   Ibid. , p. 3.
43.   Ibid. , p. 6.
44.   Ibid. , p. 9.
45.   Ibid.
46.   Ibid. , pp. 6-7.
47.   Ibid. , p. 6.
48.   Ibid.
49.   Ibid. , p. 7.
50.   Ibid. , p. 30.
51.   Ibid. , p. 32.
52.   Ibid. , p. 37.
53.   Ibid. , p. 45.
54.   Lloyd F. Sunderman, op. cit. , p. 15.
55.   Wilson and Lyall, op. cit. , p. 59.
56.   Ibid. , pp. 61-63.
57.   Richmond Bryan Brown, "Why Not Try a Biblical Cal-
            endar?" The Baptist Program (August 1959), p. 16.

REVIEW QUESTIONS FOR CHAPTER 11

(1)   Why should a choral director in a church leadership po-
        sition have a firm conviction as to the
        a) definition of the term worship?
        b) the role of music in worship?
        c) church music as an artistic form?

(2)   What should be the status of music in worship?

(3)   Relate musical performance to the act of worship.

(4)   What specific role should music occupy in the order of
        worship?

(5) Define "Ministry of Music" as it relates to the total life of a given church of your acquaintance.

(6) What specific objectives are served by the Ministry of Music?

(7) What are graded or multiple-choir programs, and how do they fit into the total church program?

(8) What specific role does the Minister of Music play in the church program?

(9) What are the needs and desires of church choir singers?

(10) What is the function of church choir administration?

(11) How can the church choir director deal most effectively with attendance and punctuality?

(12) What are some effective recruitment measures for church choirs?

(13) Cite the problems and methods of auditioning new recruits for the choir.

(14) Discuss the relationship of the choir as a body with the congregation.

(15) How can the choir serve the church throughout the entire year?

(16) What are the problems encountered with paid singers being employed to be soloists and to strengthen the choir?

(17) What are some concerns in recruiting and motivating young choir singers?

(18) What practical methods can be employed to ensure the distribution and care of musical scores in the church choir situation?

● BIBLIOGRAPHY

A. Conducting Technique and
   Choral Procedures

BAMBERGER, Carl, ed. The Conductor's Art. New York: McGraw-
   Hill, 1965.

BLACKMAN, Charles. Behind the Baton. New York: Charos Enterprises, 1964.

BOULT, Adrian Cedric. A Handbook on the Technique of Conducting.
   New ed. Oxford: Hall, 1943.

DECKER, Harold A., and Julius Herford. Choral Conducting.
   Englewood Cliffs, N.J.: Prentice-Hall, 1973.

EBERHARDT, Carl. A Guide to Successful Choral Rehearsals. New
   York: C. F. Peters, 1973.

EHMANN, Wilhelm. Choral Directing. Minneapolis: Augsburg Pub-
   lishing House, 1968.

ERICSON, Eric; Gösta Ohlin; and Lennart Spanberg. Choral Conducting. New York: Walton Music, 1976.

EWEN, David. The Man with the Baton. Freeport, N.Y.: Books
   for Libraries Press, 1936; reprinted, 1968.

FINN, William J. The Conductor Raises His Baton. New York:
   Harper and Brothers, 1944.

FUCHS, Peter Paul. The Psychology of Conducting. New York:
   MCA Music, 1969.

GARRETSON, Robert. Conducting Choral Music. 3rd ed. Boston:
   Allyn and Bacon, 1970.

GRAY, H. W. The Choir Loft and the Pulpit. New York: H. W.
   Gray, 1943.

GREEN, Elizabeth A. H. The Modern Conductor. 2nd ed. Englewood Cliffs, N.J.: Prentice-Hall, 1969.

341

HABERLEN, John. Mastering Conducting Techniques. Champaign,
    Ill.: Mark Foster Music, 1977.

HENRY, Nelson B., ed. Basic Concepts in Music Education. Chi-
    cago: University of Chicago Press; 57th Yearbook of the Na-
    tional Society for the Study of Education.

JENNINGS, John W., and Kenneth L. Neidig. Choral Director's
    Guide. West Nyack, N.Y.: Parker, 1967.

KRONE, Max T. The Chorus and Its Conductor. Chicago: Neil A.
    Kjos Music, 1945.

LAMB, Gordon H. Choral Techniques. Dubuque: William C. Brown,
    1974.

McELHERAN, Brock. Conducting Technique. New York: Oxford
    University Press, 1966.

NEWMANN, Frederick. Ornamentation in Baroque and Post-Baroque
    Music. Princeton, N.J.: Princeton University Press, 1978.

PELOQUIN, C. Alexander. Choral Precision. Toledo: Gregorian
    Institute of America, 1962.

POOLER, Frank, and Brent Pierce. New Choral Notation. New
    York: Walton Music, 1971.

_____, and Gail L. Shoup. Choralography. New York: Walton
    Music, 1975.

ROBINSON, Ray, and Allen Winold. The Choral Experience. New
    York: Harper's College Press, 1976.

_____, and _____. The Choral Experience: Literature, Ma-
    terials and Methods. New York: Harper & Row, 1976.

ROTHSCHILD, Fritz. Musical Performance in the Times of Mozart
    and Beethoven. London: Adam and Charles Black, 1961.

_____. Stress and Movement in the Works of J. S. Bach. Lon-
    don: Adam and Charles Black, 1966.

SAMINSKY, Lazare. Essentials of Conducting. London: Dennis
    Dobson, 1958.

SATEREN, Leland B. Criteria for Judging Choral Music and Those
    Straight-Tone Choirs. Minneapolis: Augsburg Publishing House,
    1963.

_____. Focus on Mixed Meter Music and Line in Choral Music.
    Minneapolis: Augsburg Publishing House, 1968.

STANTON, Royal. The Dynamic Choral Conductor. Delaware Water
Gap, Pa.: Shawnee Press, 1971.

THOMAS, Kurt. The Choral Conductor. New York: Associated
Music Publishers, English Adaptation by Alfred Mann and William
H. Reese, 1971.

WILSON, Harry R. Artistic Choral Singing. New York: G. Schirmer, 1959.

B. Vocal Production

APPELMAN, Ralph D. The Science of Vocal Pedagogy. Blooming-
ton: Indiana University Press, 1967.

BACKUS, John. The Acoustical Foundations of Music. New York:
W. W. Norton, 1969.

BRODNITZ, Friedrich S., M.D. Keep Your Voice Healthy. New
York: Harper Brothers, 1953.

BURGIN, John Carroll. Teaching Singing. Metuchen, N.J.: Scarecrow Press, 1973.

FIELDS, Victor Alexander. Foundations of the Singer's Art. New
York: Vantage Press, 1977.

_____. Training the Singing Voice. New York: Kings Crown
Press, 1947.

HAMMAR, Russell A. Singing--An Extension of Speech. Metuchen,
N.J., & London: Scarecrow Press, 1978.

HUSLER, Frederick, and Yvonne Rodd-Marling. Singing: The Physical Nature of the Vocal Organ. New York: October House,
1965.

LEHMANN, Lilli. How to Sing. Trans. from German by Richard
Aldrich. New York: Macmillan, 1924.

McKENZIE, Duncan. Training the Boy's Changing Voice. London:
Faber and Faber, 1956.

MILLER, Richard. English, French, German and Italian Techniques
of Singing. Metuchen, N.J.: Scarecrow Press, 1977.

REID, Cornelius L. Voice: Psyche and Soma. New York: Joseph
Patelson Music House, 1975.

SCOTT, Charles Kennedy. The Fundamentals of Singing. London:
Cassell, 1954.

SHEWAN, Robert. Voice Training for the High School Chorus. New
    York: Parker, 1973.

SWANSON, Frederick J. The Male Singing Voice Ages Eight to
    Eighteen. Cedar Rapids: Laurance Press, 1977.

VENNARD, William. Singing: The Mechanism and the Technic.
    New York: Carl Fischer, 1967.

WITLOCK, Weldon. Facets of the Singer's Art. Vol. 1 of Twen-
    tieth Century Masterworks on Singing, Edward Foreman, Gen-
    eral Editor. Champaign, Ill.: Pro Musica Press, 1967.

C. Music Education and Psychology

ADLER, Samuel. Sight Singing--Pitch, Interval, Rhythm. New
    York: W. W. Norton, 1979.

ANDREWS, Frances M., and Joseph A. Leeder. Guiding Junior
    High School Pupils in Music Experiences. Englewood Cliffs,
    N.J.: Prentice-Hall, 1953.

BENNETT, Roy C. The Choral Singer's Handbook. New York:
    Edward B. Marks Music, 1977.

BENWARD, Bruce. Sightsinging Complete. 2nd ed. Dubuque,
    Iowa: William C. Brown, 1973.

BERGER, Melvin. Fundamentals of Part Singing. New York: Sam
    Fox, 1969.

BERKOWITZ, Sol; Gabriel Fontrier; and Leo Kraft. A New Approach
    to Sight Singing. New York: W. W. Norton, 1960.

DEARMAN, Nancy B., and Valena White Plisko. The Condition of
    Education. U.S. Dept. of Health, Education & Welfare. Wash-
    ington, D.C.: U.S. Government Printing Office, 1979.

HALTER, Carl. The Christian Choir Member. St. Louis: Con-
    cordia Pub. House, 1959.

HOFFER, Charles R. Teaching Music in the Secondary Schools.
    Belmont, Calif.: Wadsworth, 1973.

JONES, Archie N., ed. Education in Action. Dubuque: William
    C. Brown, 1964.

KODALY, Zoltan. Let Us Sing Correctly. London: Boosey &
    Hawkes, 1952.

LLOYD, Norman; Ruth Lloyd; and Ian De Gaetani. The Complete

Sightsinger--A Stylistic and Historical Approach. New York:
Harper & Row, 1980.

MASLOW, Abraham H. Motivation and Personality. 2nd ed. New
York: Harper & Row, 1970.

MURSELL, James L. Education for Musical Growth. Boston:
Ginn, 1948.

PETERS, R. S. The Concept of Motivation. New York: Human-
ities Press, 1958.

ROE, Paul F. Choral Music Education. Englewood Cliffs, N.J.:
Prentice-Hall, 1970.

RORKE, Genevieve A. Choral Teaching at the Junior High School
Level. Chicago: Hall & McCreary, 1947.

STACEY, Chalmers, and Manfred De Martino. Understanding Human Motivation. Cleveland: Howard Allen, 1958.

SUNDERMAN, Lloyd Frederick. Choral Organization and Administration. Rockville Centre, N.Y.: Belwin, 1954.

WILSON, H. R., and Jack L. Lyall. Building a Church Choir.
Minneapolis: Hall & McCreary, 1957.

_____, and Paul Van Bodegraven. The School Music Conductor.
Chicago: Hall & McCreary, 1942.

D. Artistry

ARNOLD, Frank Thomas. The Art of Accompaniment from a
Thorough-Bass. 2 volumes. New York: Dover, 1965.

BAMBERGER, Carl, ed. The Conductor's Art. New York: McGraw-
Hill, 1965.

BLUME, Friedrich. Renaissance and Baroque Music: A Comprehensive Survey. Trans. M. D. Herter Norton. New York:
W. W. Norton, 1967.

_____. Two Centuries of Bach: An Account of Changing Taste.
Trans. Stanley Godman. London: Oxford University Press,
1950.

BROWN, Howard Mayer. Music in the Renaissance. Englewood
Cliffs, N.J.: Prentice-Hall, 1976.

CONE, Edward T. Musical Form and Musical Performance. New
York: W. W. Norton, 1968.

COOPER, Grosvenor, and Leonard B. Meyer. The Rhythmic Structure of Music. Chicago: University of Chicago Press, 1960.

DART, Thurston. The Interpretation of Music. London: Hutchin-
son University Library, 1967.

DOLMETSCH, Arnold. The Interpretation of the Music of the XVII
and XVIII Centuries. London: Novello, 1946.

DONINGTON, Robert. The Interpretation of Early Music. New version. London: Faber and Faber, 1974.

_____. A Performer's Guide to Baroque Music. London: Faber
and Faber, 1973.

DORIAN, Frederick. The History of Music in Performance: The
Art of Musical Interpretation from the Renaissance to Our Day.
New York: W. W. Norton, 1966.

E. History and Literature

AN ANNOTATED Inventory of Distinctive Choral Literature for Performance at the High School Level, Margaret Hawkins. Tampa,
Fla.: American Choral Directors Association, 1976.

APEL, Willi. Harvard Dictionary of Music. Cambridge: Harvard
University Press, 1964.

BAKER'S Biographical Dictionary of Musicians. New York: G.
Schirmer, 1940.

BISHOP'S Committee on the Liturgy. Music in Catholic Worship.
Washington, D.C.: United States Catholic Conference, 1972.

BLACKWOOD, Andrew W. The Fine Art of Public Worship. New
York: Abingdon Press, 1939.

BLOM, Eric, ed. Grove's Dictionary of Music and Musicians. 5th
ed. New York: St. Martin's Press, 1954.

BUKOFZER, Manfred. Music in the Baroque Era. New York:
W. W. Norton, 1947.

BURNSWORTH, Charles C. Choral Music for Women's Voices: An
Annotated Bibliography of Recommended Works. Metuchen, N.J.:
Scarecrow Press, 1968.

CARSE, Adam. The Orchestra from Beethoven to Berlioz. Cambridge, England: W. Heffer & Sons, 1948.

CHARLES, Sydney Robinson. A Handbook of Music and Music Literature in Sets and Series. New York: The Free Press, 1972.

COAR, Birchard. The Masters of the Classical Period as Conductors. Sarasota, Fla.: Privately published by Birchard Coar, Rt. 1, Box 91 C, n.d.

COOPER, Martin, ed. The Concise Encyclopedia of Music and Musicians. New York: Hawthorn Books, 1958.

CROCKER, Richard L. A History of Musical Style. New York: McGraw-Hill, 1966.

DARROW, Gerald. Four Decades of Choral Training. Metuchen, N.J.: Scarecrow Press, 1975.

DEISS, Lucien, C. S. Sp. Spirit and Song of the New Liturgy. Trans. by Lyla L. Haggard and Michael L. Mazzarese. Cincinnati: World Library Publications, 1970.

DEMUTH, Norman. Musical Trends in the 20th Century. London: Rockliff, Salisbury Square, 1952.

DICKINSON, Edward. Music in the History of the Western Church. New York: Charles Scribner's Sons, 1902.

ETHERINGTON, Charles L. Protestant Worship Music. New York: Holt, Rinehart & Winston, 1962.

FELLERER, Karl Gustav. The History of Catholic Church Music. Baltimore: Helicon Press, 1961.

FELLOWS, Edmund H. The English Madrigal School: A Guide to Its Practical Use. London: Stainer and Bell, n.d.

FLANNERY, Austin, O. P., gen. ed. Vatican Council II. Collegeville, Minn.: The Liturgical Press, 1975.

GROUT, Donald Jay. A History of Western Music. New York: W. W. Norton, 1973.

HEYER, Anna Harriet, comp. Historical Sets, Collected Editions, and Monuments of Music. 2nd ed. Chicago: American Library Association, 1969.

HOLSINGER, Clyde William. A History of Choral Conducting with Emphasis on the Time-Beating Techniques. Unpublished Ph.D. dissertation, Northwestern University, Evanston, Ill., 1954.

HOPPIN, Richard H. Medieval Music. New York: W. W. Norton, 1978.

HOPPIN, Richard H., ed. Anthology of Medieval Music. New York: W. W. Norton, 1978.

HUME, Paul. Catholic Church Music. New York: Dodd, Mead,
    1956.

INTERNATIONAL Committee on English in the Liturgy, Inc. The
    General Instruction and the New Order of Mass. Hales Corners,
    Wisc.: Priests of the Sacred Heart, 1969.

KJELSON, Lee, and James McCray. The Singer's Manual of Choral
    Music Literature. Melville, N.Y.: Belwin Mills, 1973.

LANG, Paul Henry. George Frideric Handel. New York: W. W.
    Norton, 1966.

LIEF, Arthur. The Choral Art, Vols. I and II. New York: Lawson-
    Gould Music, 1974.

LOVELACE, Austin C., and William C. Rice. Music and Worship
    in the Church. New York: Abingdon Press, 1960.

McGIVERN, James J. Worship and Liturgy. Official Catholic Teach-
    ings. Wilmington, N.C.: A Consortium Book, McGrath, 1978.

MACHLIS, Joseph. The Enjoyment of Music. 3rd ed. New York:
    W. W. Norton, 1970.

MAY, James D. Avant-Garde Choral Music: An Annotated Selected
    Bibliography. Metuchen, N.J.: Scarecrow Press, 1977.

PIUS TENTH School of Liturgical Music, ed. The Piux X Hymnal.
    Boston: McLaughlin & Reilly, 1950.

REYNOLDS, William J. A Survey of Christian Hymnody. New York:
    Holt, Rinehart and Winston, 1963.

ROBINSON, Ray, ed. Choral Music. New York: W. W. Norton,
    1978.

ROSENSTIEL, Leonie, genl ed. History of Music. New York:
    Schirmer Books, A Division of Macmillan, 1982.

ROUTLEY, Erik. The Church and Music. London: Gerald Duck-
    worth, 1950.

SACHS, Curt. The Rise of Music in the Ancient World East & West.
    New York: W. W. Norton, 1943.

SCHONBERG, Harold C. The Great Conductors. New York: Simon
    & Schuster, 1967.

SIMS, W. Hines. Church Music Manual. Nashville, Tenn.: Con-
    vention Press, 1957.

SPELMAN, Leslie P. "Luther and the Arts," reprinted from the

Journal of Aesthetics and Art Criticism, Vol. X, No. 2, December 1951.

TORTOLANO, William. *Original Music for Men's Voices: A Selected Bibliography.* Metuchen, N.J.: Scarecrow Press, 1973.

ULRICH, Homer. *A Survey of Choral Music.* New York: Harcourt Brace Jovanovich, 1973.

WIENANDT, Elwyn A. *Choral Music of the Church.* New York: The Free Press, 1965.

F. Phonetics and Pronunciation of
    Commonly Used Languages

ADLER, Kurt. *Phonetics and Diction in Singing: Italian, French, Spanish, German.* Minneapolis: University of Minnesota Press, 1967.

HALL, William D., ed. *Latin Pronunciation According to Roman Usage.* Tustin, Calif.: National Music Publishers, 1971.

HINES, Robert S. *Singer's Manual of Latin Diction and Phonetics.* New York: Macmillan, 1975.

MARIETTA, Sister. *Singing the Liturgy.* Milwaukee: Bruce, 1956.

THOMAS, Charles Kenneth. *Phonetics of American English.* New York: Ronald Press, 1958.

INDEX

A cappella singing 150, 151, 181, 257, 264
Abdominal breathing 72
Acoustics 203, 204, 207, 240, 241
Aesthetic expression (appeal) 34, 49
Alligator jaw 91
Ambrose (Bishop, Ambrosian Chant) 251
American Choral Directors Journal 26
Anacrusis 197
Ancient practices 3
Anglo-Saxon 254
Antes, John 270
Appetites and aversions 32
Ars antiqua 258
Ars nova 258
Articles of Religion 260
Aspiration (level of) 32
Atmospheric conditions 186, 187
Audience appeal 48, 49
Auditioning singers 145, 146, 324-326
Aural image 64, 65, 67, 80, 104, 108, 109, 127, 212
Avant-garde music 212, 213
Awareness (musical) 21, 26

Babylonian empire 4
Bach, Carl Philipp Emanuel 57, 208, 209, 268
Bach, Johann Christian 57, 208
Bach, Johann Sebastian 8, 9, 13, 15, 133, 134, 188, 206, 208,
    221, 230, 231, 232, 262, 264, 265, 266, 267, 268, 272, 273
Backus, John 148, 149
Balance 149, 170, 173, 190, 223-229
Bangert, Byron 286, 289-290, 294
Baptists 270
Barber, Samuel 212
Baroque 7, 15, 24, 56, 59, 135, 155, 205-208, 258, 261-267, 268,
    272
Barrel organ 269
Basso continuo 263
Baton 10, 11, 14, 194-195
Beethoven, Ludwig van 12, 13, 14, 118, 210, 268, 272
Bel canto 106
Benedictines of Solesmes 275

Bennett, Roy C.   128
Berlioz, Hector   13, 210, 276
Bernstein, Leonard   276
Bethlehem Bach Festival   12
Biber, Franz Heinrich   264
Billings, William   271
Binchois, Gilles   258
Bizet, Georges   274
Blend   89, 150, 170, 173, 190, 223-229
Book of Common Prayer   260, 280
Brahms, Johannes   210, 228, 273, 276
Breathing (breath management)   67-74, 214, 216-218
Brodnitz, Friedrich S.   104, 119
Broudy, Harry S.   310
Brown, Richmond B.   328
Bruckner, Anton   210, 274, 276
Buber, Martin   286
Buccalpharyngeal cavity   72, 75, 77, 78, 79, 80, 90, 102, 107
Byrd, William   205, 259, 261, 267

Caccini, Guilio   258
Caecilian Society   275, 276
Calvinism   259-260, 261
Cantata   265-266
Cantio   253
Cantor   3, 5
Cantus firmus   256
Celts   254
Chant   290
Charlemagne (Charles the Great)   252
Charles I, King   261
Chironomy   4, 5
Christ on the Mount of Olives   272
Christian Reformed Church   278
Church choirs   47
Church of England   260
Classic(al) period   15, 24, 57, 155, 208-210, 268-270, 274
Clavicular breathing   72
Codex juris canonici   276
Commonwealth Period   269
Community choruses   10
Concert pitch   13
Conductus   257
Congregationalists   270
Consonants   80, 100, 101-104, 190-191, 214, 215
Contemporary period   57, 59, 155, 212, 213, 220
Contrapuntal music   207, 217-218, 229
Copland, Aaron   212
Corelli, Arcangelo   262
Couperin, Francois   56
Cover(ing)   104, 105
Cranmer, Thomas   260

The Creation 272
Creative teaching 41
Crescendo 207, 216-217, 220, 235
Croft, William 267
Cromwell, Oliver 261
"A Crown of Grace for Man Is Wrought" 273
Crudeness to precision 50
Crüger, Johann 259

Davies, Walford 293, 305-306
Derived drives 32
Developmental teaching 19, 49, 51
Diaphragmatic breathing 72
Diminuendo (decrescendo) 207, 216-217, 219, 220, 235
Diphthongs 100-101
Discrimination (musical) 21, 22, 26
Divini cultus sanctitatum 276
Drilling 169, 173-174
Dufay, Guillame 258
Dunstable, John 258

Elizabeth I, Queen 261
Epiglottis 119
Episcopal Church 280
Equal temperament (well-tempered) 114, 115
Esteem needs 31, 33
Eustachian tubes 65

Falsetto 106-108, 226
Five-lane highway of learning 50, 174
Freud, Estes D. 63
Fundamental characteristics of adjustment 32

Gabrieli, Andreas 258, 262
Gabrieli, Giovanni 205, 259, 262
German Requiem 273
Gestalt 50, 165-167, 177, 315
Gibbons, Orlando 205, 261, 262
Gluck, Christoph 208
Grace, Harvey 293, 305, 306
Graded choir system 278
Grass roots concept 61, 62, 78, 89, 149, 211, 213, 311
Greeks 4, 248, 249
Gregorian Chant 5, 251, 252, 253, 254, 256, 257, 274, 275, 278, 279
Griffes, Charles 212
Guerro, Francisco 265
Gutenberg, Johann 7, 259

Haik-Vantoura, Suzanne 4
Halter, Carl 306, 307-308
Hand clapping (gestures) 4
Handel, George Frideric 9, 132, 136, 197, 206, 232, 262, 267,
    331-332
Handel and Haydn Society 12
Hanson, Howard 212
Hard palate 80
Harpsichord 7, 8
Hartshorn, William C. 289, 292
Hassler, Hans 259
Haydn, Franz Joseph 9, 10, 57, 208, 268, 272; see also Handel
    and Haydn Society
Haynie, William 309-310
Head voice 106-108
Hebrew people (music) 3, 4, 248, 335
Hemiola 232-234
Henry VIII, King 260
High baroque 10
Hindemith, Paul 212
Homogeneous groups 47
Homophones 77
Homophonic music 218, 224
Honor system grading criteria 154-157
Horizontal drive (movement) 207, 214, 222-223
Humming 224
Humor 159-160, 193
Husler and Rodd-Marling 107

James I, King 261
Jazz movement 277
Jewish congregations 4, 335
Josquin des Pres 258
Just tuning 113, 114, 115
Jutted jaw 91

Ictus 196, 213, 215
Individual differences 42
Initiative (musical) 21, 22, 26
Insight (musical) 21, 23, 26, 171
International Committee on English in the Liturgy 278
International phonetic alphabet (IPA) 78, 79
Interpretation 49, 178-180
Interval detection 129
Intonation problems 89, 111, 112-116, 170, 173, 215, 224, 225
Isometric exercises 186, 214

Kentucky harmony 271
Krenek, Ernst 212

"Laissez-faire" tone (concept) 26, 60-62
Lassus, Orlando de 258, 262
Learning readiness 20
Leeder, Joseph 309-310
Legato singing 190, 196
Liszt, Franz 274
Liturgical 49
Liturgical movement 247, 248, 275-276
Lotti, Antonio 276
Love needs 31
Lovelace, Austin C. 286, 290
Lully, Jean Baptiste 8, 205, 262
Luther, Martin 259, 267, 268
Lutheran tradition 11, 274, 277
Lyall, J. W. 306, 323, 324-325

Mahler, Gustav 118
Marchant (de) Guillame 258
Mary I, Queen 261
Mascagni, Pietro 274
Mass 11, 264, 266, 267-268, 273, 274, 276, 277, 278
Mass in B-minor 133, 232, 266, 268, 273
Meantone tunings 113, 114, 115
Mechanistic teaching 19, 50
Mediator Dei 278
Medieval practices 5, 6, 7
Melisma 94, 235-236
Memorization 174-177
Mendelssohn, Felix 13, 210, 265
Mensural notation 5
Merbecke, John 260
Messiah 132, 232, 331
Meter 130
Methodists 269-270
Michel, Dom Virgil 276
Minnesingers 254
"Missa de Sancto Joanne" 276
Mitropolous, Dimitri 223
Mixed voice (Voix mixte) 108
Modal notation 5
Modified vowels 99-100
Monteverdi, Claudio 205, 262, 263
Moody, Dwight L. 273
Moore, Douglas 212
Moravian influence 12, 270-271
Morley, Thomas 259, 267
Motet 257-258, 268, 269
Motivation 31, 45, 46, 48, 51
Motu Proprio (1903) 275, 276, 278, 279
Mozart, Wolfgang A. 9, 10, 11, 57, 208, 218, 268, 272
Muddy (muddied) vowels 100
Multiple-choir programs 298-299

Mursell, James   289
Music education   19
Musicae Sacrae Disciplina   278
Musical application   25
Musical awareness   21-22, 24
Musical cognition   25, 26
Musical consciousness   24, 26
Musical discernment   25, 26
Musical discrimination   22-23, 25
Musical initiative   22, 25
Musical insight   23, 26
Musical proficiency   25, 26
Musical skill   19, 23-24, 26, 27
Musicam Sacram   278

Nasal (naso-) pharynx   80
Negro spiritual   271
New York Oratorio Society   12
Nodules (vocal)   117-120
Normans   254

Ockeghem, Johannes (Jean de)   258, 264
"Open throat"   69, 74, 90, 190
Opera   263
Oral pharynx   80, 190
Oratorio   262, 265-266, 272-274
Organ   7, 8, 10
Organum   254-255, 256, 257
Orthography   77

Pacing (of rehearsals)   167-173
Paleographia Musicale   275
Palestrina, Giovanni Pierluige da   258, 262, 276
Passaggio (break)   93, 104, 105-109
Passion According to St. Matthew   265, 272
Passions   265, 272-274
Paths (avenues) of musical growth   20-26, 166
Penderecki, Krzysztof   212, 277
Pentatonic scale   248
Pergolesi, Giovanni   208
Peri, Jacapo   263
Personality (of conductor)   157-165
Peters, Flor   276
Philo   249
Phonology   77
Phrasing   217, 218
Physiological needs   31
The Pius X Hymnal   276
Pius X School of Liturgical Music   276
Placement (of voice)   81-85

Plain chant   5, 267
Plainsong   290
Polyphony   5, 14, 255, 256, 257, 259, 265, 266, 268
Polyps (vocal)   117-120
Pope Gregory (Gregorian Chant)   5, 251, 252, 253, 254, 256, 257,
    274
Pope John XXII   256
Pope Leo I   250
Pope Leo X   260
Pope Leo XIII   275
Pope Paul VI   277, 278
Pope Pius X   275
Pope Pius XII   278
Pope Sylvester   5, 252
Posture   67-74, 169, 192
Potiron, Henri   276
Poulenc, Francis   276
Pratt, Waldo W.   306
Preparatory beat   195-196
Presbyterians   270
Psalm(s)   3, 4
Psychological needs   32
Ptolemy   113
Purcell, Henry   205, 262, 267
Puritanism   261
Pythagoras   248
Pythagorean scale   113, 114

Recording rehearsals   241-243
Reformation Church   12
Reformation (English)   12, 260, 261, 267
Reformation (German)   12, 253, 258, 259
Register   105, 108
Regolamento (1912)   275
Rehearsal tips   167-171
Reinberger, Joseph   274
Religious education   300
Renaissance period   6, 7, 15, 56, 59, 155, 204, 205, 273
Requiem   264, 274
Resonance   63, 75-77, 79-80
Rhythm   4, 130, 135, 137, 192-193, 206, 207, 215, 220
Rice, William C.   286, 290
Rococo style   56, 57
Roman Catholic Church   274-280, 290-291, 294
Roman Catholic Masses   264, 266, 267-268, 278-280
Romans   4, 248-249
Romantic Period (Era)   15, 24, 57, 59, 118, 208, 209, 210-211,
    222, 273, 274
Routley, Erik   260, 273
Rubato   210, 218-219

Sacred harp 271
Safety needs 31
St. John's Abbey 276
St. Matthew Passion see Passion According to St. Matthew
Saint-Saëns, Camille 274
Sankey, Ira D. 274
Scarlatti, Domenico 56
Schoenberg, Arnold 212, 277
Schola Cantorum 5, 252
Schubert, Franz 210, 268
Schütz, Heinrich 205, 262, 264, 272
The Seasons 272
Seating arrangements 147-151
Second Vatican Ecumenical Council 278
Section rehearsals 127
Self-actualization 31
Serial (twelve-tone) 212
Shakespeare, William 261
Shaw, Robert 58, 62
Short vowel 96-99
Sight-singing (reading) 27-29, 48, 125, 126-137, 146, 169, 175,
    177-178
Silent breath 190, 191, 195
Sims, W. Hins 304
Singenberger, John B. 275
"Singet dem Herrn" 273
Singkreis 11, 211
Sistine choir 6
Society of Friends (Quakers) 293
Society of St. Gregory 276
Soft palate 80, 87, 93, 102, 103, 104
Sonorous-blend tone 26, 62, 63
Souter Liedekens 260
Southern Baptist Church 278, 307
Southern harmony 271
Spencer, John 285
Spohr, Ludwig 12
Stacey and De Martino 32, 33
Stage department 180-182
Staccato 214-215
Stoughton Massachusetts Musical Society 12
"Straight tone" 26, 58, 59, 60, 63, 112, 204
Stravinski, Igor 276
Strophic songs 217
Sub-vowel 97-99, 214
Succentor 5
Sumerians 4
Symonds, Percival M. 311, 312, 313
Synthesis-analysis-synthesis (SAS) 38, 39, 50, 129, 165-167, 170,
    171, 177, 315, 316

Tact 6

Tallis, Thomas 258, 260, 261
Telemann, Georg Philipp 262
Tenuto 217-218
Terpander 248
Thomas, Edith Lovell 288, 299, 300, 302
Thompson, Randall 212
Tomkins, Thomas 261
Tone placement 105
Tongue 80
Trope 252, 253
Troubadours 254
Turtle neck 91
Tye, Christopher 258, 260, 261

Untempered scale 113

Vaughan Williams, Ralph 276
Ventilation 112
Verdi, Giuseppe 210, 274
Viadana, Lodovico 276
Victoria, Tomas Luis 265, 276
Violin bow 10, 11
Vocal abuse 117-120
Vocalises (vocalizing) 75, 170, 173, 186, 187-188, 224
Voice classification 109-111
Volume 64, 225
Vowel (purity, focus, diction) 55, 64, 65, 72, 75-80, 86, 87, 88,
    91-102, 187, 190-191, 214, 215, 216, 227, 235, 241
Vowel derivations (derivatives) 91, 92-93
Vowel migration 93
Vowel spectrum 88

Wagner, Richard 211
Webern, Anton 212
Weelkes, Thomas 261
Wesley, Charles 269
Wesley, John 269
Westminster Presbyterian Choir School 302
Willaert, Adrian 258
Wilson, Harry R. 306, 323, 324-325
Witt, Franz Xaver 275
Wolle, Frederick 12
Worship 285-297

Zimmerman, Heinz Werner 277